In this thought-provoking study, Silvina Milstein proposes a reconstruction of Schoenberg's conception of compositional process in his twelve-tone works, which challenges the prevalent view that this music is to be appropriately understood exclusively in terms of the new method.

Her claim that in Schoenberg we encounter hierarchical pitch relations operating in a twelve-tone context is supported by in-depth musical analysis and the commentary on the sketch material, which shows tonal considerations to be a primary concern and even an important criterion in the composition of the set itself.

Arnold Schoenberg: notes, sets, forms addresses the conflicting interaction between theory and practice in Schoenberg exploring the extent to which the techniques of developing variation, the notion of formal prototypes, and the use of balancing phrase-construction, as described in his didactic writings, represent the elements of his actual compositional thought.

The core of the book consists of detailed analytical studies; yet its heavy reliance on factors outside the score (such as the sketch material, the composer's theoretical and philosophical writings, his musical development, and cultural milieu) places this work beyond the boundaries of textual analysis into the field of the history of musical ideas.

Music in the Twentieth Century

GENERAL EDITOR: ARNOLD WHITTALL

Arnold Schoenberg: notes, sets, forms

Music in the Twentieth Century

GENERAL EDITOR: ARNOLD WHITTALL

This series offers a wide perspective on music and musical life in the twentieth century.

Books included will range from historical and biographical studies concentrating particularly on the context and circumstances in which composers were writing, to analytical and critical studies concerned with the nature of musical language and questions of compositional process. The importance given to context will also be reflected in studies dealing with, for example, the patronage, publishing and promotion of new music, and in accounts of the musical life of particular countries.

PUBLISHED TITLES ·

Robert Orledge *Satie the composer*
Kathryn Bailey *The twelve-note music of Anton Webern*

Arnold Schoenberg: notes, sets, forms

SILVINA MILSTEIN

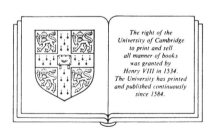

The right of the
University of Cambridge
to print and sell
all manner of books
was granted by
Henry VIII in 1534.
The University has printed
and published continuously
since 1584.

CAMBRIDGE UNIVERSITY PRESS

CAMBRIDGE

NEW YORK PORT CHESTER MELBOURNE SYDNEY

CAMBRIDGE UNIVERSITY PRESS
Cambridge, New York, Melbourne, Madrid, Cape Town, Singapore, São Paulo, Delhi

Cambridge University Press
The Edinburgh Building, Cambridge CB2 8RU, UK

Published in the United States of America by Cambridge University Press, New York

www.cambridge.org
Information on this title: www.cambridge.org/9780521106924

First published 1992
This digitally printed version 2009

A catalogue record for this publication is available from the British Library

Library of Congress Cataloguing in Publication data
Milstein, Silvina.
Arnold Schoenberg: notes, sets, forms / Silvina Milstein.
      p.   cm. – (Music in the twentieth century)
Includes bibliographical references.
ISBN 0 521 39049 4
1. Schoenberg, Arnold, 1874–1951 – Criticism and interpretation.
2. Twelve-tone system. I. Title. II. Series.
ML410.S283M55 1991
781.2′68′092 – dc20   90–21851 CIP

ISBN 978-0-521-39049-1 hardback
ISBN 978-0-521-10692-4 paperback

Contents

Illustrations

Between pages 184 and 205

In order to provide the fullest information, the MSS listed above are presented in their entirety, untrimmed.

Preface

At the very beginning, when I used for the first time rows of twelve-tones in the fall of 1921, I foresaw the confusion which would arise in case I were to make publicly known this method. Consequently I was silent for nearly two years. And when I gathered about twenty of my pupils together to explain to them the new method in 1923, I did it because I was afraid to be taken as an imitator of Hauer, who, at this time, published his *Vom Melos zur Pauke*.[1] I could show that I was on the way to this method for more than ten years and could prove so by examples of works written during this time. But, at the same time, already I did not call it a 'system' but a 'method', and considered it as a tool of composition but not as a theory. And, therefore I concluded my explanation with the sentence: 'You use the row and compose as you had done it previously.' That means: 'Use the same kind of form or expression, the same themes, melodies, sounds, rhythms as you used before.'[2]

More than half a century after Schoenberg enthusiastically proclaimed that his method would 'assure the supremacy of German music for the next hundred years',[3] his twelve-tone works remain as exhilarating but almost as little understood as in his own time. Even putting aside the intrinsic difficulties of the extreme conciseness of Schoenberg's mode of expression, evident even in his early tonal works,[4] the precise nature and scope of twelve-tone thought in his compositions remain largely unexplained. For although the particular twelve-tone set and the operations for its systematic transformations are readily available to the analyst, the syntactical relevance and the precise levels at which the set determines the composition are not explicit and often require explanation outside twelve-tone theory itself.

---

1 'Schoenberg most likely means *Vom Wesen des Musikalischen*, which was published in 1923, rather than *Vom Melos zur Pauke*, which appeared in 1925 – and was dedicated to Schoenberg.' Editor's note, Schoenberg, *Style and Idea*, p. 523
2 Schoenberg, 'Schoenberg's Tone Rows', in *Style and Idea*, p. 213
3 Quoted by Rufer, in *The Works of Arnold Schoenberg: A Catalogue of His Compositions, Writings and Paintings*, p. 48
4 See Berg, 'Why Is Schoenberg's Music So Difficult to Understand?'

A glance at the various efforts to deal even just with the genesis of the method shows the complexity of the subject. Existing accounts range from Reich's historical approach,[5] and Goehr's inquiry into its philosophical motivation,[6] to Babbitt's textual analysis, which is geared towards describing the self-referential elements in Schoenberg's atonal works and their relation to the twelve-tone idea.[7]

On the strictly musical side, the problematic nature of the relation between the systematic aspects of the twelve-tone method and the particular way in which Schoenberg achieved musical continuity has been the subject of extensive controversy. Initially the discussion of these compositions was restricted to the identification of set forms, and to the enumeration of their formal analogies with traditional models, which were regarded as self-evident proof of the artistic worth of the music.[8] But since the late forties the systematic aspects of these compositions have been generalized in a series of articles by Babbitt and other American theoreticians.[9] Babbitt abstracted constructional principles latent in Schoenberg's music, and proposed new extensions to them, which inspired a generation of American analysts and composers. His writings on the twelve-tone method provided the theoretical basis for dealing with its constructional aspects. But perhaps more fundamentally they constitute the basis for a theory of the twelve-tone system which American composers have been exploring 'since Schoenberg'. Babbitt's comments on 'Composition with Twelve Tones (1)' illustrate the abyss separating the post-War generation from Schoenberg:

> On the basis of Schoenberg's preoccupation with questions of historical derivation, and his insistence on negative rather than positive aspects of the system, one is obliged to conclude that the system's demonstrable consistency is an astounding fortuity, and that Schoenberg, like many other great innovators, was not, at least at this point, entirely aware of the implications of his own discovery. This is, in no sense, to minimize his achievement; on the contrary, it makes the achievement appear all the more remarkable.[10]

It is a truism that in his music Schoenberg integrated traditional principles of musical discourse with the constructional potential of the method, but there

5 Reich, *Schoenberg: A Critical Biography*, pp. 130–1. See also Smith, *Schoenberg and His Circle: A Viennese Portrait*, pp. 173–219.

6 See Goehr, 'The Idea behind the Music: Schoenberg and Karl Kraus'.

7 See Babbitt's analysis of Op. 23/III in 'Since Schoenberg', pp. 3–7.

8 See Rufer, *Composition with Twelve Notes Related to One Another*, and Leibowitz, *Schoenberg and his School*. For a critique of Leibowitz's approach see Babbitt's review of *Schoenberg et son école* and *Qu'est ce que la musique de douze sons?*, p. 58.

9 See in particular: Babbitt, 'Some Aspects of Twelve-Tone Composition', 'Twelve-Tone Invariants as Compositional Determinants', and 'Set Structure as a Compositional Determinant'; Lewin, 'A Theory of Segmental Association in Twelve-Tone Music', 'A Study of Hexachordal Levels in Schoenberg's Violin Fantasy', and 'Inversional Balance as an Organizing Force in Schoenberg's Music and Thought'; Rochberg, 'The Harmonic Tendency of the Hexachord'; and Perle, *Serial Composition and Atonality*.

10 Babbitt, review of *Quatrième Cahier (n.d.): Le Système dodécaphonique*, p. 266

are conflicting views as to the nature and extent of such integration. Boulez and Perle maintain in different ways that archaic tonal idioms and twelve-tone procedures stand in a capricious relationship. Yet Schoenberg's practice has been justified from two radically different angles. On one hand, Rufer and Leibowitz consider the twelve-tone method itself as a vehicle of historical continuity. Since their analyses do not explore the relationship between detail and the whole, they fail to expose the constructional scope of the twelve-tone method in Schoenberg's conception. On the other hand, Hyde claims that the generative force of detail in Schoenberg relies solely on the twelve-tone method itself. Since Hyde regards thematic and formal elements exclusively as vehicles for twelve-tone relations, her work constitutes more an account of coherence between music and a generating set than an explanation of musical thought.[11]

The eighties have witnessed an impressive development of research on the systematic aspects of Schoenberg's music.[12] While occasionally displaying genuine historico-analytical concerns, this work generally exhibits a marked preoccupation with matters of mainly theoretical interest. Schoenberg's music has proven an inexhaustible well of compositional procedures, which have been generalized, formalized, and turned into the core of the corpus of twelve-tone theory. A survey of this literature reveals a wide spectrum of theoretical preoccupations ranging from the interpretation of sets in multiple dimensions[13] and isomorphic partitioning,[14] to the function of recurring pitch-class collections for establishing long-range connections,[15] and the comparison of twelve-tone with tonal large-scale formal strategies.[16] But common to the new generation of American twelve-tone scholars is the conviction that behind the immediate fact that

> Schoenberg's twelve-tone compositions display surface features that strikingly invoke large-scale tonal forms

lies a much deeper truth:

> despite surface similarities to tonal idioms, Schoenberg's twelve-tone music represents a distinctly different form of musical life.[17]

Much of the recent American research deals with the compositions discussed in this book and often touches on matters obviously related to my task. Nevertheless I have chosen not to deal directly with each of these studies one by

11 See in particular: Hyde, *Schoenberg's Twelve-Tone Harmony: The Suite Op. 29 and the Compositional Sketches*.
12 See the bibliography in Mead's 'The State of Research in Twelve-Tone Music', which provides a comprehensive survey of recent American writings on the subject.
13 Peles, 'Interpretations of Sets in Multiple Dimensions: Notes on the Second Movement of Arnold Schoenberg's String Quartet no. 3', pp. 303–52
14 Haimo and Johnson, 'Isomorphic Partitioning and Schoenberg's Fourth String Quartet', pp. 47–72
15 Mead, 'Large-Scale Strategy in Arnold Schoenberg's Twelve-Tone Music' and '"Tonal" Forms in Arnold Schoenberg's Twelve-Tone Music'
16 Mead, '"Tonal" forms in Arnold Schoenberg's Twelve-Tone Music'
17 Ibid., p. 67

one; my discussion is addressed almost exclusively to the ideas of Babbitt, which seems pertinent given their seminal position in the development of twelve-tone theory.

Schoenberg's dismissive statement that 'you use the row and compose as you have done it previously'[18] is at least partly responsible for the idea that set-theoretical analysis is irrelevant to the appreciation of his music. Although Schoenberg discouraged 'note-counting', the distinct mark left by the twelve-tone method on the music suggests that we are not dealing with a mere pre-compositional prop but with a powerful 'means to fortify the [musical] logic'.[19]

Central to Schoenberg's preoccupation with matters of musical logic is the question of 'comprehensibility'. This question refers to the relationship between compositional idea and listener's response, the subject addressed by Berg in 'Why is Schoenberg's music so difficult to understand?' I shall deal with this area only indirectly when commenting on the motivations behind Schoenberg's conception of the twelve-tone method. A critical assessment of matters of comprehensibility would probably question the perceptibility of many aspects of Schoenberg's practice: whether it is possible to comprehend aurally large-scale tonal relationships in chromatically saturated music, or to perceive complex principles of twelve-tone association. These considerations are concerned with psychology, and therefore lie beyond the scope of my enquiry, which aims at explaining the genesis of the music.[20] Successful reconstruction of musical structure involves complex and multifarious paths between real-time auditory experience and analysis. As an attempt to characterize the lines of thought – the type of musical logic and syntax – manifested in the compositions, this book may ultimately contribute to developing sympathetic modes of listening to Schoenberg's dodecaphonic works.

This study does not purport to be an account of either my own phenomenological experience, or that of an idealized listener; and though primarily based on standard twelve-tone analytical procedures, its heavy reliance on factors outside the score itself – such as the composer's own statements, his musical development and cultural mileu – extends its scope beyond the boundaries of textual analysis. My aim is to reappraise the extent and nature of the integration of traditional principles of musical discourse and twelve-tone principles of association in Schoenberg. I have also attempted to establish whether the categories described by Schoenberg in his philosophical, theoretical, and didac-

---

18 Schoenberg, 'Schoenberg's Tone Rows', in *Style and Idea*, p. 213

19 The full passage from 'Schoenberg's Tone Rows', p. 214, reads:

> Although I have warned my friends and pupils to consider this as a change in compositional regards, and although I gave them the advice to consider it only as a means to fortify the logic, they started counting the tones and finding out the methods with which I used the rows.

20 Recent studies on the perception of twelve-tone music include Krumhansl, Sandell, and Sergeant, 'The Perception of Tone Hierarchies and Mirror Forms in Twelve-Tone Serial Music', and Lerdahl, 'Cognitive Constraints on Compositional Systems'.

tic writings apply to his twelve-tone music. An important part of this study has involved the examination of sketch material, which has proven a fascinating route into Schoenberg's own understanding of the music. In short, this book proposes a hypothetical reconstruction of Schoenberg's conception of compositional process. It does not belong, at least in the first instance, to the debate on either the 'purity' or perceptibility of twelve-tone structures in Schoenberg; it belongs to the field of the history of musical ideas.

My interest in Schoenberg's music and ideas originated during my undergraduate studies with Stephen Arnold. Early versions of the manuscript were improved by suggestions from Oliver Neighbour, Julian Rushton, Hugh Wood, and an anonymous reviewer. I am particularly indebted to David Lambourn and Neil Boynton for their comments on sections of this book. Remaining errors are, of course, entirely my responsibility.

My thanks are due to both Jesus College and King's College, Cambridge, for their financial support and special intellectual environment.

Finally, I am especially grateful to Alexander Goehr for his criticism and encouragement.

Acknowledgements

Photographs of Schoenberg's manuscripts are by Susan Einstein and are reproduced by courtesy of the Arnold Schoenberg Institute, Los Angeles.

Music examples are reproduced by kind permission of the copyright owners: Music Sales Ltd/J.W. Chester Ltd; Universal Edition (London); and Boelke-Bomart.

Symbols and conventions

The integers 0 to 11 are used to indicate pitch-classes as well as the order number of an element within a set.

Order numbers are always in italics; e.g.: *0* signifies order number 0 (i.e. the first element of a set), and *3* signifies order number 3 (i.e. the fourth element of a set).

The following pairing between pitch-class numbers and pitch-class names was adopted: 0=C, 1=C♯, 2=D. . .and 11=B. Thus,

P_0 the prime form beginning on C
I_0 the inversion beginning on C
R_0 the retrograde ending on C
RI_0 the retrograde inversion ending on C

Therefore, P_0 (*3–5*) symbolizes the segment of P_0 starting with the pitch-class with order number 3 and ending with the pitch-class with order number 5.

Pitch-levels are indicated in relation to the C two octaves below middle C; e.g.:

C^0 = the C two octaves below middle C
C^1 = the C one octave below middle C
C^2 = middle C
. . .
C^5 = the C three octaves above middle C
C^{-1} = the C three octaves below middle C

Thus, G^2 symbolizes the G a perfect fifth above middle C.

A succession of arabic numerals separated by a colon indicates step progression in terms of an implicit diatonic scale; e.g., 5:1 denotes linear progression from the fifth to the first degree.

A succession of roman numerals in italics indicates in some instances bass-line progression and in others large-scale formal relation in terms of an implicit diatonic scale.

Bar numbers are indicated by 'b.'. When reference is made to an event which does not coincide with the beginning of the bar a stroke followed by a roman numeral indicates the beat where it occurs; e.g., b. 3/ii = second beat of bar three.

'Trichord' refers to any collection of three different pitch-classes, while 'triad' specifically refers to the common three-note chords of the tonal system, i.e. major, minor, diminished, and augmented triads.

Pitch-class sets are said to be 'equivalent' when their normal order forms reduce to the same prime form by transposition, or inversion followed by transposition. This study adopts Forte's method for deciding on the best normal order of sets and his list of prime forms and interval-vectors.[1]

I refer to 'interval-class' when the distinction between complementary intervals is irrelevant, and refer to 'interval' when referring to a specific interval.[2]

'Interval' refers to the absolute (positive) distance in semitones between two pitch-classes.

In the graphs dealing with pitch hierarchies, which should not be confused with voice-leading graphs, the following conventions have been adopted (unless otherwise specified):

> open and beamed notes: pitch-level representing a principal pitch-class centre and the pitch-class a perfect fifth apart
>
> darkened notes: pitch-level representing a subsidiary pitch-class centre and the pitch-class a perfect fifth apart, and pitch-level functioning as a leading-note
>
> darkened and beamed notes: pitch-level representing a subsidiary pitch-class centre and the pitch-class a perfect fifth apart which are locally prominent
>
> slurs: fifth support (i.e. 5:1)
>
> ----⌐ : lower leading-note relation
>
> ⌁ : upper leading-note, often as an appoggiatura

The following books by Schoenberg are referred to by their shorter or original titles:

> *Theory of Harmony/Harmonielehre*
> *Fundamentals of Musical Composition/Fundamentals*
> *Structural Functions of Harmony/Structural Functions*

Full publication details of books and articles quoted in footnotes can be found in the bibliography (pp. 205–10).

1 See Forte, *The Structure of Atonal Music.*
2 For a definition of 'interval class' and 'intervallic vector', see ibid., p. 210.

Editorial method for the presentation of sketch material

In most instances, I have chosen to present the sketch material in diagrammatic transcription. In order to show the different layers in the development of the material, the transcriptions often combine on a single sheet extracts from different sketch sheets while trying to convey the original layout of the autograph as much as possible. Photographs of the majority of autographs discussed are included for reference (Plates 1–20, between pp. 184 and 205). The Arnold Schoenberg Institute reference number appears on the upper left corner of the transcriptions and autographs preceded by 'MS'. Editorial additions and comments are indicated by brackets, i.e. [ ]. Deletions in the autograph are indicated in the transcription by a double stroke over the originally crossed-out area.

In the sketches for the Septet, Schoenberg indicated set forms with the following abbreviations: *T*: prime, *TK*: retrograde, *U*: inversion, *UK*: retrograded inversion. Transposition levels were identified by the interval formed between the pitch-classes with order number 0 of the untransposed prime and the other set form (retrograded forms are regarded as starting on the pitch-class with order number 11). Schoenberg's transposition figures refer to the generic size (e.g., +3: major third, and 5: perfect fifth) as opposed to the distance by semitones. Schoenberg indicated transpositions in two different ways:

when the interval of transposition is to be added, a figure follows immediately the set form either at the same level or above, or is placed over an oblique stroke (e.g. T5K: T^5K: T^5/K: retrograde ending a fifth above the prime);

when the interval is to be subtracted, it is in some cases written as a subscript and in others placed under an oblique stroke (e.g. U_{-7}: $U/_{-7}$: inversion starting a minor seventh below the prime)

1

Towards a general theoretical framework (1)

Introduction

Schoenberg published very little on the twelve-tone method and only discussed twelve-tone composition with a selected group of pupils of the calibre of Webern or Berg. Before attempting to deal theoretically with the subject, he considered it a prerequisite to write an all-embracing study of musical logic:

> For nearly twenty years I have been collecting material, ideas and sketches for an all-inclusive textbook of composition. When I shall finish it, I do not know. In any case: I have published nothing about 'composition with 12-tones related to one another' and do not wish to do so until the principal part of my theory was ready: the 'Study of Musical Logic'. For I believe that meaningful advantage can be derived from this composition when it is based on knowledge and realization that comes from musical logic. And that is also the reason why I do not teach my students: '12-tone composition', but 'composition', in the sense of musical logic; the rest will then come, sooner or later, by itself.[1]

This project, which preoccupied him intermittently for several long periods from the time of the completion of the *Harmonielehre* onwards, eventually failed to reach fruition, and three years before his death, Schoenberg wrote:

> One day there will be a theory which abstracts rules from these compositions. Certainly the structural evaluation of these sounds will again be based upon their functional potential.[2]

In view of the absence of a guiding theoretical statement from Schoenberg himself, a general framework for dealing with the dodecaphonic works may be inferred by interpreting Schoenberg's fragmentary statements in the light of his compositional practice and assessing their significance in terms of their value in reconstructing musical structure. Schoenberg's only three extended essays on the method, though of a general and introductory nature, indicate

---

1 Quoted in Goehr, 'Schoenberg's *Gedanke* Manuscript', p. 4.
2 Schoenberg, *Structural Functions of Harmony*, p. 194.

his preoccupation with various problematical questions.[3] The substantial amount of extant sketch musical material showing not only the manipulation of sets but often various stages in the conception and development of material, provides another primary source for studying the manner in which Schoenberg viewed and worked with the new method. The analysis of the compositions supported by the notions which can be inferred from these writings and sketches provides the basis for constructing a conjectural account of Schoenberg's conception of twelve-tone composition.

In his writings Schoenberg dealt with the technical aspects of the method in an unproblematic and largely pragmatic manner, while exhibiting a constant concern as to the desirability and consequences of integrating tonally laden material and twelve-tone procedures. In a manuscript of 1923, he wrote that the introduction of

> consonances (major and minor triads) and also the simpler dissonances (diminished triads and seventh chords) – in fact almost everything that used to make up the ebb and flow of harmony – are, as far as possible, avoided.[4]

According to Schoenberg, the avoidance of tonal material was not a requisite of the new method but arose from the desire

> to try out the new resources independently, to wrest from them possibilities of constructing forms, to produce with them alone all the effects of a clear style, of a compact, lucid and comprehensive presentation of the musical idea.[5]

Twenty-five years later, Schoenberg reviewed his position:

> It seemed in the first stages immensely important to avoid a similarity with tonality. The feeling was correct that those free combinations of simultaneously sounding tones – those 'chords' – would fit into a tonality. Today's ear has become as tolerant to these dissonances as musicians were to Mozart's dissonances.[6]

The twelve-tone method provided in the early stages a regulating technique for organic composition with non-tonal configurations, as is more explicitly stated in the following passage, written around 1948:

> The third advantage of composition with a set of twelve-tones is that the appearance of dissonance is regulated. Dissonances are not used here as in many other contemporary compositions as an addition to make consonance more 'spicy'. For the appearance of such dissonant tones there is no con-

---

3 These are Schoenberg, 'Twelve-Tone Composition', 'Composition with Twelve Tones (1)', and 'Composition with Twelve Tones (2)', in *Style and Idea*. See also 'Vortrag/12TK/Princeton', an early version of 'Composition with Twelve Tones (1)'.
4 Twelve-Tone Composition', in *Style and Idea*, p. 207
5 Ibid.
6 Composition with Twelve Tones (2)', in *Style and Idea*, p. 246

ceivable rule, no logic, and no other justification than the dictatorship of taste. If dissonances other than the catalogued ones are admitted at all in music, it seems that the way of referring them all to the order of the basic set is the most logical and controllable procedure toward this end.[7]

In the 'Addendum' of 1946 to 'Composition with Twelve Tones (1)', Schoenberg admitted that in the course of the previous ten years the strict avoidance of 'octave doubling and prominent appearances of fundamental chords of harmony. . .[had] been loosened to some degree' and justified their incorporation into twelve-tone composition on the grounds that their presence in the context of 'the characteristic melodies, rhythms, phrasings and other formal devices which were born simultaneously with the style of the freedom of the dissonance' would not recreate tonality.[8] The style of the freedom of the dissonance – the sound world of *Erwartung* and *Herzgewächse* – is, however, far removed from the pre-1946 American dodecaphonic works, which achieved a distinct set of idiomatic features more akin to some of the late tonal works. In this respect Samson noted that in the Scherzo of the Second String Quartet

> by couching such unorthodox harmonies in a traditional rhythmic language of Beethovenian energy and drive, Schoenberg created in this movement a sound world which presents close analogies with some of his later serial music. If we compare the movement to passages from the Fourth String Quartet, composed some twenty years later and itself often suggesting D minor, we find that in both instances the on-going energy is generated as much by rhythmic as by harmonic means.[9]

The examination of the European twelve-tone works also reveals that the incorporation of tonal functions and tonally laden material took place at a much earlier stage than that admitted by Schoenberg in the 'Addendum', and even suggests that it was never totally absent.

The new method provided Schoenberg with a concise system of 'self-defined' musical relations which, in a constructional sense, could replace those formerly given by tonality. Yet unlike tonality, the twelve-tone method has no recourse to generalized functionality, in the sense that it does not prescribe functional relations which are constant for all compositions, such as the hierarchy of tonal distance provided by the circle of fifths in tonal music. But progression is 'associative' and 'non-functional' since no tonal motivation, hence no tonal function, can be inferred without recourse to the connotations of a generalized system of functions, such as tonality.[10] On the contrary, in twelve-tone composition 'the normative factor is determined without any reference to means of

7 Ibid., p. 247
8 'Addendum' to 'Composition with Twelve Tones (1)', in *Style and Idea*, p. 244
9 Samson, *Music in Transition*, p. 108
10 See Babbitt, 'The String Quartets of Bartók', pp. 377 and 380.

its being so recognized other than by internal structure, which is not true in tonal music, and by priority, which is not necessary in tonal music'.[11]

Schoenberg's twelve-tone works generally show that he was unwilling to relinquish completely the functional relations of tonality and often concentrated implications formerly pertaining to a tonal region or key on single pitch-classes or pitch-levels. This compositional approach is not exclusive to the dodecaphonic works and has been described in relation to the Expressionist compositions as the replacement of 'a harmonically valid form by an overall melodic one, [which] though it could not have the significance of the old forms, nevertheless enabled the composer to differentiate between sections which return to their starting-point and those which move away from it'.[12] In order to achieve functional differentiation within the context of the continuous permutations of the total chromatic, Schoenberg developed a variety of procedures for delineating structural hierarchies by integrating twelve-tone relations and traditional means for articulating musical discourse. Although some of these procedures are common to several works, each composition comprises a unique syntactical constellation exhibiting varying degrees of dependence on traditional tonal functions and idioms.

The tonal implications of the twelve-tone works of the early American period have come to the attention of several writers, such as Newlin and Cone,[13] while the earlier twelve-tone works have generally been regarded as uncompromisingly devoid of tonal connotations. In these earlier works, though the deployment of tonal functionality is relatively less extensive, the large-scale unfolding of the composition is mainly controlled by the tonally directed motion of certain individual lines and line complexes. Similarly, the abandonment of classical balancing phrase-construction in some of the later works, such as the String Trio, and its replacement with a kind of 'musical prose', reminiscent of that of the Expressionist period, has been viewed as the counterpart of a more autonomous type of twelve-tone syntax. In this respect, it is most illuminating to examine tonal motion and association in those works generally regarded as exhibiting rather attenuated tonal motivation; for it reveals the procedures for establishing pitch hierarchies in extreme conditions, as will be shown in the discussion of the third movement of the Wind Quintet later in this chapter, and in the examination of the String Trio in the final chapter.

Schoenberg's music exhibits a comparatively high degree of consistency in the use of the twelve-tone method, yet analysis occasionally reveals 'licences' or deviations from strict twelve-tone criteria in order to accommodate events which seem to arise from outside the domains of twelve-tone relations. This

---

11 Babbitt, review of *Quatrième Cahier (n.d.): Le Système dodécaphonique*, p. 265
12 W. and A. Goehr, 'Arnold Schoenberg's Development towards the Twelve-Tone System', p. 91
13 Newlin, 'Secret Tonality in Schoenberg's Piano Concerto', pp. 137–9, and Cone, 'Beyond Analysis', pp. 86–7

tendency is even more pervasive in Berg, where the large diversity of integrative devices and the many musical and dramatic motivations stretch and obscure the boundaries of Schoenberg's method.[14]

The presence of gestures and sonorities which do not derive directly from the particular integrative devices of the work, but often characterize technically dissimilar compositions, is not exclusive to Schoenberg. The inter-War period saw the emergence of music in which elements derived from traditional tonality were integrated with new means of structuring music. The works of Stravinsky, Bartók, Berg, and Webern retain to a certain extent tonal functions as well as a variety of tonal idioms. Similarly, some of Schoenberg's earlier twelve-tone compositions drew heavily on the sound world of his late atonal works.[15] For instance the repertoire of textures and harmonies, and the reliance on formal prototypes in the Piano Suite, Op. 25, were anticipated in *Pierrot lunaire*. Generally the new methods did not immediately generate unprecedented sonorities, but often recreated musical contexts which preceded their conception. In this respect, before engaging in a discussion of the works composed with the twelve-tone method, it seems appropriate to examine in the course of this chapter the type of syntax involved in his earlier music. The cursory discussion of certain aspects of the Second String Quartet, *Erwartung*, and 'Valse de Chopin' from *Pierrot* which follows aims at characterizing lines of continuity and attempts to establish whether those events which seem to respond to other than twelve-tone criteria can be explained by tendencies already present in the tonal and atonal works.

'Composing with notes' (1)

In many of Schoenberg's atonal and twelve-tone works, tonal function is not abandoned completely, but single pitch-classes or pitch-levels, rendered prominent by virtue of their position as boundaries of groupings, are often made to bear implications formerly pertaining to tonal regions or keys and therefore function as true tonal centres displaying centricity within a given context without necessarily carrying all the implications of the tonal system.[16] It is important to distinguish these pitch-class and pitch-level centres from the analogies to, or substitutes for, tonal functions found in the music of some composers.

14 For a detailed account of Berg's twelve-tone practice see Perle, *The Operas of Alban Berg*, vol. 2: *Lulu*, pp. 85–207. The possibility of conceptualizing some of Berg's recondite schemes has been questioned by Babbitt in *Words about Music*, p. 24.

15 Schoenberg's explanation of the twelve-tone method to a group of pupils in 1923 concluded with the following remark:

> You use the row and compose as you had done it previously. That means: Use the same kind of form or expression, the same themes, melodies, sounds, rhythms as you used before.
>
> ('Schoenberg's Tone-Rows', *Style and Idea*, p. 213.)

16 Berger's 'Problems of Pitch Organization in Stravinsky' deals with a similar concept, which he calls 'pitch-class priority'.

Substitutes for tonal centres are frequently found in Bartók, whose music often exhibits the use of novel elements performing functions analogous to large-scale tonal relations.[17] Schoenberg's music indicates that he also was interested to some extent in devising such analogies, but these will be discussed as special cases. The use of individual pitch-levels and pitch-classes as tonal centres has also been identified in Berg. Perle commented in relation to *Wozzeck* that 'though one notes the occasional presence of tonic functionality in this otherwise "atonal" work. . .the centricity of a given pitch or collection of pitches is no less unmistakable in many of the "atonal" sections of *Wozzeck*'.[18] Perle explained in relation to the tonal centre which he identified as being the primary linear focal element in scene 1 in *Wozzeck* that 'its priority was expressed through repetition, durational preponderance, and prominence at registral and temporal boundaries'.[19]

In Schoenberg the structural importance of tonal centres and the manner in which they are used varies not only among different works but also among different sections of a single work. However, many of Schoenberg's compositions share certain devices for creating hierarchies; namely, the structure of regular metre and the prominence of those pitch-levels or pitch-classes which appear at the boundaries of groupings, often reinforced by leading-note and appoggiatura-like semitonal figures, and frequently supported by perfect fifths and by the use of idiomatic cadential gestures. While the nature of conventional metric structure remains essentially unaffected by the new situation, the retention of pitch-class centres or pitch-level centres unsupported by tonal progression creates a new syntactical context in which tonal motion is achieved through the polyphonic unfolding of hierarchically structured lines.

Even in the case of *Erwartung*, a work characterized by its tonal elusiveness, Walter and Alexander Goehr identified a melodic framework connecting important events and thus enabling 'the composer to differentiate sections which return to their starting-point and those which move away from it'. Although the very nature of the musical language of *Erwartung* seems to resist analysis, it is possible to observe even here certain tendencies which would recur in a much more systematic manner in later music.

An examination of *Erwartung* from this point of view reveals that the overall design of the vocal line at the beginning of each scene has many elements in common with the opening of scene 1. As shown in ex. 1, at the opening of each scene, boundaries of groupings tend first to emphasize C♯, then E♯/F, and finally E♭. The comparison of the opening bars of the first three scenes

---

17 For instance, in the third movement of the Fourth String Quartet, the pitch-class content of the chord which is slowly built up in the opening bars (A–B–C♯–E–F♯–G♯) reappears at the end of the first section, b. 31–34, transposed at the perfect fifth (E–F♯–G♯–B–C♯–D♯), and is restated in its original transpositional level in the coda, b. 64 to end. The manner in which this harmony is used suggests that an analogy to a tonic–dominant relation was intended.

18 Perle, *The Operas of Alban Berg*, vol. 1: *Wozzeck*, p. 130

19 Ibid., pp. 134–5. In the original Perle uses the term 'tone centre'.

shows that in each case the vocal line freely permutes some of the pitch-levels of the opening gesture and either starts from or aims towards C♯ (ex. 1). Some

Ex. 1.1

⌒ groupings

○ boundaries of groupings

▭ pitch-classes present in the opening vocal gesture

of these pitch-levels are also present in the opening bars of the fourth scene and the closing section (b. 418), but in these two cases C♯³ is replaced by C♯². In this sense, the opening vocal fragment defines a 'harmonic area', which performs an 'articulating' role.[20] Some of these melodic shapes recur in highly

20 Discussing Bartók's string quartets, Babbitt commented on the 'articulative role' of harmonies recurring at a fixed tonal level in different contexts in such a way that the harmonic structure itself possesses different implications; see 'The String Quartets of Bartók', pp. 381–2. See also his comments on the articulative function of the E minor chord in *Symphony of Psalms* in 'Remarks on the Recent Stravinsky', p. 168.

dissimilar contexts. For example, the vocal line at the opening of the third scene follows the overall pattern of the last vocal phrase which closes on E♭ in the first scene; yet the contexts are dissimilar:

scene 1, b. 23–24   C♯³   D²   D♭²   F♯³   E³   D²   E♭²
scene 3, b. 90–93   C♯³   B²   C³   F♯³   E³   D³   E♭²

A reference to the gestures of the original context occurs after a further close on E♭² (b. 95), in another fragment similarly closing on D♯² (E♭²), b. 101, which is followed by a *tremolando-sul-pont.* figuration reminiscent of the one in scene 1 (b. 24). The diagonal lines in ex. 1 draw attention to some of the many vocal phrases which follow the same overall pattern in terms of their points of arrival and departure. W. and A. Goehr refer to such cross-references and continuous reinterpretations of the material when they write:

> In *Erwartung* we experience a sense of being overwhelmed and lost in a maze of variation and juxtaposition of elements which are hardly memorable and result in a seeming structural incoherence. . .Though the chordal structure is complex and the individual parts are heavily doubled in augmented fourths, sevenths, etc. (which in this case tend to loosen the vertical coherence), an arc is circumscribed and the basic tonal principle of movement away from and towards a point or centre is retained. . .One feels that Schoenberg here already starts 'composing with notes'; that is, that he tended to replace triads as the functional agents with the identity of individual tones.[21]

Schoenberg's writings on the twelve-tone method give ample evidence of his concern with the problems involved in integrating tonally laden material and the new resources. But the deployment of only certain aspects of tonality creates a new and complex situation, for tonality is an integrated system, in which form, metric structure, voice leading, dissonance treatment, and harmonic progression explain each other. From the standpoint that regards twelve-tone music and tonality as constituting totally separate and well defined systems, the acknowledgement of tonal elements in a twelve-tone context raises the problematic issue of 'mixed systems'. Dealing with this, Boretz pointed to the incongruities in construing 'a twelve-tone trichord as also a tonal triad in the same piece under the same explanation'.[22] Since the premises in Boretz's conception are at the basis of much current research on Schoenberg, it is important to examine them in detail.

Boretz considers 'the total constructional hierarchy of each single piece to be inferable from its data alone, without recourse to a conventional lexicon or grammar'.[23] For him the shared aspects between different pieces of music are 'not best understood as a "common practice" or "common language"', because

21 W. and A. Goehr, 'Arnold Schoenberg's Development towards the Twelve-Tone System', p. 89
22 Boretz, 'Meta-Variations, Part IV: Analytic Fallout (1)', p. 150
23 Ibid., p. 147

8

he considers such an approach only appropriate to a construction where the individual's importance is mainly that of an *instance* of structure in a domain of such structures.[24] The construction of an 'individual-syntactical' model for each piece has the advantage that it is more likely to account for its singularity than an analysis based on a 'general-syntactical' model for a literature, such as that proposed by Forte for atonal music.[25] Yet, dismissing the notion of common language or practice is problematic on various accounts. Its first corollary is the possibility of music which exhibits no continuities with the past, and can only be understood in terms of totally novel rules. Once the notion of a 'common language' is discarded, the cognitive mechanisms involved in the process of inferring the syntactical rules of musical structures are reduced to the analysis of the set of measurements of the data of the piece. Consequently, the gap between pre-analytical perception of the music, with its reference to past experience, and analytical reconstruction widens. Moreover, Boretz's mode of inquiry cannot be concerned with questions of historical derivation, modelling, and reference. Schoenberg's own view was that he was working within a tradition from which he derived modes of musical thought and an array of common musical elements, conventional techniques (such as development and variation) and a repertoire of formal prototypes. Even a cursory examination of his music reveals it to be imbued with references to the music of the past. The problems, rightly pointed out by Boretz, arising out of the idea of 'mixed systems' only exist if we think that twelve-tone music constitutes an autonomous musical system. On the other hand, if we regard the twelve-tone method, as Schoenberg did, as a means for fortifying musical logic in place of a weakening tonality, we need not exclude the possibility of remnants of tonal thought or of any other element of continuity derived from earlier music. Although, as Boretz points out, one should be wary of assigning words 'like "cadence" and "phrase" in their tonal sense (or without specified alternative sense) to non-tonal pieces',[26] I believe that one should not dispense with such terminology altogether.

Babbitt's characterization of the way in which Bartók integrates self-defined structural devices with the conventions of tonality in his string quartets provides a seminal model for this type of enquiry.[27] His remarks on the question of contextuality and tonal motivation are particularly relevant to Schoenberg's compositional attitude. Babbitt considers that Bartók was 'unwilling to abandon completely the employment of generalized functional tonal relations, existing prior to a specific composition'.[28] For, even though Bartók was aware of the 'hazards inherent in the use of a language overladen with connota-

---

24 Ibid., p. 146
25 See the discussion of Forte's analysis of Webern Op. 5/IV in Boretz, pp. 218–23
26 Ibid., p. 149
27 Babbitt, 'The String Quartets of Bartók'
28 Ibid., p. 377

tion, in which the scarcely suggested is perceived as the explicitly stated', he knew that 'the exclusive employment of unique, internally-defined relationships, which can avoid this danger, leads to a considerable sacrifice of tonal motivation'.[29] According to Babbitt, Bartók tackled the problem of achieving a balance between these two methods, without oversimplifying the problem by assigning separate areas of control to each, that is, substituting segmentation for integration.[30] While Babbitt recognizes the relative independence of these two organizational principles in Bartók's music, his discussion of the third movement of Schoenberg's Fourth String Quartet – his only published extended analysis of a twelve-tone work – focuses exclusively on the set-determined aspects of the music.[31] For he considers that Schoenberg's extensive use of the serial method establishes a context, while its sporadic use as an integrative device in the detail – as in Bartók's string quartets – is determined by the context in which it occurs.[32] Babbitt's analysis implies that elements originally belonging to a tonal context provide a conventional framework, a vehicle, for the articulation of twelve-tone relations but disregards their function in reciprocally determining the choice of twelve-tone procedures and their role in the structuring of large-scale continuity.

The notion of 'composing with notes' can be traced back to the practice in much classical music of treating certain notes in such a way that they perform the associative function ordinarily attributed to keys. The reinterpretation of harmonic function of individual notes explains certain large-scale enharmonic changes, such as the famous Db/C♯ alteration in the *Eroica*. According to Walter Goehr, Schoenberg used to analyse the *Eroica* in his classes in terms of individual notes carrying the implication of keys.[33]

Composing with formal prototypes and their idioms

Integration of tonally evasive material and historical forms

The 'style of the freedom of the dissonance' involved a kind of 'musical prose' almost devoid of a sense of metre, in which intuitively associated musical gestures evoking a world of traumatic images combined into a web of free-moving melodies punctuated by overlapping cadences in the individual parts. In the twenties, Schoenberg came to regard the dependency of this type of music on text and free association as a serious limitation.[34] Such constructional qualms would have been utterly unacceptable to Schoenberg in the previous

29 Ibid., p. 377
30 Ibid., p. 378
31 Babbitt, 'Set Structure as a Compositional Determinant'
32 Babbitt, 'The String Quartets of Bartók', pp. 382–3
33 This information was passed to me by Alexander Goehr.
34 See Schoenberg, 'Analysis of the Four Orchestral Songs Op. 22', p. 27.

decade, when he criticized Liszt for not having 'the courage to explore the dark region of the unconscious, in order to bring up content and form as a unity'.[35] At that time, Schoenberg defiantly advocated unmediated comprehension and believed that through artistic intuition it was possible to attain complex formal continuity in an undeliberate manner. A letter to Kandinsky dated 24 January 1911 reads:

> Every formal procedure which aspires to traditional effects is not completely free from conscious motivation. But art belongs to the *unconscious*! One must express *oneself*! Express oneself *directly*! Not one's taste, or one's upbringing, or one's intelligence, knowledge or skill. Not all these *acquired* characteristics, but that which is *inborn, instinctive*. And all form-making, all *conscious* form-making, is connected with some kind of mathematics, or geometry, or with the golden section or suchlike. But only unconscious form-making, which sets up the equation 'form = outward shape', really creates form; that alone brings forth prototypes which are imitated by unoriginal people and become 'formulas'.[36]

Schoenberg's radical change of rhetoric in the twenties with its focus on construction, comprehensibility, and objectivity (*Sachlichkeit*) is the counterpart to striking changes in musical style. According to Neighbour,

> in January 1915 Schoenberg wrote to Zemlinsky that his new symphony would be 'worked' (*'ein gearbeitetes Werk'*) in contrast to his many 'purely impressionistic' recent works.[37]

The thematicism of *Jakobsleiter* reflects the change of emphasis from the 'one must express oneself directly' of the letter to Kandinsky to an uncompromising attitude towards clarity, coherence, and directness, corresponding to a time when Schoenberg was consolidating his personal, somewhat theosophical, outlook, and considered it his task 'to define his thoughts and to compose coherently out of them'.[38]

The commitment to 'carry on a logical and comprehensible argument in which Idea gives rise to related ideas through the agency of musical structures'[39] resulted in the integration of the 'style of the freedom of the dissonance' into a pre-established hierarchy of formal prototypes and balancing phrase-construction. Catalogued forms – such as dance-forms, rondo, and sonata – as well as established textures – such as fugue and passacaglia – provided not only a set of patterns of expectation but a repertoire of idioms traditionally associated with them. The 'Valse de Chopin' from *Pierrot* will serve to illustrate

35 Schoenberg, 'Franz Liszt's Work and Being', in *Style and Idea*, p. 444
36 In Hahl-Koch, *Arnold Schoenberg, Wassily Kandinsky: Letters, Pictures and Documents*, p. 23
37 Schoenberg is referring to his plan for a choral symphony incorporating texts from Dehmel, Tagore, and the Old Testament, which included *Die Jakobsleiter* in its final section. Quoted by Neighbour, 'Schoenberg', in *The New Grove Dictionary*, p. 713.
38 Goehr, 'Schoenberg and Karl Kraus: The Idea Behind the Music', p. 69
39 Ibid., p. 67

the type of interaction between tonally evasive material, and the idiomatic gestures and formal expectations of the quoted historical model.

The Waltz idioms in the opening five bars insinuate triadic groupings and tonally centred linear motion (ex. 2a & b). The piano constantly interchanges

Ex. 1.2

~~~ upper neighbour-note
L‿♪ semitonal leading-note
☐   triadic grouping

12

the registral placement of upbeat melodic fragments and block chords, as indi-cated by the white arrows in ex. 2a. The bass line delineates *I:V*, C–G, while the treble initially unfolds a G♯ minor triad and eventually arpeggiates F♯ minor. The treble F♯ in turn becomes the leading-note to G, whose function as a point of arrival is reinforced by the G–G♯–G neighbour-note figure at b. 5. The entry of the clarinet on F♯ completes two familiar groupings: it adds the minor seventh to the G♯ minor triad and the fifth to B–D♯. The arrows in ex. 2b show that in these five bars many of the groupings reappear in reverse order and are associated by common tones. This type of triadic progression defies tonal conventions, for the unfolding of motifs imposes its own condi-tions of containment disregarding the boundaries of tonality. The function of such progressions is associative and articulatory in addition to supporting and colouring strongly profiled polyphonic strands, whose linear implications often conflict with the connotations of the triads that result from their combination.

In 'Linear Counterpoint: Linear Polyphony', Schoenberg refers to this use of chords in the atonal works as articulatory and colouring elements:

> It can easily be shown that in the earlier works the chords are designed to have at least an accentual, articulating and colouring effect, and that their mutual conduct is full of regard for the relationships of the parts as they move. However, what is even here not under discussion – not, at least, in the way found in the *Harmonielehre* – is the harmonic progression. This, however, was never under discussion in counterpoint; but still one must pay a certain amount of attention to chordal progression, insofar as there is a prevalent tendency to avoid tone repetition as much as possible, or to disguise it.[40]

Babbitt's characterization of Bartók's tonality provides a hypothetical premise adequate for approaching 'Valse'. According to Babbitt, Bartók's polyphony progresses

> tonally in terms of the successive elaborations of a tonal area controlled by single thematic elements. At the same time, the polyphonic lines are co-ordinated and given unified harmonic direction through the relationships existing among the simultaneously elaborated central tones. This procedure often appears to be an organic employment of what has been mistermed 'polytonality', a self-contradictory expression which, if it is to possess any meaning at all, can only be used as a label to designate a certain degree of expansion of the individual elements of a well-defined harmonic or voice-leading unit.[41]

Unlike Bartók's lines, which are unified by small collections of pitch-classes, Schoenberg's tend to involve a rapid circulation of the total chromatic and a high rate of motivic transformation. In addition, while harmonic progression is

40 Schoenberg, *Style and Idea*, pp. 295–6
41 Babbitt, 'The String Quartets of Bartók', p. 380

not truly tonal, individual polyphonic lines often rely on creating amongst the tonal centres a hierarchy based on the circles of fifths. Thus a linear movement from C to G in the bass line, such as the one in b. 1–4 (ex. 2a), appears as a less distant movement away from the 'home' pitch-class centre, C, than the progression from C to D which occurs between b. 1 and 10. This reading is supported by the fact that Schoenberg subordinates the section centred on D to that centred on G by closing the setting of the first stanza with a bass descent by semitones and octave transfers to G (ex. 2a & c):

bar	1	2–4	8	9–10	11		12		13		14
	C^0	G^0	$C\sharp^1$	D^0	C^0 (B^0)		$B\flat^0$	$(B\flat^{-1})$	A^0	$(A\flat^{-1})$	G^{-1}
	I	*V*	⌊⌐⌐⇢	*II*	*(I)*						*V*

⌊⌐⌐⇢ leading-note

In 'Valse', Schoenberg uses non-literal repetition of themes and figures in combination with referential pitch collections and pitch-level centres to create a kind of formal ambiguity unattainable in the early through-composed atonal works. The main formal divisions of 'Valse' are marked by a bass-line strand centred on C combined with the presence in the treble of chords involving D♯–F♯ (ex. 3a, b & d): the opening (b. 1–4), the section leading to the recapitulation and the beginning of the recapitulation proper (b. 21–26), and the close of the coda (b. 40–42). In all these instances, the quaver figure in the bass and the block chords remain constant, while the other intervening elements are modified. At the beginning of the recapitulation, syntactical ambiguities arise from the fact that elements associated with the opening of the piece overlap with the close of the second stanza (ex. 3b). The recapitulation proper begins at b. 23, the piano playing a free permutation of the opening rising figure accompanied by the original block chords and followed by a compressed restatement of the piano treble from b. 2–3. The rising figure at b. 21–22 is also recapitulatory, recalling the two initial pitch-levels of the piano, C^0–$B\flat^0$, while the combination of flute, clarinet, and voice includes the $G\sharp^2$, $D\sharp^3$, and $F\sharp^3$ of b. 1–2. The reprise of the opening clarinet melody starts two bars earlier than in the opening (b. 22), but the initial fragment is subsequently repeated at b. 25 so as to coincide with the piano right-hand descent D–C♯–B, as was the case in b. 3. Towards the end of the coda the initial referential pitch-classes recur once more (ex. 3d). In this instance D♯–F♯ becomes part of a B major ninth chord (b. 40). The C^0 from b. 1 appears at b. 40 (preceded by G^1), as part of the arpeggiation of a transposition of the quartal collection[42] (C–G–D) which previously featured at b. 32–33 (B–E–A) (ex. 3c & d).

In 'Valse', we have observed the presence of freely permuted pitch-class collections, as in the restatement of the rising figure of b. 1 at b. 23–24 (ex. 3a

---

42 Quartal is used here to refer to collections resulting from cycles of either perfect fifths or fourths.

Ex. 1.3

& b), and also intervallic sets, as the linear statement of the quartal collection at b. 32–33 (piano left-hand), which appears articulated by a different figure at b. 40–42 (ex. 3c & d). These two forms of association are accounted for by the type of analysis which correlates set-theoretic operations and motivic relations. In 'Valse', however, there is another form of association not explained by the set-theoretic method: untransposed ordered pitch-class collections are used as a frame within which further elements are attached. For instance, the last line of the first stanza (ex. 2c) involves a double statement of D♯–A–D–F♯, the second of which embeds a further collection:

```
voice b. 10–11              b. 12–13
(neighbour-note)
     |
 D♯  (E)  D♯  A  D  F♯   D♯  A  G  E  F  E  B♭  D  F♯
 └_____ └__ └__ └___┘  └___ └_____ └___┘
```

Similarly, the descending figure played by the flute at b. 12 incorporates the figure played by the piano at b. 4 (ex. 2a & c):

```
piano, b. 4      E   D♯      C♯   A   F♯
flute, b. 11–12  E   E♭  D   C♯   A   F♯
```

The use of referential collections as boundaries of groupings to which other elements are freely attached suggests a wider repertoire of techniques for motivic association than those generally attributed to Schoenberg. It also re-inforces the hypothesis that boundaries of groupings, such as final notes and high points, should be regarded as relatively stable elements, a kind of frame-work, to which others of a more transient function are attached.

Schoenberg's model of musical unity and the twelve-tone method

In *Pierrot*, the use of formal prototypes and established contrapuntal textures is generally motivated by the imagery of the poems. Imitative textures, as in 'Der Mondfleck', and ground-bass techniques, as in 'Nacht', are particularly well suited to a compositional method largely based on motivic cohesion. Yet the integration of pre-classical and classical idioms and forms with material which originally operated in the context of virtually unrestricted free association is also symptomatic of a shift to a more conscious compositional attitude.

It would however be misleading to take the view, held by Rosen amongst others, that 'Schoenberg's most pressing concern, after World War I, was to return to the great central tradition of Western music'. Rosen thinks that 'the problem was, above all, to integrate the advances of 1908–13 with the inheritance of the eighteenth and nineteenth centuries', incorrectly implying a rupture and consequent reconciliation between Schoenberg's compositional practice and tradition.[43]

43 Rosen, *Arnold Schoenberg*, p. 79

On the contrary, it is possible to trace many paths between the sound world of *Erwartung* and *Die Glückliche Hand* and the idiomatic tradition and syntax of much late Romantic music. Schoenberg admired in Brahms and Wagner those elements which contributed towards 'musical prose', which he defined as 'a direct and straightforward presentation of ideas, without any patchwork, without mere padding and empty repetition'.[44] The late-nineteenth-century tendency towards formal asymmetry, overlapping phrase construction, and the avoidance of the cadence became much emphasized in Schoenberg's tonal and Expressionist works. Moreover, the 'style of the freedom of the dissonance' evolved from those self-contained tonally evasive passages often found in the music of Strauss, Liszt, and Mahler amongst others, for which, according to W. Goehr, Schoenberg coined the general category of *Inselbildung* (island formations), referring to their structural isolation.[45] The adoption of pre-Classical and Classical idioms in the early twelve-tone works severed Schoenberg's music from tradition more radically than 'the advances of 1908–13', for the introduction of archaic elements effected a stylistic break with the prevailing mode of expression.

Webern's account of the path which led to the twelve-tone method points to the connection between Karl Kraus's and Schoenberg's preoccupations:

> Finally I must point out to you that this is so not only in music. We find an analogy in language. . .Karl Kraus's handling of language is also based on this; unity also has to be created there, since it enhances comprehensibility.[46]

Schoenberg's statements in 'Composition with Twelve Tones (1)' similarly places the question of 'comprehensibility' as the central issue:

> Form in the arts, and especially in music, aims primarily at comprehensibility. The relaxation which a satisfied listener experiences when he can follow an idea, its development, and the reasons for such development is closely related, psychologically speaking, to a feeling of beauty. Thus, artistic value demands comprehensibility, not only for intellectual, but also for emotional satisfaction. However, the creator's *idea* has to be presented, whatever the *mood* he is impelled to evoke.
>
> Composition with twelve tones has no other aim than comprehensibility.[47]

The fusion of the twelve-tone method with Baroque and Classical forms furnishes a composition with a repertoire of fixed relations existing prior to the particular composition, thus providing a more stable context of reference and expectation than that which existed in the atonal works. Therefore, to view Schoenberg's post-World-War-I works as archaic shells filled with twelve-tone

---

44 Schoenberg, 'Brahms the Progressive', in *Style and Idea*, p. 415
45 This term appears in the prospectus for the *Gedanke* MS.; quoted in Goehr, 'Schoenberg's *Gedanke* Manuscript', p. 22.
46 Quoted in Reich, *Schoenberg: A Critical Biography*, p. 135
47 Schoenberg, 'Composition with Twelve Tones (1)', in *Style and Idea*, p. 215

content would be to misunderstand their motivation and position in history; for, on the contrary, they represent an organic response to an urge for rational and disciplined musical discourse, an attempt at reconstructing a syntax in a state of dissolution.

Schoenberg's theoretical efforts fall into two distinct categories. On one side, he endeavoured 'to find the rules of form which govern musical works by raising the question of coherence',[48] on the other, he dealt with the structure of the separate elements of music individually. The latter preoccupation resulted in the all-embracing *Harmonielehre* and the series of didactic books posthumously compiled from material written in connection with his teaching at the University of California, Los Angeles. The coexistence of both modes of enquiry is evident in the title given to the first document which Rufer lists in relation to Schoenberg's preoccupation with *Gedanke* – 'Coherence, Counterpoint, Instrumentation and Theory of Form' – dated 1917.[49] This indicates that Schoenberg viewed the two tasks as complementary, despite the obvious discrepancies in their theoretical stances. The closest that Schoenberg ever came to a model of musical coherence was the formulation of the principle of developmental variation, which regards form as proceeding primarily from pitch factors.[50] The organic concept of developmental variation inherently conflicts with the attempt to generalize processes in each separate domain. The difficulties in finding a point of convergence between these conflicting viewpoints may have motivated the change of rhetoric in the prospectus of 1934 for the *Gedanke* project. The shift from the original plan of dealing with each musical element separately to a synthetic approach is evident from the titles listed, which include exclusively global categories such as 'coherence', 'development', 'variation', and 'differentiation and characterization of the parts and their functions'.[51] *Structural Functions* replaces the abstract harmonic progressions devoid of rhythmic and motivic features of the *Harmonielehre* by fully fleshed examples from the literature. *Fundamentals* on the contrary treats form as a separate vehicle, possibly representing a rudimentary version of what the proposed *Formenlehre* of 1917 might have been like.[52] Accounts by some of Schoenberg's pupils suggest that both approaches coexisted in his teaching. In this regard, Greissle commented that Schoenberg's analysis was more of a synthesis than an analysis: 'he composed it before your ears'.[53] The other side of this dichotomy is represented by the theoretical premises implied in the published analyses of

48 Quoted by Rufer, *The Works of Arnold Schoenberg: A Catalogue*, p. 137
49 Ibid., p. 136. This document is labelled 'Zusammenklang, Kontrapunkt, Instrumentation und Formenlehre'.
50 Dahlhaus, 'Some Models of Musical Form', p. 20
51 The full prospectus is shown in Goehr, 'Schoenberg's *Gedanke* Manuscript', p. 8 (German) and pp. 21–2 (English translation).
52 See Goehr, 'The Theoretical Writings of Arnold Schoenberg', pp. 94–5.
53 Quoted in Smith, *Schoenberg and His Circle*, p. 155

Schoenberg and his pupils, such as Ratz, Stein, and Greissle,[54] which reflect the type of reification of musical forms derived from Adolf Marx.[55]

The conflict inherent in attempting to construct a theory of musical coherence from an organicist standpoint while at the same time dealing with the structure of each musical element in isolation, led to a creative confrontation responsible for much of the individuality of Schoenberg's music. His commitment to organic integration with its intimate links with the notion of developmental variation, and his adoption of a repertoire of catalogued forms, which relates to the view of musical structure as a composite of distinct elements, constitute, from a theoretical and stylistic viewpoint, the most distinctive features of Schoenberg's twelve-tone practice. These ambivalences are evident in the Piano Suite, Op. 25. The use of historical dance-forms indicates his reliance in the idioms, hierarchies and expectations of the prototype.

After the first movement, the ordering of the set is no longer strictly maintained. Schoenberg justified this as a consequence of

> the subdivision of the BS into three groups of four notes. No change occurs within any of these groups; otherwise, they are treated like independent small sets. This treatment is supported by the presence of a diminished fifth, db–g, or g–db, as third and fourth tone in all forms of the set, and of another diminished fifth as seventh and eighth tones. This similarity functioning as a relationship makes the groups interchangeable.[56]

P_{10}	Bb	B	Db	G		C	A	D	Ab		F	Gb	Eb	E
P_4	E	F	G	Db		Gb	Eb	Ab	D		B	C	A	Bb
I_{10}	Bb	A	G	Db		Ab	B	Gb	C		Eb	D	F	E
I_4	E	Eb	Db	G		D	F	C	Gb		A	Ab	B	Bb

In the Menuett these tetrachords not only appear in various orderings in relation to each other but their elements are often freely permuted. For instance, the rhythm of the treble at b. 9 is stated in augmentation at b. 28, articulating in both cases a free permutation of a trichord contained in the second tetrachord of P_4 (ex. 4b). The pitch-classes involved in this motif (Gb–Eb–D) first appeared in the middle part at b. 1, preserving the original ordering of elements within the tetrachord (ex. 4a). Although at b. 9 and b. 28 the tetrachord retains its content identity by virtue of the registral placement of its elements, it is freely reordered in a manner reminiscent of the treatment of

54 For instance see Ratz's analysis of the first movement of Beethoven Op. 59/I, in his *Formenlehre*, pp. 167–83 and the introductions to the Universal Edition scores of Schoenberg's Second String Quartet and Wind Quintet by Stein and Greissle respectively.
55 Marx, *Dr Marx's General Musical Instruction*, pp. 88–94
56 Schoenberg, 'Composition with Twelve Tones (1)', in *Style and Idea*, p. 234

Ex. 1.4

a)

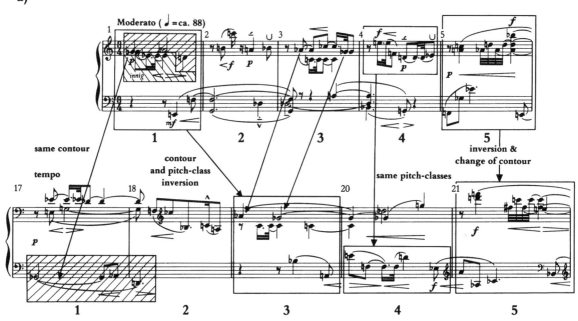

b)

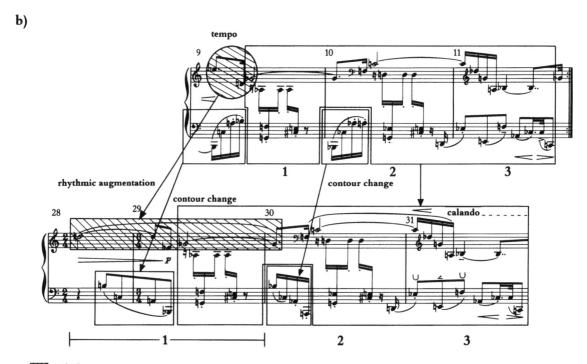

pitch-class motifs in *Erwartung* and *Pierrot*. Even in those cases where the re-elaboration of material responds to twelve-tone operations, often Schoenberg unsystematically shifts the placement of the elements of each tetrachord. For instance, the inverted reprise of b. 5–6 at b. 21–22 is not strict: at b. 5 the first note in the treble is the fifth element in P_{10} (order number *4*) while at b. 21 it is the sixth element in I_4 (order number *5*) (ex. 5a). Yet, other features of the work are uncompromisingly determined by strict association through twelve-tone invariants, such as the left-hand figures at b. 28–30, which project the invariant pitch-classes between the first tetrachord of P_4 and the third one of RI_4 by retaining the registral disposition of G–C♯–E (ex. 5b).

The familiar idioms and procedures associated with the Baroque dance-forms are well suited to the type of free elaboration and inexact repetition mentioned in relation to 'Valse'. In the Menuett, a major reprise starts at b. 17 commencing on the first pitch-class of the piece, G♭. Ex. 4 shows a variety of recapitulatory procedures, ranging from the almost literal reprise of b. 9–11 at b. 28–31, which involves rhythmic augmentation and contour inversion, to the less immediate reference to b. 3 in the third bar of the recapitulation (b. 19). The constructional tightness and economy of this music is such that often a single event simultaneously refers to various originally diachronic ones. For instance, b. 19 is a strict contour and pitch-class inversion of b. 1, but the A♭ and G♭ in the treble appear in the same order as at b. 3. Moreover b. 19 occupies the same relative position as b. 3 with relation to the beginning of the section and the following reference to the treble of b. 4 in the bass leads to a quasi-sequential passage, as in the exposition.

The overall four/five-part texture of the Menuett is punctuated by several unaccompanied notes occurring at the beginning and end of phrases. For example, the E♭² which closes the first phrase (b. 4), the B♭² at the end of the second phrase (b. 7–8), and its reprise at b. 24–25, as well as the G♭² which opens the first phrase and the second half of the Menuett (b. 1 & 12), and the D³ at b. 28, which introduces the recapitulation of the quasi-sequential passage from b. 9. All these are treble notes, with the exception of the G♭⁰ at b. 17, where the role of the textural components is momentarily reversed. Although these unaccompanied notes delineate an arpeggiation of an E♭ minor major seventh, the only close on E♭ is a relatively secondary event (b. 4). Throughout the Menuett the treble repeatedly closes on B♭ (b. 7, 16, 24, and 33); and in almost all the cases, these linear cadences are approached by an ascending semitonal leading-note (the only exception being the semitonal descent at b. 24), making B♭ the main cadential pitch-class of the piece. G♭ also performs a prominent referential function, appearing as the first pitch-class of the exposition and reprise.

Ex. 1.5

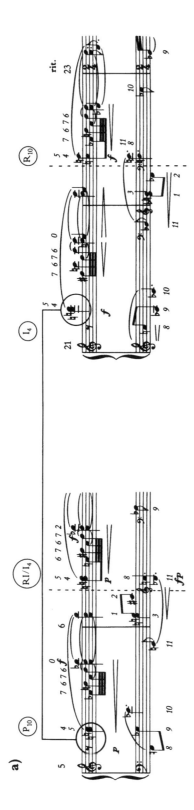

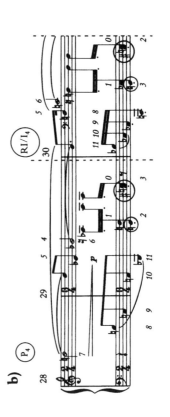

We have observed that the Menuett exhibits an extensive repertoire of formal and motivic procedures associated with the contrapuntal Baroque dance, such as bipartite design, the punctuation of the various sections by a hierarchy of linear cadences, and the use of sequence and cadential formulae. Since Schoenberg, in his theory, regarded music as the composite sum of its various elements, it can be seen that he would, by extension, have regarded single elements as being detachable from their original context. The organicist side of Schoenberg's outlook is represented by the twelve-tone method itself and the techniques for motivic integration and developmental variation, which provide unity, consistency, and solidity of detail. The creative tension between these two conflicting stances is reflected in the mode of expression which underlies Schoenberg's twelve-tone works.

Towards a new 'Doric architecture of sound'

According to Schoenberg's 'Notes on the Four String Quartets', in certain movements of his Third and Fourth String Quartets, conventional musical forms prescribe the 'order of appearance of their functional constituents (themes, melodies, units, motives and other functional elements)' and determine whether these are 'repeated, elaborated or abandoned'.[57] In addition, these catalogued forms 'involve methods which provide for coherence and comprehensibility (that is, the methods by which the functional constituents connect, add, introduce, contrast, juxtapose and prepare for fluent continuity)'.[58] Schoenberg explains that the third and fourth movements of the Third String Quartet and the second and third of the Fourth comply with the requirements of the traditionally developed forms, but the other movements obey different laws.[59] The justification offered for these freely conceived movements implies that the catalogued forms had validity *per se*, while continuity and coherence in the case of the non-fixed forms have to rely on the composer's intuition:

> There is no key to an analysis, tracing these forms to traditionally developed organizations. This fact entitles one to question an author: What made him do this?
>
> There are many causes, but only one answer: a composer must possess a full, unshakable confidence in the logic of his musical thinking. . . With the subject to be expressed undisruptedly in mind, a composer might 'copy' from his vision like from a mode[l] – one detail after another.[60]

Thus, for Schoenberg a limited repertoire of conventional forms accounted for most music, but the possibility also existed of the work which proceeds entirely from the composer's 'vision'.

57 In Rauchhaupt, *Schoenberg, Berg, Webern: The String Quartets, a Documentary Study*, p. 51
58 Ibid.
59 Ibid.
60 Ibid.

Reflecting on his development as a composer (c. 1950), Schoenberg wrote:

> My technique and style have not been developed by a conscious procedure. Reviewing this development today, it seems to me that I have moved in many roundabout ways, sometimes advancing slowly, sometimes speedily, sometimes even falling back several steps. The most decisive steps forward occurred in the Two Songs, Op. 12 [14?], and the Three Piano Pieces, Op. 11. Next to them comes the Suite for Piano, Op. 25. Then comes a turn – perhaps you would call it to the Apollonian side – in the Suite for Seven Instruments, Op. 29.[61]

It seems that after the initial experimental phase of composition with the new method, the twelve-tone technique turns into a norm, a new 'Doric architecture of sound'.[62] Hence, in terms of Schoenberg's personal development the Piano Suite, Op. 25, and the Wind Quintet, Op. 26, stand on the Dionysiac side of the duality – to which Nietzsche metaphorically attributes 'the heart-shaking power of tone, the uniform stream of melody, the incomparable resources of harmony'.[63] In musical terms, however, the turn towards the normative occurs within *Pierrot* and is further consolidated in the Piano Pieces, Op. 23, to culminate with the first twelve-tone works.

The normative aspect of Schoenberg's attitude on the question of form reflects Adolf Marx's ideas. *Fundamentals* is in many respects an amalgamation and expansion of the sections from *Dr Marx's General Musical Instruction* entitled 'Homophonic and mixed forms' and 'The peculiar forms of instrumental music'. The order of presentation of topics in parts II and III of *Fundamentals* coincides with that in Marx's treatise (1 – song form, including trio and variation, 2 – rondo form, and 3 – the sonata form), which further suggests that the latter may have served as a direct model. Marx's concluding remark summarizes Schoenberg's reification of form:

> These are the most important forms of art: all others that we may meet with in vocal and instrumental music, are either a selection of these or a combination from them.[64]

The second movement of the Fourth String Quartet is one of the works which exhibits the methods for coherence and comprehensibility attributed to the catalogued forms:

> The 'comodo' is closely related to the Intermezzo type. It is an A–B–A form. Its B section brings new thematic material, but has otherwise a certain resemblance to a Durchführung (elaboration) because it combines its own themes with the preceding ones, in many ways.[65]

---

61 Schoenberg, 'My Technique and Style', in *Style and Idea*, p. 110
62 See Nietzsche, *The Birth of Tragedy*, p. 27
63 Ibid.
64 Marx, *Dr Marx's General Musical Instruction*, p. 60
65 In Rauchhaupt, *Schoenberg, Berg, Webern: The String Quartets, a Documentary Study*, p. 60

A brief thematic examination of the first section A (b. 285–429), taking into account Schoenberg's own categories for describing it, will indicate how traditional procedures account for the detail of the music. The analysis will focus on the outline of the *Hauptstimme*, for this is the part most immediately referable to traditional thematic procedures, though elements from the accompaniment are discussed in those instances where their function is prominently thematic.

According to Schoenberg,

> its main theme. . .[b. 285–287], in the viola, is accompanied by a dance-like character in the first and second violin and cello. . .After a repetition and an extension, a contrasting phrase. . .[b. 306–308, viola], leads by means of the little motif. . .[b. 311, first violin and 312, viola], to a partial repetition of. . . [the opening theme], finishing thereby this section. A subordinate theme follows whose sonority is produced by the lightning flashes of harmonics which accompany a 'cantabile' on the G string of the first violin [b. 324–329, first violin]. A repetition of this. . .is clothed in an even richer colour.[66]

In fact, the main theme is not repeated literally but b. 285–298 involve an antecedent–consequent period (ex. 6). Both parts start with the same pitch-levels, D–A–B♭, which constitute a derived sequence in the antecedent and a set segment in the consequent. The first four bars of the antecedent and the complete consequent involve 'secondary sets'[67] (ex. 6):

first secondary set, antecedent, viola, b. 285–289

P_2	0	2	3	6	8	9	1	4	5	7	10	11
	D	A	B♭	E	G♯	G	D♭	F	E♭	C	F♯	B

L___ hexachord *a* ___J L___ hexachord *b* ___J

second secondary set, consequent, first violin, b. 292–298

R_5	11	10	9	5	4	3	0	1	2	6	7	8
	D	A	B♭	G♭	A♭	D♭	F	E	C	G	E♭	B

L___ hexachord *c* ___J L___ hexachord *d* ___J

RI_{10}	8	7	6	2	1	0	3	4	5	9	10	11
	E	C	A♭	E♭	C♭	B♭	D	G	A	F	G♭	D♭

L___ hexachord *d* ___J L___ hexachord *c* ___J

In the Comodo the hexachords of these secondary sets are treated as motifs. Although throughout section A these secondary sets feature in the main thematic statements, only the basic set itself accounts for the majority of events in the movement. Since the *Hauptstimme* and the accompaniment both unfold secondary sets or aggregates structured by the secondary set respec-

---

66 Ibid., p. 60. Bar numbers in brackets refer to the musical excerpts shown in the original.
67 A 'secondary set' is a twelve-tone aggregate which results from the juxtaposition of segments from discrete forms of the basic twelve-tone set of the work.

Ex. 1.6

antecedent

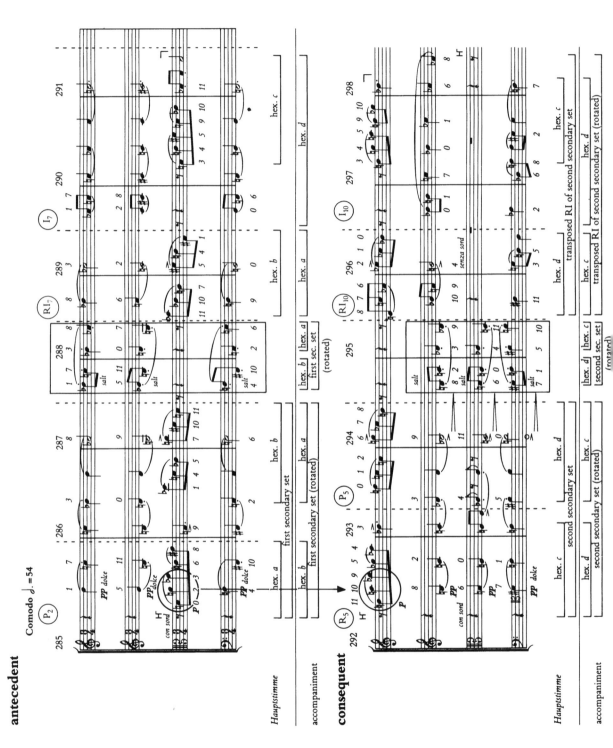

tively, the separate appearance of either of these reinforces the distinctive identity of the secondary sets. For instance, see b. 287–288 and 294–295, where the accompaniment of b. 285–287 and b. 292–294 respectively is stated on its own, i.e. independently of the basic twelve-tone set (ex. 6). At the large-scale level the thematic prominence of these secondary sets is further manifested in the manner in which Schoenberg recapitulates the opening theme. The recapitulation commences with the 'dance-like' accompaniment without its original *Hauptstimme* (b. 518), whose restatement is delayed until b. 592.

The examination of symmetries and asymmetries in the *Hauptstimme* of the first period reveals some of the ways in which this music relates to traditional categories. The consequent exhibits a simple symmetrical construction – its second half is a retrograde inversion of its first half – but the antecedent is asymmetrical in the sense that its second half (b. 288/ii–291) introduces a rhythmic and intervallic variant of the opening motif which uses a new hexachord, hexachord *c* (ex. 6). This asymmetry corresponds to criteria which Schoenberg associates with periodic phrase construction:

> The construction of the beginning determines the construction of the continuation. . .The first phrase is not repeated immediately, but united with more remote (contrasting) motif forms, to constitute the first half of the period, the *antecedent*. After this contrast repetition cannot be longer postponed without endangering comprehensibility.[68]

> Since the consequent is a kind of repetition, the antecedent should be completed with more remote motif-forms in m. 3–4.[69]

In the case of the fourteen-bar period of the Comodo, b. 6–7 substitute the third and fourth bars of a standard eight-bar period. At the local level, the presence of a variant of the motif at the end of the antecedent (b. 290–291) responds to the need to introduce 'more remote motif forms' mentioned above. Though the consequent also exploits this variant (hexachord *c*), the requirement of repeating for the sake of comprehensibility is fulfilled both by the fact that the antecedent and consequent each start with D–A–Bb, and by 'THE PRESERVATION OF THE RHYTHM [which] ALLOWS EXTENSIVE CHANGES IN THE MELODIC CONTOUR'.[70] In this instance, however, the contour is retained while only the intervals are altered. Moreover, in terms of the overall structure of section A, the asymmetries and relative motivic remoteness of the last two bars of the antecedent relate to the construction of the 'extension' (b. 298/ii–306). The *Hauptstimme* of the first part of the extension (b. 299–303) exclusively features hexachord *c* (*3, 4, 5, 9, 10, 11*) (ex. 7). In the first part the viola plays exclusively the hexachords of the P_2/I_7 combinatorial area, as in the antecedent

---

68 Schoenberg, *Fundamentals*, p. 25
69 Ibid., p. 27
70 Ibid., p. 30. The capitals are Schoenberg's.

Ex. 1.7

of the first period, and the first violin those belonging to P_5/I_{10}, as in the consequent (exx. 6 and 7). In this sense, the beginning of the extension is almost an overlapping statement of the first and final bars of the consequent and the final bar of the antecedent, with the sole addition of the viola hexachord at b. 298/ii–299 (ex. 7). The second part of the extension features similar symmetries, but in this instance the first violin consists entirely of the trichords from hexachord *d* (*0, 1, 2, 6, 7, 8*), while the viola plays once more the trichords of the ending of the antecedent at their original pitch-level (ex. 7). In short, the ending of the antecedent of the first period introduces the motivic material of the consequent which in turned is developed in the extension balancing the asymmetry of the antecedent.

The exposition of the principal theme of the first section of the work (section A) involves only two hexachordal areas:

the 'home' hexachordal area,

P_2	D	C♯	A	B♭	F	E♭	E	C	G♯	G	F♯	B
I_7	G	G♯	C	B	E	F♯	F	A	C♯	D	E♭	B♭

and

P_5	F	E	C	C♯	G♯	F♯	G	E♭	B	B♭	A	D
I_{10}	B♭	B	E♭	D	G	A	G♯	C	E	F	F♯	C♯

As explained above, the antecedent and consequent of the first period associate these areas through the trichord D–A–B♭, which is contained in the first hexachord of P_2 and is a segment of P_5. Similarly the other expository sections of the movement consist of a small group of sets, often a group of two combinatorial pairs. Such is the case of the exposition of the 'subordinate theme' (b. 324–338) and its elaboration (b. 353–364), which characteristically involve only two hexachordal pairs:

P_{10}	B♭	A	F	F♯	C♯	B	C	G♯	E	E♭	D	G
I_3	E♭	E	G♯	G	C	D	C♯	F	A	B♭	B	G♭

and

P_1	C♯	C	G♯	A	E	D	E♭	B	G	F♯	F	B♭
I_6	F♯	G	B	B♭	E♭	F	E	G♯	C	C♯	D	A

The initial bars of the subordinate theme are constructed so that when inverted the pitch-class content of the first pentachord and the last two of the subsequent trichord of the original remains invariant (ex. 8):

Ex. 1.8

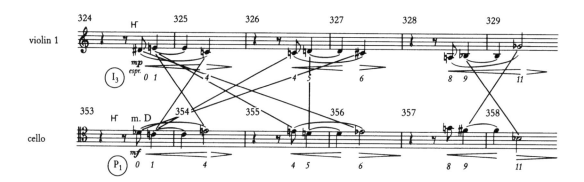

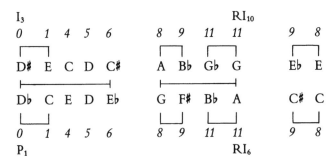

Hence, the use of the violin G and cello A strings, respectively in the exposition and elaboration of the 'subordinate theme', is not merely for colouristic effect – as one may infer from Schoenberg's account – but is related to the registral fixing of invariant pitch-classes, which establish strong links between the two appearances of the theme (ex. 8).

The thematic statements marking the principal sections of the movement are tightly constructed according to principles of set association, but in those sections involved in motivic liquidation the balance between traditional motivic procedures and twelve-tone constructional motivations tends to be relatively less stable. For example, the detail of the four bars preceding the statement of the subordinate theme (b. 320–323) and the passage leading to its elaboration (b. 345–352) seems to respond primarily to traditional principles of motivic liquidation. Yet twelve-tone invariants still provide a further level of association. At the large-scale level the collection D–C♯–A – the first trichord of the basic set – associates the ending of the exposition of the first theme (b. 425– 428), the close of section A, and the opening of the *Nebenstimme* of the Trio (section B, b. 430):

ending of the exposition of the first theme b. 321–323	P_2	*0* D	*1* C♯	*2* A
close of section A b. 425–428	I_6	*9* C♯	*10* D	*11* A
opening of the *Nebenstimme* of the Trio b. 430	I_9	*0* A	*2* D	*3* C♯

In this sense, the *Nebenstimme* motif at the beginning of the Trio relates to the ending of section A, in a way similar to that in which the beginning of the antecedent of the first period relates to the beginning of the consequent, for in both instances a trichord which is a set segment in one case appears as a derived sequence in the other.

The analysis of this movement shows how Schoenberg's thinking on formal matters crystallized in a fully integrated mode of discourse, in which the associative function formerly provided by tonality is replaced (at least analogously) by association through set invariants. In this context thematic continuity, procedures for motivic transformation and liquidation, and the formal articulation of exposition, elaboration, and recapitulation are not merely textural events but are intimately intertwined with the particular structure of the twelve-tone set and systematic criteria for association. The set engenders the motif, which progresses according to principles of developmental variation, having no longer tonality but rather the set as its absolute boundary.

Trying out the new resources independently

The Wind Quintet realizes in many respects 'the unconscious urge to try out the new resources independently, to produce with them alone all the effects of a clear style, of a compact, lucid and comprehensive presentation of the musical idea', which Schoenberg discussed in his essay of 1923.[71] As one of the earliest twelve-tone works, it may serve both to assess whether the new method resulted in a shift of emphasis from 'composing with notes and motifs' to 'composing with intervals', and to determine what kind of effect it had on the large-scale tonal structure of the composition.

The Quintet extensively features the type of tonally evasive collections which had increasingly attracted Schoenberg since the First Chamber Symphony. Comparing the First Chamber Symphony to the First String Quartet, Samson concluded that

---

71 Schoenberg, 'Twelve-Tone Composition', in *Style and Idea*, p. 207

> in the chamber symphony, the chief alternatives to the central tonality are not contrasting tonal regions (though they exist) but 'non-tonal' passages which are organized contrapuntally or in symmetrical harmonic structures. Both contrapuntal and symmetrical structures embody form-giving principles which are no longer dependent upon tonality and which actually serve to weaken it.[72]

The distinctive features of these non-tonal passages also apply to the Adagio from the Wind Quintet. Its freely moving lines devoid of tonal connotations, contrapuntally congested textures, and almost exclusive use of symmetrical formations make it one of the most uncompromising instances of extended non-tonal writing amongst Schoenberg's early twelve-tone works.

The set of the Quintet features a whole-tone segment in each of its hexachords:

0	1	2	3	4	5	6	7	8	9	10	11
E♭	G	A	B	C♯	C	B♭	D	E	F♯	G♯	F

These whole-tone segments permeate the movement and are often prominently articulated as in the *Nebenstimme* at b. 1–2. The set further embeds a complete whole-tone collection, C–B♭–D–E–F♯–G♯, but in the Adagio Schoenberg generally does not project this whole-tone hexachord, possibly to avoid the undesirable homogeneity which could result from the extensive exclusive use of this collection. In this regard he wrote in the *Harmonielehre*:

> The exclusive use of this [the whole-tone] scale would bring about an emasculation of expression, erasing all individuality (*Characteristik*).[73]

In 'Composition with Twelve Tones (1)', our attention is drawn to the 'regularity in the distribution of tones' in the first seven bars of the Adagio.[74] Schoenberg is pointing to the fact that the *Hauptstimme* forms a secondary set, which consists of a succession of three symmetrical formations: two quartal collections (tetrachords *a* and *b*) and a third one containing two fifths interlocked by a semitone (tetrachord *b*: ex. 9a).

In the Adagio the unordered content of tetrachords *a*, *b*, and *c* performs a major associative role; e.g.:

The *Nebenstimme* at b. 15–19 involves a reordering of each of these tetrachords, resulting in the second secondary set (ex. 9b).

The clarinet at b. 15–19 plays another form of the second secondary set extracted in an identical manner to the above but from the untransposed inversion (ex. 9b).

The quasi-isorhythmic statement of the opening theme played by the flute starting at b. 22 consists of a further reordering of these tetrachords (ex. 9c).

---

72 Samson, *Music in Transition*, pp. 102–3
73 Schoenberg, *Harmonielehre*, p. 394
74 Schoenberg refers to bars 1–7 but the horn theme actually ends in b. 8. In *Style and Idea*, p. 230

Ex. 1.9

a)

first secondary set extracted from P₃, H b. 1–8 (horn)

b)

second secondary set extracted from P₃, N b. 15–19 (bassoon)

second secondary set derived from I₃, b. 15–19 (clarinet)

c)

first secondary set extracted from R₃, H b. 22–29 (flute)

first secondary-set extracted from I₃, N b. 22–29 (horn)

d)

first secondary set extracted from R₃, H b. 82–89 (oboe)   first secondary set extracted from RI₃, H b. 90–96 (flute)

In this case, R₃ is partitioned on the same pattern as that used to obtain the first secondary set, resulting in the retrograde of each of the tetrachords of the original secondary set (ex. 9a). The latter reappears in several places throughout the movement, such as the beginning of the recapitulation of first-subject material at b. 82–89 (oboe R₃), and is inverted in its continuation (flute b. 89–96: ex. 9d).

All the tetrachords from these secondary sets consist of elements symmetrically disposed in the basic set, e.g. in the case of the first secondary set:

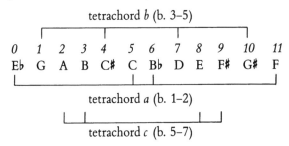

Schoenberg's sketches and set tables for the Quintet confirm that he was deliberately working with symmetrical partitions of the set. In MS 525, after a draft of the opening theme of the third movement, there is a small diagram (ex. 10a) which represents in geometric form the pattern of partitioning which resulted in the secondary set (ex. 10b).[75] MS 1110 is a comprehensive set table showing four different groups of secondary sets (see Plate 3).[76] Each of these groups results from applying the pattern of partition indicated by the diagram in MS 525 (ex. 10a) to rotations of the set, starting successively with the first element of each trichord:

```
1           2           3           4
Eb  G   A   B   C#  C   Bb  D   E   F#  G#  F
```

___ first element of the prime form of the secondary sets

75 Various explanations to this diagram and the inscription beside it ('I believe Goethe would have been quite pleased with me') are published in 'Correspondence', *Journal of the Arnold Schoenberg Institute*, pp. 181–90. E. Newman relates the 'doodle' in Schoenberg's sketch to a 'sign' which is mentioned in Goethe's *Faust*:

> MEPH[ISTOPHELES]. I must admit, my exit from the scene
> Is discommoded by a trifling thing;
> The devil-charm above your door, I mean.
> FAUST You find my pentagram embarrassing?
> If that forbids you, tell
> How came you in, you child of hell?
> And how is such spirit caught or cheated?
> MEPH. Beg pardon, Sir, the drawing's not completed
> For here, this angle on the outer side
> Is left, you notice, open at the joint.
> FAUST Thus fortune sometimes scores a lucky point.
> (translation by Philip Wayne)

Since the figure sketched by Schoenberg consists of five horizontal planes (lines) joined together as one, it qualifies as a 'pentagram', and, of course, it is clearly 'open at the joint' (p. 180).

76 Note that Schoenberg designates set order numbers with numerals 1 to 12, while I use 0 to 11, and that he

Ex. 1.10

a)

interpretation of the diagram in MS 525

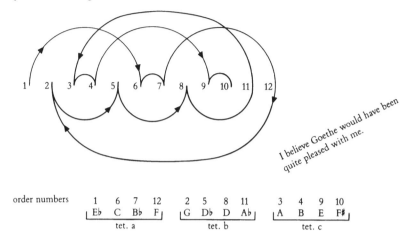

I believe Goethe would have been quite pleased with me.

order numbers	1	6	7	12		2	5	8	11		3	4	9	10
	Eb	C	Bb	F		G	Db	D	Ab		A	B	E	F#
		tet. a					tet. b					tet. c		

b)

transcription of a section of MS 1110 showing the first secondary set

set of the Wind Quintet with order numbers according to Schoenberg's designation

Each of the four groups of secondary sets shown in MS 1110 consists of the sets which result from applying the same pattern of partition to P, I, R, and RI of the untransposed basic set. Note that the secondary sets extracted in this manner from P and R, as well as those extracted from I and RI, are not a retrograde of each other (Schoenberg listed the retrograde of several of the secondary sets in the top half of MS 1110 immediately after some of the secondary sets). All these sets involve permutations of only six tetrachords with different pitch-class content.[77]

calls the first and last order number of the retrograde 1 and 12 respectively, while I refer to them as *11* and *0* respectively.

77 For a formal treatment of segmental and non-segmental partition in this movement see Mead, 'Large-Scale Strategy in Arnold Schoenberg's Twelve-Tone Music', pp. 131–40.

These procedures result in the systematic limitation of the number and type of collections used in the main thematic statements of the Adagio. The manner in which Schoenberg associates sets and derives themes intimately relates to the symmetries of the set, indicating a concern for devising systematic procedures, both to assign the elements of the set to the different polyphonic constituents and to control continuity. For this reason, it is striking from a theoretical viewpoint that, even in the earliest stages of the movement, Schoenberg deviates from what, according to the sketches, was a laboriously devised scheme. The first phrase of the Adagio unfolds three complete sets plus the final $E\flat^0$ played by the bassoon, which is the first pitch-class of the following set. In this way, the carefully achieved symmetry is broken. This deviation indicates that other criteria besides strict twelve-tone ones are in operation.

The changes in the three preliminary drafts for this phrase provide evidence for reconstructing the lines of thought underlying this compositional decision. In the earliest extant draft – dated 10 May [1923] – MS 508 (ex. 11), the lower

Ex. 1.11

partial transcription of MS 508

N.B. bar numbers do not appear in the original

part starts with the whole-tone segments, as in the final version, but the top part contains pitch-class repetitions. Besides being less accomplished in its construction than the final scheme, the first version is also less effective in terms of its voice leading and motivic treatment. Schoenberg's changes in the two subsequent drafts included in MS 525 (ex. 12) – dated 1 June 1923 – considerably

Ex. 1.12

partial transcription of MS 525

N.B. bar numbers do not appear in the original

1/6/1923

improve the linear profile of the first draft. In MS 508 the lower line of the first phrase, b. 1–8, reaches its lowest points at b. 4 and 6 with D^1 and $C\sharp^1$ respectively, before closing on $E\flat^1$ at b. 7–8; while in the second draft in MS 525, the descent to $E\flat$ is more convincingly attained by gradual downward motion followed by a semitonal ascent to $E\flat$:

bar	1	2	4	5	6		8
	$C\sharp^1$	$G\sharp^0$	E^0	G^0	C^0	D^0	$E\flat^0$

In the first draft the top voice starts on $E\flat$ and closes on G, and the bottom part does the reverse. In the third draft the top voice closes on $F\sharp$ (b. 7), and the bottom one closes on $E\flat$ (b. 8) while the top voice has a rest (ex. 12). The sounding of the $E\flat$ against the $F\sharp$ only occurs in the final version (b. 7–8). As I shall later explain, $E\flat$ and $F\sharp$ perform an important articulative role in the Adagio, comparable to the function of those pitch-classes and pitch-levels in *Erwartung*, 'Valse de Chopin' and the Menuett from Op. 25 which were found to 'serve to differentiate between sections which return to their starting-point and those which move away from it'.[78] Moreover, the lower voice in the final version tightens the number of intervening shapes by repeating several times the contour of the first four notes. The various stages in the sketching of this theme indicate a concern for constructional consistency, motivic tightness, balanced voice-leading, and finally the establishment of referential pitch-classes.

Despite the exhaustive listing of sets in MS 1110, the exposition and recapitulation of the first subject – b. 1–30, 82–96, and 110–113 – employ exclusively the four sets of the first group of secondary sets, and the prime and inversion of the second one, often in conjunction with their transposition at the fifth. In addition, the second subsidiary subject unfolds a tritone transposition of the third set in the third group of secondary sets (b. 53–60, flute). All the secondary sets employed feature $E\flat$, A, or $F\sharp$ as their first or final elements; and these appear in the composition as important points in the linear unfolding. $E\flat$ and $F\sharp$ (respectively the first and last pitch class of the secondary set at the opening of the movement) function as the main or 'home' pitch-class centres of the whole movement and the group of subsidiary subjects respectively.

Certain pitch-classes are made prominent by placing them at extreme points of the two principal parts. For instance, in the opening phrase, the *Hauptstimme* starts on $E\flat$ and closes on $F\sharp$, while $E\flat$ is also the final pitch-class of the *Nebenstimme* (b. 1–8). As explained above, this phrase unfolds three complete sets plus the final $E\flat^0$, whose introduction seems motivated by the use of $E\flat$ as a referential pitch class throughout the movement. The *Hauptstimme* of the second phrase ends on C^2 (b. 15) and that of the following phrase on A^2 (b. 19), which was also prominent in the flute part at b. 15. C^2 is also the final pitch-level of the clarinet

---

78 W. and A. Goehr, 'Arnold Schoenberg's Development towards the Twelve-Tone System', p. 91. The authors refer here only to *Erwartung*.

and oboe *Hauptstimme* in the final phrase (b. 20–21), and F#/Gb^2 becomes the point of arrival of the flute cadential figure. Thus, these points of arrival and departure in the *Hauptstimme* – Eb^2, F#/Gb^2, C^2, and A^2 – which are further associated by being within the same tessitura, outline another symmetrical collection: a diminished seventh. Besides these pitch-levels, only Db receives special emphasis as the final note in the *Nebenstimme* of the second phrase (b. 14), the beginning of the *Hauptstimme* of the third (b. 15), and finally in the closing flute melody, where it gives fifth support to Gb (b. 21). This prominent linear cadence on Gb^2, which is followed by a long pause in all parts, recalls the F#^{2} which closes the opening phrase (b. 7–8). The *Hauptstimme* of the final phrase of the first subjects (b. 22–30) initially expands the registral span of the treble to close eventually on F^2, preparing for the F#^{2} which opens the first subsidiary subject (b. 34, bassoon). All these referential pitch levels, with the exception of the bassoon Eb^0 at b. 8, are further associated by being within the same tessitura.

The procedures used in the first subsidiary subject (b. 34–52) also exhibit Schoenberg's concern with giving prominence to particular notes. Its opening melody unfolds a rotation of the twelve-tone set, starting on F# and closing on Ab, respectively the tenth and ninth elements of I$_9$:

I$_9$	9	10	11	0	1	2	3	4	5	6	7	8
	F#	E	G	A	F	Eb	Db	B	C	D	Bb	Ab

Other rotations of the basic set also feature extensively in this section, e.g.:

bassoon, b. 42–44

R$_9$	2	1	0	11	10	9	8	7	6	5	4	3
	D#	C#	A	B	D	C	A#	G#	E	F#	G	F

and horn, b. 47–49

I$_2$	9	10	11	0	1	2	3	4	5	6	7	8
	B	A	C	D	Bb	Ab	Gb	E	F	G	Eb	Db

———— invariant dyads

These rotational procedures, when applied to a pair of sets related by either transposition at the fifth or untransposed inversion, result in sets with a large number of dyadic invariants, as indicated in the three sets listed above. In addition, the choice of set forms used and their compositional presentation indicate a concern with giving prominence to particular pitch-classes. The majority of rotations either start or end on Gb/F# and Db/C#, and are combined with non-rotated segments of the set starting and/or ending on these pitch-classes, e.g.:

Hauptstimme b. 46–47, clarinet

I$_9$	9	10	11	0	1	2	3
	F#	E	G	A	F	Eb	Db

Hauptstimme b. 47–48, horn

I_2	9	10	11	0	1	2	3
	B	A	C	D	Bb	Ab	<u>Gb</u>

Hauptstimme b. 48–49, oboe

I_9	3	4	5	6	7	8	9
	<u>C#</u>	B	C	D	Bb	Ab	<u>Gb</u>

The sketches also confirm a link between the mode of derivation of the secondary sets and the rotational procedures in the first subsidiary subject. MS 1112b shows preliminary drafts of the beginning of the bassoon theme, b. 34–39 in the final version, unfolding a rotation of I_2 commencing on F# (ex. 13). On the

Ex. 1.13

partial transcription of MS 1112b

same page, Schoenberg partitions rotations of I_2 starting respectively on B and F#, according to the pattern shown in the diagram in MS 525 (ex. 10a). The resulting secondary sets are transpositions of the inversion of the second and fourth secondary sets of the first group of four secondary sets in MS 1110.

In 'Linear Counterpoint: Linear Polyphony' Schoenberg explained that in the earlier atonal works chords were used for 'their accentual, articulating and colouring effect'.[79] The emphasis between these functions varies substantially amongst different works. Non-tonal simultaneities are used mainly for their colouring effect in the opening bars of *Erwartung*, where a transposition of the same collection which appears as tetrachord *b* in the set of the Wind Quintet is heard on the first downbeat, F♯–B–C–F played by the clarinets, bassoon, and horn. Here its function is mainly to colour the B of the *Hauptstimme*, which, together with the following oboe, cello, and harp lines, anticipates the pitch-levels of the first bar of the vocal part. The use of such chords mainly for their articulative effect within a largely tonal context is evident in the Second String Quartet, whose associative deployment of quartal harmonies to articulate a multi-movement work will be discussed in detail later on in this chapter.

A distinctive feature of the Adagio of the Wind Quintet is the high degree of differentiation between its textural components. The extreme diversity of individual lines, which coincide only momentarily, immediately to diverge, makes the few chordal passages of the movement stand out as caesuras within the continuous linear flow. For this reason, sustained simultaneities, such as the closing quartal chord accompanying the flute cadencing figure at b. 21, become prominent events. The presentation of this material towards the end of the recapitulation, b. 103, performs an important associative function. It refers to the event which marked the beginning of the large-scale shift towards the pitch-class centre of the subsidiary subjects, i.e. the linear cadence on F♯² at b. 21. Yet in this case E♭³ is held over the quartal chord (E♭ being the tritone above the bass note, while previously F♯ was the tritone above the top note of the chord), instead of F♯.

```
               ┌──┐
b. 21   A   D   G   C   F♯
b. 103  A   D   G   C   E♭
        └──────────────┘
```

The original F♯² is not sounded until the very end of the bar, and is immediately followed by the reprise of the opening theme at its original pitch-level (starting at b. 104).[80] After the first note of the Adagio, no structurally significant *Hauptstimme* event either starts or ends on E♭² until this point. This further confirms that specific pitch-levels play a crucial articulative role in the syntax of this movement.

In terms of the large-scale structure of the Quintet, the untransposed tetrachord *a*, E♭–C–B♭–F, in combination with the whole-tone segments,

---

79 Schoenberg, in *Style and Idea*, pp. 295–6
80 According to MS 566 and to serial ordering, the last note of the bassoon at b. 110 should be F♮ and not F♭♮ as it appears in the Universal edition.

also performs a powerful associative function, appearing at major articulative points:

The coda of the first movement (b. 205–227) first comes to a close on a sustained C–Bb–F–Eb chord accompanying a flute melody consisting of whole-tone segments (b. 209–212).

The second movement is punctuated by two appearances of tetrachord *a* accompanying a cadenza-like rendering of the whole-tone segments by the piccolo (b. 142 and 359). This tetrachord is also present at the climactic sequential passage at b. 400–405, where the whole-tone material is played as an ascending scale by the horn and then by the flute. In addition, tetrachord *a* appears at less prominent cadences such as b. 188–190, where it is followed by its linear statement, played by the horn (b. 191–192).

The second movement closes with a chordal presentation of tetrachord *a* and a whole-tone piccolo descent; the same pitch collections featured in the opening two bars of the Adagio. At the beginning of the Adagio the minor ninth descent of the *Nebenstimme* is reminiscent of the flute melody in the coda of the first movement (b. 209–212). The association was stronger in the earliest extant draft for this phrase, MS 508 (ex. 11) – dated 10 May [1923] – which shows a twofold statement of the flute shape from the coda of the first movement.

The sequential passage towards the end of the second movement involving these referential collections (b. 400–405), reappears in the fourth movement at b. 223–225. The connection is evident despite the fact that in the fourth movement the direction of the scalic figures is reversed as a result of the derivation of the referential tetrachords from an inversion of the set (I_0).

The Adagio relies to a much lesser degree on semitonal leading-notes, appoggiatura figures, cadential formulae, and other similarly traditional means to create pitch hierarchies than the Menuett from Op. 25. But, though its lines express relatively attenuated tonal motion, we have observed that referential pitch-levels and pitch-classes play an important articulative role. Similarly the function and effect of prominent chords cannot be said to be colouristic; on the contrary, they function as landmarks associating distant events. In this sense, they perform a function similar to that of the first vocal fragment of *Erwartung* discussed above. Furthermore, the use of set rotation, as in the group of subsidiary subjects, is also symptomatic of a mode of pitch discourse which focuses on particular notes. In earlier works free permutations of pitch-class collections, as in *Erwartung* and 'Valse' from *Pierrot*, and the free reordering of set segments in the Menuett of Op. 25, assure variety while serving an associative function by making reference to specific pitch-classes. The secondary sets of the Adagio of the Wind Quintet represent a systematic realization of this procedure, resulting in a small number of pitch-class collections – only six tetrachords – which account for all the themes of the first group of subjects.

In the third movement of the Wind Quintet the functional differentiation of the outer voices is highly attenuated. In later twelve-tone works, as will be shown in the following chapters, the structural function of the outer voices is retained in the form of hierarchically differentiated bass and treble lines, whose interaction controls the large-scale tonal motion of the composition. Yet in the later twelve-tone compositions the bass tends to contribute only intermittently to the tonal direction of the composition, which is largely controlled by an overall melodic conception.

Roots of Schoenberg's later musical syntax

Reflecting on the changes in his musical language which resulted from the abandonment of tonality, Schoenberg wrote in 1949 that

> usually when changes of style occur in the arts, a tendency can be observed to overemphasize the difference between the new and the old. Advice to followers is given in the form of exaggerated rules, originating from a distinct trend 'épater les bourgeois', that is, 'to amaze mediocrity'. Fifty years later, the finest ears of the best musicians have difficulty in hearing those characteristics that the eyes of the average musicologist see so easily.
>
> True, new ways of building phrases and other structural elements had been discovered, and their mutual relationship, connection, and combination could be balanced by hitherto unknown means. New characters had emerged, new moods and more rapid changes of expression had been created, and new types of beginning, continuing, contrasting, repeating, and ending had come into use.[81]

Schoenberg insisted that strong lines of continuity run not only through his music and the music of the past but through the various facets of his evolution as a composer. In this respect it is particularly interesting to examine the Second String Quartet, a work which stands at the crossroads between the new and the old.

An early precedent for the type of 'melody-oriented composition' occurs in the introduction to the last movement of the Second String Quartet. The passage unfolds five three-bar units. The first group consists of a motif which ascends by perfect fifths, followed by an ostinato on part of this figure, on which a cadential figure in descending fourths is superimposed in the third bar. In the first bar of the second group, every alternate step in the chain of descending fourths is omitted, leading to a descending pattern which outlines a whole-tone scale closing with a variant of the final bar of the previous group. The third unit opens with a two-bar ostinato on the cadencing figure of the first group, leading to an unexpected chord in harmonics on D to which the cello adds a descent from G to C. The same bass-line descent D–G–C reappears in

81 Schoenberg, 'My Evolution', *Style and Idea*, pp. 87–8.

the fifth unit in conjunction with a fragment from bar 6 now played by the violins. Meanwhile the fourth three-bar unit retains the sustained E and D from the third group (first violin and cello). In short, this section uses a small number of motifs disposed within a flexible symmetrical frame of three-bar units. These motifs tend to be disposed according to patterns based on either superimposed fifths or fourths, and whole-tone scales. The continuous circulation of the total chromatic is counterbalanced by pedal points and recurring cadential patterns, while major cadences are punctuated by descending fifths. The texture generally involves two components, each consisting of a pair of lines. Even though the bass occasionally provides pedal points and conventional cadential patterns, the overall design responds to an essentially melodic conception.[82]

The use of quartal harmonies as landmarks articulating a multi-movement work, which we have observed in the Wind Quintet, has a precedent in the first three movements of the Second String Quartet. At this stage tonally elusive material, mainly whole-tone and quartal harmonies, still coexists with extensive triadic passages. A seminal passage featuring such formations occurs towards the end of the exposition of the first movement (b. 58–89). Here, the emphasis on Eb and Bb, brought about by placing them as extreme notes of grouping and their position within the metric structure, is confirmed by the cadence at b. 89, a half close in Eb minor. Yet the tonal expectations of this passage are contradicted by the subsequent statement of the head motif of the first theme in D minor (b. 90). This tonal progression is recalled in the second movement by the altered reappearance of the quartal chords (b. 31–34), leading once more to D minor (b. 35). The resolution of the interrupted tonal motion in the exposition of the first movement is delayed until the third movement, a set of variations in Eb minor on a theme entirely based on material from the previous movements, which begins with the notes of the treble of the first theme, transposed to Eb minor.[83]

Tonally Eb minor is quite distant from F# minor; however, the connection becomes less remote when viewed in terms of the interaction of motif and harmony, which in this instance is also that of treble and bass lines. In the *Harmonielehre*, which is contemporary with the Second String Quartet, we find the key to even the most adventurous harmonic events in this work. At the centre of Schoenberg's harmonic theory lies the notion that tonally interesting progressions often exploit the fact that chords can be reinterpreted as simultaneously belonging to several tonal areas. The functional ambiguity afforded

---

82 See Samson's discussion of this work in *Music in Transition*, p. 110–13.

83 Webern wrote in 1912:

> Despite its four movements this Quartet has a formal connection with Opp. 7 and 9, as we have mentioned; here too, a large-scale development follows the Scherzo, namely the 'Litanei'. It is a variation movement; the theme is a combination of motives from the first and second movements.

In Rauchhaupt, *Schoenberg, Berg, Webern: The String Quartets, a Documentary Study*, p. 15

by the reinterpretation of tonal triads and their interaction with tonally evasive chords and non-tonal formations led Schoenberg to conceive an all-embracing monotonal system based on the twelve tones of the chromatic scale.[84] Schoenberg's reference to the motif as the 'motor' that drives the movement of voices suggests that harmony is to some extent a realization of the exigencies of the motif.[85] The characterization of the interaction between motif and harmony is particularly relevant to understanding the origins of the idea of 'composing with notes' as manifested in the atonal and twelve-tone works.

In the Second String Quartet we can observe that the reinterpretation of function through common tones applies not only to chords but to motifs. At the large-scale level this is manifested in the reappearances in different harmonic contexts of the untransposed opening motif. After appearing twice in the context of F# minor (b. 1–2 and b. 35–36), it is eventually harmonized in D minor at b. 90–91. Although the opening motif unfolds an F# triad, its first note initiates the arpeggiation of an A major/minor triad in the treble (b. 1–12: ex. 14). The tension resulting from the simultaneous arpeggiation of A major/minor in the treble and a *I–V* progression in the bass, F#–C#, has far-reaching consequences. This initial A/F# opposition seems to motivate the transposition of the opening motif so that it starts on F# (Gb), the fundamental of the home key; a process which would involve the first three movements of the Quartet. The Eb minor passage in the first movement (b. 58–89), can be interpreted as a preparation for the eventual transposition of the motif a minor third down, but as explained above, the tonal expectations of this passage are contradicted and the motif is once again stated untransposed in the context of D minor. The transposition a minor third down does not occur until the third movement, where the motif starting on Gb (F#) is stated in the context of Eb minor, which can be seen as a large-scale resolution of the tensions in the original relation between treble and bass:

movement	opening motif starting on	
first	A	F# minor
third	Gb (F#)	Eb minor

In the first three movements of the Quartet, Schoenberg 'composes with notes' in the sense that he draws large-scale structural implications from the tension arising between bass and treble, a practice which goes back to the tradition of chorale harmonization.

A recurrent device in Schoenberg's tonal writing is the stabilization of a dissonant event in terms of overall structure by its incorporation into a triad. For instance, in the first movement of the Quartet, the Ab major/A minor triad

---

84 See Schoenberg, *Harmonielehre*, pp. 384–9.
85 Ibid., p. 34

at b. 5–9 prolongs the C from the essentially unstable tritone progression from F♯ to B♯/C in the treble of the opening four bars (ex. 14). Another instance of this procedure occurs at b. 10–12, where the resolution of the appoggiatura, A–G♯, is delayed for two complete bars. Meanwhile the dissonant A is momentarily stabilized by being incorporated first into an F major triad, and then into a C♯ augmented triad, before resolving onto G♯ (ex. 14). The procedure of giving stability to a dissonant event by making it part of a triad may have led to the type of triadic writing discussed in relation to 'Valse', and is also related to the kind of progression found in the first movement of the Suite Op. 29 and the *Ode to Napoleon*, which will be discussed in the following chapters.

This procedure had its origins in diminution technique as exemplified by Beethoven's large sets of variations, such as the third movement of Op. 135. In the first movement of Beethoven's Piano Sonata Op. 109, the second theme (b. 9–15) exhibits diminution procedures which invite comparison with Schoenberg's practice. The exposition of the second theme proper (b. 9–11) is followed by its embellished repetition at b. 12–14. Forte noted that at b. 13 the F𝄪 in the soprano, stabilized by a D♯ triad, is to be equated with G♯ at b. 10, and commented that 'the remarkable aspect of the equivalence resides in the fact that, in m. 10, F𝄪 occurs as an embellishment to G♯'.[86] A similar procedure is evident in the recapitulation (b. 58–65), where the ornamental B♯ generates the C major arpeggio at b. 62. Moreover, Beethoven's reinterpretation of the untransposed B–B♯–C♯–B–A–C♯ treble succession of b. 58–59 in the opening bars of the closing section of the reprise (b. 66–68), exemplifies the associative use of referential pitch-levels, which, as we have observed in the preceding sections, is a major structural device in Schoenberg's music.

Schoenberg's theoretical writings indicate his fascination with deviations from standard symmetrical phrase construction;[87] while Berg has commented upon the pervasive use of irregular groupings and phrases in Schoenberg's early music.[88] However, it has not been sufficiently stressed that irregular and overlapping phrase construction is possibly the key to the dissolution of tonality, for it leads to the blurring and eventual abandonment of the cadence, which, until then, kept, tonally evasive material within the boundaries of the system. In the first movement of the Second String Quartet such irregular phrases are often the result of prolonging a dissonant or harmonically unstable event. For instance, the opening theme consists of a seven-bar followed by a five-bar phrase, which according to Schoenberg's views should be regarded as a highly irregular construction. The fourth bar of the first phrase could have been immediately followed by b. 8. The three bar connection serves the function of

---

86 Forte, *The Compositional Matrix*, p. 21
87 For instance, see 'Brahms the Progressive', *Style and Idea*, pp. 409–41.
88 See Berg, 'Why is Schoenberg's Music so Difficult to Understand?', p. 191.

Ex. 1.14

momentarily prolonging B♯/C. The five-bar phrase similarly involves an essentially four-bar structure. The fifth bar results from the first violin delaying the resolution of the dissonant A.

Many other features of Schoenberg's atonal and twelve-tone works are already present in the Second String Quartet; such as the characteristic use of appoggiatura-like gestures where traditional treatment of dissonances is not necessarily observed. In the first movement this can be observed at b. 15–16 where the viola and cello appoggiaturas result in an interrupted chain of dissonant sevenths. A type of combinatorial texture which is extensively used in later works, particularly in the second movement of the Fourth String Quartet and in the String Trio appears in the E♭ passage of the exposition of the first movement. At b. 72–75 textural components are interchanged between instruments in order to create the illusion of animation without effectively introducing new elements. In the case of the Second String Quartet the pitch content of each segment is fixed, whereas in the extract from the String Trio shown in ex. 15 only the mode of partitioning the sets is fixed, while hexachordal pairs change in every bar but the last.

We have observed in this chapter the progressive emancipation of idiosyncratic tendencies in the detail of Schoenberg's earlier music and their promotion to the role of structural agents in subsequent compositions. Major changes in Schoenberg's philosophical outlook have been shown as crucial determinants in his musical development. From these emerges an hypothetical theoretical framework for dealing both with the origins of 'the style of the freedom of the dissonance' and the turn to a normative standpoint in the inter-War period, which culminated in his conception of the twelve-tone method.

Ex. 1.15

String Trio, Part II, bars 148–153

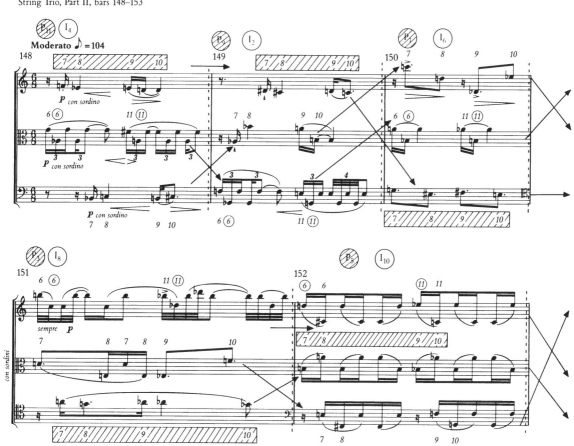

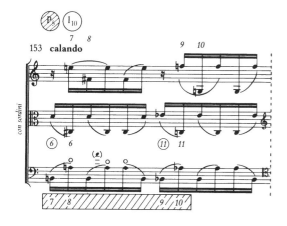

primes

inversions

2

Structural hierarchies in the 'Ouvertüre' of the Septet (Suite), Op. 29

Introduction

Schoenberg's legacy at the *Arnold Schoenberg Institute* includes a vast quantity of sketch and autograph material for the Septet.[1] The large number of extant early drafts affords us a unique opportunity to explore the modes of thought involved in the genesis of the music and to observe the interaction of tonal motivation, thematic procedures, and twelve-tone logic in the early stages of composition.

Most of this material remains unpublished, with the exception of those sketches showing the manipulation of sets, which have been discussed and reproduced in Hyde's *Schoenberg's Twelve-Tone Harmony: The Suite Op. 29 and the Compositional Sketches*. In this study Hyde argues that in Schoenberg's twelve-tone compositions harmony is entirely regulated by the basic set. With the aid of Schoenberg's sketches, Hyde is able to illustrate Schoenberg's well-known preoccupations with constructional consistency and his fascination with symmetrical pitch formations, particularly in the detail of local thematic statements. Hyde concludes that

> Schoenberg uses harmonies of the basic set to integrate all dimensions of harmonic structure. By expanding the definition of harmony to include nonsimultaneous events occurring in both horizontal and vertical dimensions, by allowing harmonic events to overlap, and by identifying the relating harmonies primarily by total intervallic content, Schoenberg legitimately asserts

---

1 The sketch and autograph material of the Septet is partly included in *Skizzenbuch V* and partly in a lot consisting of a combination of bound and loose sheets. *Skizzenbuch V* includes the final sketches of the complete Septet (MS 580–99 and MS 601–72), five pages of preliminary sketches (MS 576–9 and MS 600) and a set-table pasted on cardboard (MS 671–2). The remainder consists of a combination of bound and loose sheets (MS 1113–206) which are included in *Filmfile No. 5 – Chamber Music 'Manuscripts of Arnold Schoenberg, Suite op. 29'* and comprises:

> fair copies of all four movements (MS 1113–78); a thorough description of the format of this material can be found in Rufer, *The Works of Arnold Schoenberg: A Catalogue of His Compositions, Writings and Paintings*, pp. 50–1;
> set-tables and sketches dealing with combinations of sets (MS 1176–85, MS 1188, and MS 1206); material related to a new form of musical notation on three-line staves (MS 1187, MS 1204–5 and an articulated set-table (no reference number)).

that his twelve-tone compositions are totally integrated, because every feature is derived from a single source, the basic set.[2]

But 'harmony' implies a hierarchical relation between structures in a composition, so even if, as Hyde claims, we were to establish that all pitch events in the Septet are reducible to the source sets contained within the set, we would have described only a method for producing intervallic patterns. The concept of 'harmony' is of value when it implies the existence of configurations in a work which can be systematically or contextually recognized as being 'nonharmonic'. In this respect, Babbitt commented that

> The distinction between those aggregates which are sets and those which are less extensive in their interrelational scope is the process contextually involved in rejecting eventually as a 'set' such an aggregate as that which unfolds in the opening ten measures of the Op. 31 Orchestral Variations or that which occurs so compactly and strikingly in the first measure of the String Trio (invitingly delineating all-combinatorial hexachords by both temporal and registral projection).
>
> May it not be then that the hierarchically derived concept of a set 'can replace the structural differentiation provided by tonal harmonic structure' in that the twelve pitch-class set, like a 'tonic', is distinguished from other aggregates not simply by internal content or even interval relations. . .just as a 'tonic' is determined not sufficiently by its triadic structure (or representation thereof) but by its relation to other such structures within and over a composition?[3]

Such evaluation of hierarchical relations is however missing from Hyde.

My study of the sketches aims at the appraisal of the constraints involved in the moulding of gesture into compositional idea. Accordingly, it focuses on those sketches found to be relevant to the development of compositional ideas and restricts the discussion of those relating to manipulation of sets to those instances which I have traced to be the origin of significant ideas in the 'Ouvertüre'.

What modes of musical continuity do we find in the 'Ouvertüre'? How are structural hierarchies established? What is the interrelation between texture and processes in the pitch domain? What are the compositional implications of the structure of the set? Before proceeding to a discussion of the sketch material, I will put forward some tentative answers to these questions.

The relational kernel

The opening three bars of the 'Ouvertüre' contain in embryonic form the harmonic relations of the movement and the elements of its prolongational

---

2 Hyde, *Schoenberg's Twelve-Tone Harmony: The Suite Op. 29 and the Compositional Sketches*, pp. 17–18
3 Babbitt, 'Since Schoenberg', pp. 7–8

syntax.[4] The harmonic discourse involves the establishment, prolongation and shift of pitch centres which are pitch-levels or pitch-classes, acting as points of departure, frames or goals of linear gestures within hierarchically structured lines. In these three bars the pitch-class Eb is predominant, but F♯ also functions to a lesser degree as a centre (ex. 1). Local hierarchies are determined by the following means:

(a) The grouping of tones into triads: the set divides into two inversionally related hexachords, each of which is partitioned into two trichords through the vertical spacing of its elements, yielding in both cases a major and a minor triad related by a minor sixth, as in the upbeat to b. 1:

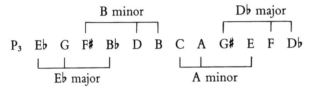

(b) The emphasis of pitch-class centres which function both as members of triads and independently of them (ex. 1). This is achieved by:

registral disposition: the predominant lines of chordal textures being the highest and lowest;

the bass line supporting the overall tonal movement in a manner analogous to that of tonality;

---

4 My use of the term 'prolongation' in relation to Schoenberg's twelve-tone works is unrelated to the idea of Schenkerian *Ursatz*, and does not imply structural levels integral to one another. In this context prolongation refers to pitch-levels, pitch-classes, or referential configurations whose position of priority within the structure is exercised even when they are not literally present. Tonal prolongation involves a small number of prolongational types (namely the passing-note, the neighbour-note, and the arpeggiation), which provide a consistent set of relationships between tones of lesser and greater structural weight (see Straus, 'The Problem of Prolongation in Post-Tonal Music', p. 4). Although such simplicity and consistency of prolongational types has no equivalent in Schoenberg's twelve-tone music, this does not imply that prolongation as embellishment or diminution is totally absent. On the contrary, the music abounds in gestures reminiscent of tonal melodic modality. Often contour, rhythm, and articulation contribute to evoke conventionalized formulae, such as cadential leading-notes, appoggiatura gestures, and 'nota-cambiata' figures. The hierarchies delineated by these figures are however unsupported by a consonance–dissonance syntax. In view of the absence of many of the fundamental features of tonal prolongation from much post-tonal music, Straus proposes that a more reliable basis for describing its voice leading is that of contextually associated as opposed to prolonged pitch-levels (ibid., p. 13). The 'associational model' makes no a priori claims regarding the pitches that intervene between the associated ones (ibid., p. 15), and can operate in music which makes no reference to any common practice of harmony or voice leading (ibid., p. 8). Straus's model can deal with procedures which have their roots in two different areas of traditional practice: tonal prolongation and motivic association (ibid., pp. 15–17). Yet since this study is particularly concerned with matters of historical derivation, and since in Schoenberg's twelve-tone music, remnants of tonal voice leading (primarily in the form of characteristic gestures, large-scale semitonal leading-notes, and fifth support to tonal centres) play such an important part in defining structures, I prefer to retain the term 'prolongation' stripped of its strict technical characteristics for discussing procedures concerning hierarchical pitch organization in order to distinguish them from those which have their origin in motivic association.

Ex. 2.1

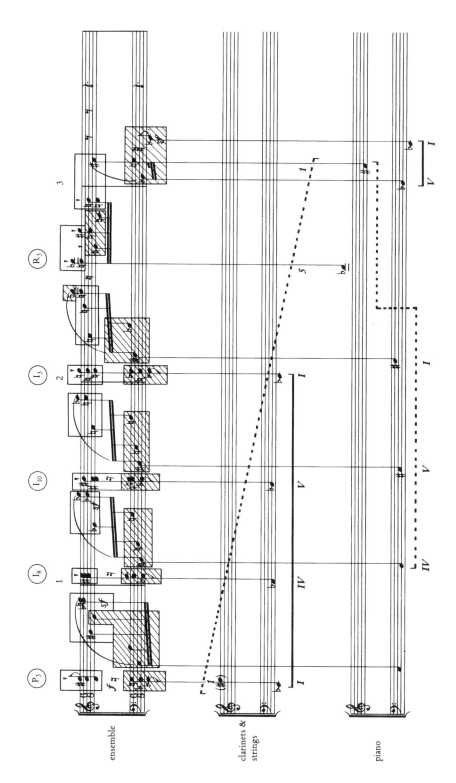

progression supporting E♭ as pitch-class centre
progression supporting F♯ as pitch-class centre
triads

the functional deployment of an implied 5:1 linear relation to support pitch-class centres;

the borrowing of the bass line idiom of tonal cadence; e.g., the bass progression *IV–V–I* on strong beats reinforces E♭, while the same progression on weak beats strengthens F♯, the secondary pitch-class centre;

the consistent deployment of the hierarchical relations of metric structure; e.g., those elements which support the establishment of E♭ as a pitch-class centre occur on the beat while those which tend to a lesser extent to reinforce F♯ are off the beat;

the functional use of timbre; e.g., at b. 1–2, E♭ elements are played by clarinets and strings, F♯ elements by the piano;

the functional deployment of textures consisting of contrasting components; e.g., at b. 1–2, chord progressions support E♭ while arpeggios articulate F♯ elements;

placing pitch-class centres at the extreme points of groupings; e.g., in b. 1–3, E♭ and F♯ appear respectively both as the first and final notes of the top and bass lines (ex. 1).

In the 'Ouvertüre', the fifth is used as an interval capable of giving support to pitch-class centres, as in tonal music. The linear deployment of the relation 5:1 or *V:I* in terms of an implicit scale is central to many sections of this movement. Yet, since no explicit scale is established as a stable referential background, since tonal centres are not fundamentals of triads, and since the circle of fifths – the standard measure of distance in tonality – has no significance in this context, the emphasis of pitch-class centres does not have the functional implications of harmonic degree associated with the tonal system. For instance, the displacement of the tonal predominance of E♭ in the first subject group by F♯ in the second subject group is not to be understood as having the functional implications of a tonal modulation from *I* to *III* but only as a relative change in the hierarchy of the elements which have a referential function within the chromatic aggregate.

The first full draft of the opening of the 'Ouvertüre' – dated 28 October 1924 – does not show b. 1–4, but commences on b. 5 of the final version and stops half-way through a different version of the first stretto (ex. 2). This draft starts with a phrase which includes the only presentation of the twelve-tone set in melodic form in the 'Ouvertüre', b. 5–7 in the final version. This melody with its accompanying voices, which are based on I_8 and I_{10}, contribute to the unfolding of the sets involved in the first bar of the final version (cf. exx. 1 and 2).[5] But none of the preliminary sketches contains any indication of the function of F♯ as a secondary pitch-class centre. Schoenberg resumed work on

---

5 A set matrix is included in ex. 11.

Ex. 2.2

partial transcription of MS 576

the movement on 17 June 1925, after completing the 'Tanzschritte', starting with b. 1–3 in the final version. The absence from the first draft of the central harmonic idea of the movement may be the reason behind the long interruption which separates the first sketches from their continuation, supporting the interpretation that b. 1–3 are a synthesis of those relations which will be developed in the composition.

Prolongation and development in the first group

The identification of the first group as the section extending from b. 1 to b. 28 is supported both by changes in the local hierarchy of pitch-class centres which occur at b. 29–35, where the relative predominance of F$\sharp$ is eventually established, and by changes in the type of thematic material. Here, the term 'prolongational' is used in relation to relatively unambiguous, and therefore stable sections which establish the predominance of a single pitch-class centre or referential configuration,[6] and the term 'developmental' in relation to more dynamic sections where the pitch-class centre hierarchy is ambiguous or in constant change.

The first twenty-five bars of the first group only use those forms of the set and their retrogrades which appear in b. 1–3 (i.e., P_3, I_3, I_8, and I_{10}).[7] From b. 7 to b. 28, the unfolding thematic material alternates between contrapuntal and chordal textures.[8] These two contrasting types shape the section by successively focusing on particular prolongational or developmental processes.

Contrapuntal type

The three predominantly contrapuntal passages of the first group can be classed as stretti in view of their combinatorial treatment of motivic material.[9]

First stretto   The first stretto (b. 7/ii–14) gains its intensity from the gradual diversification of its textural constituents (ex. 3):

6 The defining elements of a 'referential configuration' in the pitch domain can be pitch-class, registral pitch, intervallic content, and/or spacing of chords. A 'referential configuration' may include a pitch-class centre, but not all the members in a configuration need be of the same hierarchical status; e.g. in the second group of subjects of the 'Ouvertüre', F$\sharp$ is the predominant pitch-class centre but functions as part of a 'referential configuration' which also includes B (this is further discussed on p. 61 of this chapter).

7 This interpretation is supported by Schoenberg's set labelling in the manuscript. As explained on p. 71, given the unusually high number of invariant segments of the set other interpretations are also possible.

8 The terminology adopted for the discussion of texture is based on that coined by Berry (*Structural Functions in Music*) and Hall ('Texture in the Violin Concertos of Stravinsky, Berg, Schoenberg and Bartók'). A 'textural component' comprises all those lines and strands which function as a group within a texture. The defining characteristic of a textural component is that its lines contextually function as a group. The term 'textural strand' is used here as an intermediate category between 'line' and 'component' to refer to those lines which function as a group within a single component. In the discussion of textural types, the term 'contrapuntal' indicates 'a condition of interlinear interaction involving intervallic content, direction, rhythm and other qualities or parameters of diversification'. Berry, *Structural Functions in Music*, p. 192

9 The characterization of these passages as stretti has been previously made by Hugh Wood in his thematic analysis of the 'Ouvertüre' included in the miniature score of the Septet published by Universal Edition.

56

Ex. 2.3

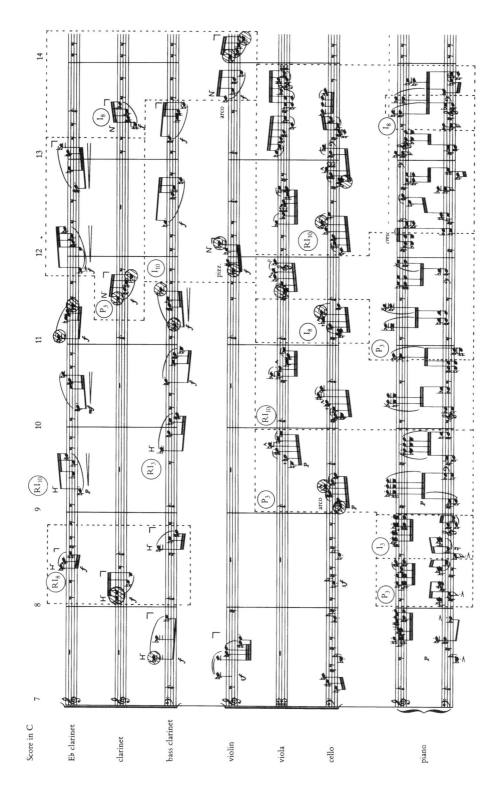

from b. 7/ii to 10, the three clarinets contribute to a single textural line successively, but from b. 10/ii their entries overlap;

similarly, the successive entries of the viola and cello which initially contribute to a single textural line overlap at b. 12;

the violin line starting at b. 11 as an extension of the clarinet line in turn overlaps with the E♭ clarinet, further contributing to the creation of textural complexity.

Each textural strand consists of distinct rhythmic groupings repeated at varying distances which continuously change their position in relation to the beat. The rhythmic web which results from the combination of the various strands causes the blurring of the basic metre. The progressive contraction of the entry-point of each rhythmic grouping contributes to the intensity of the passage, providing a contrast to the more stable rhythm of the previous section.

The predominant placement of E♭ and B♭ at the beginning and end, and/or at the highest or lowest points of rhythmic groupings, occurring in more than one octave, results in the saturation of the texture by this dyad (see the circled notes in ex. 3). The prolongation of E♭ is primarily achieved through a process of rhythmic and textural animation. The relatively stable pitch-centre hierarchy of this passage counterbalances its rhythmic and textural drive.

Second stretto   The second stretto (b. 17–21) is relatively more stable due to the reduction of textural strands: while the first stretto involves two textural components one of which consists of two textural strands, the second stretto has two components each consisting of a single homogeneous strand. The motif played by the clarinets and strings is based on the dotted-quaver figures of the *Hauptstimme* at b. 6–7. The distance of imitation is regular with only one change at the end of b. 18, where the B♭ entry is deferred by a quaver, resulting in the metrical displacement of the complete pattern of imitative entries.

Although entries of the motif occur on seven different pitch-classes, the E♭–B♭ pair becomes predominant as a consequence of its registral placement at the highest points of the *Hauptstimme* (violin b. 17–18 and E♭ clarinet b. 19 and 21). Furthermore E♭ is given prominence by the articulation of D–E♭ as a leading-note relation between the last note of the *Hauptstimme* of the chordal section and the first one of the second stretto (b. 17, E♭ clarinet & violin).

The semiquaver figures at the end of this stretto provide a reference back to the ending of the first stretto; cf. the clarinet and violin figures indicated in ex. 4. The first stretto ends on a B♭, but by exploiting segmental invariants between set forms, Schoenberg brings the second stretto to a close on E♭, thus creating a large-scale *V:I* relation (ex. 4).

Ex. 2.4

ending of stretto 1 (E♭ to B♭)

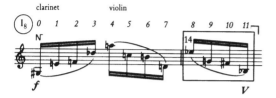

ending of stretto 2 (B♭ to E♭)

Third stretto The third stretto (b. 21–27) focuses on the movement from E♭ to F♯ and in this sense functions similarly to a transition section in classical sonata form. The recessive textural and rhythmic tendencies started in the second stretto are further stressed here.[10] Its beginning (b. 21–22) is texturally similar to that of the second stretto. The motivic material, which relates to the *Hauptstimme* at b. 5, appears in overlapping imitations at the distance of five quavers. Although the *Hauptstimme* of this passage leads to E♭ (b. 24), the piling up of motivic entries reaches its highest point on F♯⁴ (E♭ clarinet at b. 23). F♯ is further projected by the passage starting at b. 25, in which the accompanimental motif of the clarinet, viola, and cello parts of b. 23–24 is sequentially repeated until F♯⁴ is reached once more by the E♭ clarinet, b. 27.[11]

10 According to Hall, 'a directed series of changes within a certain texture can have either the effect of growth (accumulation of tension) or recession (relaxation) in one or more aspects of texture' (Hall, 'Texture in the Violin Concertos of Stravinsky, Berg, Schoenberg and Bartók', p. 10). 'In general, processes of growth or intensification involve an increase in complexity and diversification, while reduction in the number of textural constituents and homogeneity contribute towards relaxation. . .[However,] no general classification according to degrees of complexity is possible, because the factors creating complexity, even when they are measurable, are incommensurable.' (ibid., p. 7)

11 According to Buccheri, 'sequence' 'is evident when, in a succession of row statements, each statement is disposed in the same pattern but at different pitch levels' ('An Approach to 12-Tone Music: Articulation of Serial Pitch Units in Piano Works of Schoenberg, Krenek, Dallapiccola and Rochberg', p. 51). In this instance, each half of the *Hauptstimme* at b. 25 is a retrograde of hexachord (6. . .11), while the *Hauptstimme* at b. 26–27 consists of transpositions and inversions of hexachord (3. . .8).

Chordal type

The bass line of the chordal introduction to the 'Ouvertüre' contains an interlocking presentation of two transpositions of a four-note motif characterized by ending with a major second followed by a fifth, imitating the stereotyped bass line of tonal cadence, hence referred to as the 'cadential motif' (see b. 1–2 in ex. 5). Since major seconds are not available within the hexachord and fifths are

Ex. 2.5

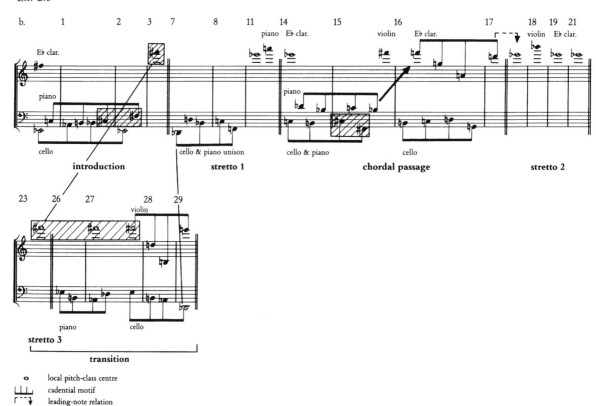

not present as a succession in the set, Schoenberg always extracts the cadential motif from combinations of sets. This motif is primarily associated with the chordal sections which elaborate the vertical thematic elements, e.g. b. 1–2 and 14–17, but it also appears in combination with imitative textures, e.g. b. 7–8 (cello and piano in unison) and a variant of the motif at b. 26–29 (piano and cello successively).

At the beginning of the movement the pair of interlocking cadential motifs appears in the low register, but only the lower one remains in its original registral position throughout (ex. 5). The upper member of the pair gradually moves upwards until it reaches the highest register at b. 16, where it performs a leading-note function as opposed to its original bass-line cadential role (ex. 5).

The appearances of the motif in the bottom register between b. 7 and 29 tend to project either D♭ and/or F♯ giving bass-line support to the establishment of F♯² at b. 23. Ex. 5 shows that following the opening bass-line cadence at b. 3, bottom D♭ becomes the absolute lower limit of the arch described by the appearances of the motif.

At b. 14, the registral distribution of pitch-class centres of the opening chordal section is reversed, so that E♭– formerly the pitch-class centre of the lower line – becomes that of the top line of the pair, and conversely F♯ – formerly the pitch-class centre of the top line – becomes that of the lower one. Note that the figure projecting F♯ at b. 14–15, C–B–C♯–F♯, which formerly appeared on weak beats in the middle register at b. 1–2, here appears on strong beats in the bass line, contributing to the shift in the pitch-class hierarchy (ex. 5).

The material of the second group

Unlike the first group, which focuses on the establishment of a hierarchy of pitch-class centres and the gradual displacement of the originally predominant pitch-class centre by the secondary one, in the second group the tendency is to prolong a referential configuration around which subordinate ones revolve. Although F♯ is the predominant pitch-class centre at the beginning of the second group, it is constantly associated with B as boundaries of linear groupings; therefore, it seems more appropriate to regard this section as prolonging the referential configuration F♯–B and not only F♯. The unfolding of lines centred on F♯ introduces new set forms and up-beat-like gestures which strongly project the final pitch of groupings; e.g. at b. 32, F♯² is approached as the last member of RI₆. Until this point the 'Ouvertüre' uses exclusively the group of set forms, and their retrogrades, presented in the introduction.

The melodic line which articulates the F♯² pitch-level centre swiftly covers one and a half octaves, b. 29–32, delineating multiple lines which will be given independent continuations (ex. 6). After projecting the movement from F♯²

Ex. 2.6

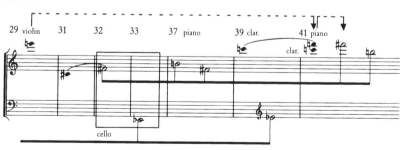

♪	prolonged pitch-class centre or referential configuration
⌢	fifth support
⌐ ¯ ¬	registral association
⌐ ¯ ↓	leading-note relation

to B² (b. 35–37), the treble branches into a pair of lines: one of its members setting out from the F#² centre functions as the bottom line of a strand consisting of repeated chords played by the piano, while the other triggers a series of quasi-sequential imitative continuations which repeatedly reach C⁴. C⁴ provides fifth support to F⁴, which in turn retrospectively gives a leading-note function to the prominent E⁴ at b. 29. F⁴, supported by C⁴ and C⁵, becomes the secondary pitch centre of the second group (b. 41–43 and 53–58).

The first theme of the second group (b. 29–35) introduces two non-triadic chordal types. One of these results from the tetrachordal segmentation of the set. Since the last tetrachord of the set is a transposed retrograde of the first, there are only two distinct tetrachords in the set in terms of intervallic content (ex. 7a). Here, these two tetrachords are analogically treated as 'stable harmonic formations' while all the other chords are treated as if 'dissonant'. At b. 33, the first G of the *Hauptstimme* functions as a foreign note within the chord (ex. 7b, chord 2a). Similarly, the first Db of the *Hauptstimme* at b. 34 functions as a 'dissonant anticipation' which resolves on the following chord (ex. 7b, chord 1b). Thus, the relation between the vertical and horizontal elements involves metaphoric references to dissonant suspension and melodic ornamentation in traditional counterpoint.

The other non-triadic stable chordal type, which characterizes b. 41–46 and b. 53–62, results from the combination of trichordal segments from pairs of sets. Since the set consists of a succession of equivalent trichords (ex. 8a), the one-to-one combination of trichordal segments of any pair of set forms invariably results in a succession of four hexachords which share the same interval vector (e.g., ex. 8b).[12] The resulting hexachords are presented here as if they were stable or 'consonant' harmonic formations. Since the succession of trichordal segments from each set is articulated by a single textural component, the rhythmic coincidence or displacement of the trichords of one textural component in relation to those of the other results in either 'consonant'/stable or 'dissonant'/unstable formations, and thus creates functions which resemble traditional 'dissonant suspension' and 'resolution'; e.g., b. 42 (ex. 8b).

In the second group, the most significant bass-line events in terms of its large-scale structure occur at the beginning and end. The placement of Eb as the bass note of the chord which harmonizes the F# pitch-class centre (ex. 6: b. 33), represents a large-scale continuation of the basic harmonic relations of the first group. The other structurally important bass-line event is the *V:I* cadence on D (b. 65–66) which prepares for the bass-line pitch-class centre of the beginning of the 'Ländler'. But, unlike the first group, the tonal unfolding of the new thematic material in the second group proper generally does not involve bass-line support.

12 In this case these are hexachord 1a [0, 1, 2, 3, 6, 9] and hexachord 1b [0, 1, 3, 4, 6, 7], which are Z-related, i.e. they share the same interval vector though they are not equivalent under transposition or inversion; see Forte (*The Structure of Atonal Music*).

Ex. 2.7

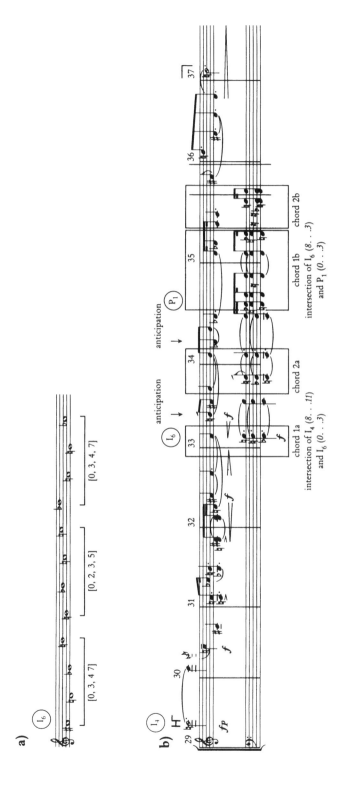

Ex. 2.8

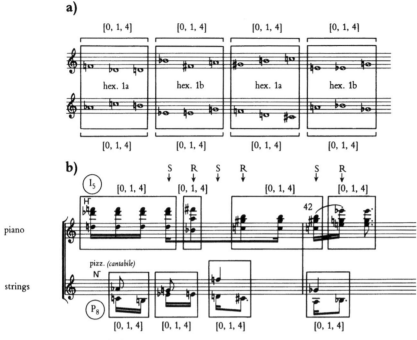

S   'suspension'

R   'resolution'

The fact that the second group, unlike the first group, does not involve cadential formulae based on fifths seems related to the decision to present an almost literally inverted version of this material in the recapitulation (b. 141–161).[13] Axial inversion precludes the use of cadential formulae based on fifths, since their character is radically distorted under inversion. Since the inversion takes place across a single inversional axis, there is only a single set of inversional dyads, as follows:

$$D \quad C\sharp \quad C \quad B \quad B\flat \quad A$$

interval-class   1   3   5   5   3   1

$$E\flat \quad E \quad F \quad F\sharp \quad G \quad G\sharp$$

The general linear pattern of the exposition of the second group is the movement away from F♯ via B, while in the recapitulation the reverse process (i.e. the movement from the pitch-class centre B via F♯) is systematically accomplished by virtue of the properties of twelve-tone inversion (ex. 9). As

---

13 The term 'recapitulation' is used here to refer to the section usually towards the end of a movement where the restatement of thematic material from previous sections takes place. The term 'reprise' is used for the procedures of almost strict, and/or functionally modified, restatement and the term 'elaboration' for restatements which involve a further degree of thematic transformation.

Ex. 2.9

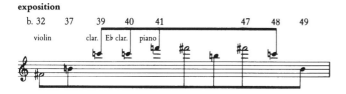

explained above, F♯–B is the main referential configuration of the second group, while F–C is the secondary referential dyad. An examination of the above diagram shows that the dyads C–F and F♯–B both invert as interval-class five, which seems related to the choice of these two dyads as the two referential pitch-class configurations in the second group. Thus, the recapitulation reverses the linear movement of the exposition by reaching F♯ via B and C via F (ex. 9).

Continuity and textural types

The first and second groups of subjects unfold in phrases defined by duration, distinct textural treatment, motivic material, and cadential gestures. Melodic statements, which are relatively short, only occur at the beginning of the first and second groups (b. 4–7, 29–35 and 47–49) and are followed by more extensive passages overflowing with contrapuntal activity. A substantial part of the first and second groups of subjects consists of combinatorial textures exhibiting a great variety of modes of continuation. Generally, these textures consist of at least two distinct components defined by a combination of distinctive elements such as harmony, type of figuration, motivic material, registral lines, and/or timbre.

Multi-layered texture

The texture of the first stretto (ex. 3: b. 7/ii–14) exemplifies one of the most characteristic types in the movement:

E♭ clarinet and bass-clarinets articulate imitations of tetrachord (*0. . .3*) or its equivalent (i.e. tetrachord (*8. . .11*)) and a single rhythmic motif;

the viola and cello imitatively combine in the presentation of pairs of equivalent segments related either by transposition or inversion articulated by a figure consisting of five or six semiquavers;

the clarinet and violin strand consists of groups of four semiquavers, which articulate tetrachordal segments. This strand does not exhibit strong distinctive features and is in this sense subordinate to the others;

the piano articulates two pairs of lines moving in sixths and delineating pairs of semiquaver groupings differing from each other in their articulation and contour. These pairs, which are organized as either imitative or contour-inverted repetitions do not radically differ from the material of the other strands but stand apart as a consequence of the distinctive colour of the parallel sixths.

The overall texture comprises two main components: clarinets and strings contribute to one component, while the piano material constitutes the other. Each component articulates a set of contrapuntal strands, which contribute to its identity and shaping. The passages extending from b. 17 to b. 22 and from b. 36 to b. 40 respectively are other instances of this type of multi-layered texture.

Interchange of textural components

Another important textural type in the 'Ouvertüre' involves the timbral and/or registral interchange of textural components. This type characterizes large sections of the movement, in particular the second group; e.g., in the section marked 'grazioso' (b. 41–46), an inversion of the material of the string pair is transferred to the piano and an inversion of the piano material is immediately passed to the clarinets, while the strings introduce a new component. This type of textural process also takes place at the level of large-scale organization, affecting the elaboration of texture in the recapitulation; e.g., in the reprise of the b. 37–46 at b. 149–158, the repeated chord component which first appears on the clarinets is immediately taken over by the strings and finally by the piano. Textural continuation within single phrases is also affected by this process, as can be observed towards the end of the first group (b. 23–27). The melodic lines articulated by the viola and cello are inverted by the piano, which repeats them interchanging their registral placement.

Stationary and moving types

The categories of 'stationary and moving types' are useful for classifying the function of textural types in Schoenberg's works.[14] Although these categories

---

14 The categories 'stationary and moving types' appear in the prospectus to the *Gedanke* MS., dated 5 June 1934. A facsimile and a transcription are given in Goehr, 'Schoenberg's *Gedanke* Manuscript', p. 8.

overlap in many ways with those of 'prolongational and developmental processes' discussed on p. 56 of this chapter, the latter refer strictly to processes in the pitch domain. The textures discussed on pp. 65–6 could be classified as moving types. In *Fundamentals*, Schoenberg described a specific instance of what I call 'stationary type', the pedal point, as follows:

> Though the *pedal point* is often used in masterpieces for expressive or pictorial purpose, its real meaning should be a constructive one. In this sense one finds it at the end of a transition or an elaboration, emphasizing the end of a previous modulation and preparing for the reintroduction of the tonic. In such cases the effect of the pedal point should be one of retardation: it holds back the forward progress of the harmony. Another constructive use of such retardation of the harmonic movement is to balance remote motival variation (a method paralleled by the balancing of centrifugal harmony with simpler motival variation).[15]
>
> The end of the liquidation is generally marked by a combination of repose and suspense: repose through the cessation of the modulatory movement; suspense in anticipation of the re-entrance of the theme. At this point, the retarding effect of a pedal point is appropriate; it keeps at least the bass from progressing. As an inverted pedal, it can also be a sustained or repeated note in another voice. The pedal can be developed into a pedal figure (. . .an ostinato-like figuration).[16]

In the context of the 'Ouvertüre', the 'effect of retardation' of pedal textures does not refer to an implied or expected resolution. Its function is similar to that of a long *fermata* on a 'roving' or ambiguous harmony in tonality. According to Schoenberg, the effect of such a long hold or 'pause resides in the suspense created by the question: "What will happen now that is different from before?"'.[17] Such a turning point is the passage extending from b. 52 to b. 62. The piano continues the stretto started at b. 51 (based on the accompanying motifs of b. 5 and 6), which in combination with the string chords turn into an ostinato by the end of the bar. In the following bar, one strand of the piano figuration is transferred to the E♭ clarinet and clarinet, and the other is taken by the viola and cello, while the piano itself starts an ostinato on a contracted version of the motif. Two harmonic features characterize the whole passage:

each textural line revolves around a limited collection of pitch-classes and/or projects a single pitch-class; e.g., at b. 53–54 E♭ clarinet and clarinet play only F♯–A–F–A♯–C♯–D, while the piano figures always start with a G♯–E–B–G chord, which strongly projects its bass note;

15 Schoenberg, *Fundamentals*, p. 31
16 Ibid., p. 153
17 Schoenberg, *Harmonielehre*, p. 209

the 'cadential-motif' pervades b. 55–63, delineating a multiplicity of pitch-class centres, e.g., E–F♯–A♭–D♭ played by the piano and cello at b. 55–56.

The combination of ostinato and pedal-tone technique with motivic imitation results in an extreme type of textural activity in which linear and motivic tendencies tend to cancel each other. This process of textural and harmonic saturation concludes in a twelve-tone pedal, at b. 59–62, which neutralizes the 'roving' linear tendencies and loosens motivic identity, fixing the registral placement of each pitch class and momentarily suspending linear activity.

The formal crux: the retransition

In Schoenberg's writings, the term 'retransition' appears in two different connections: the small connecting segments, which act as both 'bridges' and 'spacers' in the return from subordinate to principal themes in rondos,[18] and the section towards the close of the sonata-allegro *Durchführung* which prepares for the appearance of the recapitulation.[19] In *Fundamentals*, Schoenberg described the technique of tonal retransition as involving 'the reduction of motive-forms to minimum content, and the presence of relatively long sections stressing the dominant or some other suitable upbeat chord'.[20] The substantial passage which links the 'Ländler' elaboration and its reprise, b. 125–140, involves similar procedures to those of a tonal retransition.

The recapitulation starts with an almost literal contour and pitch-class inversion of the first three phrases of the second group. In the inverted reprise, the pitch-class centre of the exposition, F♯, is replaced by B; accordingly, the principal referential configuration, formerly F♯ leading to B, becomes B leading to F♯. In the exposition, the F♯ pitch-class centre is introduced as the last pitch-class of the inversion starting with E (I_4). According to the inversional scheme of the reprise, B is to be reached as the last pitch-class of the prime starting with D♭ (i.e. P_1) and for that reason the bass gives prominence to D♭ (ex. 10a).

In b. 125–131, the first and third *Nebenstimme* figures start and end with D♭ and C♯ respectively, while the *Hauptstimme* revolves around an A♭$^{-1}$ pedal (ex. 10c). According to the largely symmetrical harmonic construction of phrases in the 'Ländler', two bars projecting D♭ followed by four bars centred around A♭ should have been complemented by a two-bar return to D♭. But the cadence on D♭ is interrupted by a two-bar stretto based on first-group material, which projects E♭, b. 131–132.

Had the upbeat gesture led straight into b. 141, two important requirements of the retransition as defined above would not have been achieved. The first requirement concerns the 'liquidation' of motif-forms, which according to Schoenberg can be achieved by 'gradually depriving' them 'of their characteris-

18 Schoenberg, *Fundamentals*, p. 181
19 Ibid., p. 209
20 Ibid., p. 209

Ex. 2.10

tic features and dissolving them into uncharacteristic forms'.[21] The second arises from the dynamic harmonic scheme of the elaboration of the 'Ländler', which as explained in Schoenberg's description of retransition, demands stabilization by a substantial section.[22] The establishment of D♭ starts within the 'liquidation' of the 'Ländler' theme with the piano left-hand figuration at b. 114–121. From b. 114 to the final cadence, b. 141 inclusive, there are twenty-eight bars, the same duration in bars as the complete first group. Therefore the interpolation of the two-bar stretto fulfils the requirement for formal balance in terms of

21 Ibid., p. 152
22 Schoenberg refers to this requirement when stating that the retransition should be a 'relatively long section' in the aforementioned quotation from *Fundamentals*.

the symmetries of the movement while referring to the E♭ priority at the beginning of the movement before the recapitulation proper begins.

The movement towards D♭ is resumed in the next phrase (b. 133–140), which initially embarks on the imitative treatment of the E♭ clarinet and bass-clarinet motif of the first stretto (b. 8–14), in combination with a sequence of chords, which have the 'cadential motif' on D♭ as bass (ex. 10b). Linear features become 'liquidated' in the continuation, b. 137–140, thus fulfilling the first requirement set by Schoenberg for the retransition. This passage consists of a succession of pairs of complementary six-note chords distributed among the three instrumental groups according to a fixed pattern which delineate a bass progression on strong beats leading towards D♭ (ex. 10b). The upbeat drive of this intense cadential gesture is interrupted on the fifth semiquaver of b. 139 on a chord a semitone higher than its final goal, i.e. the downbeat of b. 141 (ex. 10b), giving rise to a further interpolation. This is an almost literal contour and pitch inversion of the bar which precedes the exposition of the second group, i.e. bar 28. The very skilful construction of this link is based on the exploitation of the derivational properties of the set.[23] The link is so constructed that when pitch and contour inversion are applied, the two passages intersect on the same final chord. The inversional derivation of b. 141 is projected registrally through the use of the bottom D♭ – instead of the previous top E – as the pitch which carries the *Hauptstimme*; cf. b. 29 and b. 141 (ex. 10a & b).

The series of interpolations starting on the 'interrupted cadence' at b. 131, which elaborate first-group material and function as a sonata-allegro *Durchführ-ung*, and the important axes of formal symmetry which meet in the retransition contribute to make this section the point of convergence for a great variety of thematic processes, and the most intricate section of the work in terms of thematic diversity and formal structure.

Set invariants and phrase construction in the 'Ländler' theme

This section first examines some of the general features of the set which deter-mine the particular type of harmonic syntax of the 'Ouvertüre', and then explores the manner in which the symmetries of the set are turned into a constructional feature in the 'Ländler' theme.

The source hexachord of the set, [0, 1, 4, 5, 8, 9], is the third-order all-combinatorial hexachord (ex. 11).[24] This hexachord does not contain interval-class 6 and is the only all-combinatorial hexachord which excludes interval-class

---

23 The derivational properties of the set are discussed on pp. 71–4 of this chapter.
24 For an informal definition of Babbitt's four categories of all-combinatorial hexachords, see Babbitt, 'Some Aspects of Twelve-Tone Composition', pp. 57–8. For a more formal treatment of the subject, see Babbitt, 'Set Structure as a Compositional Determinant', p. 135.

Ex. 2.11

| | | U8 I₃ | | | | | | | | | | | |

T	P₃	Eb	G	F♯	Bb	D	B ‖	C	A	Ab	E	F	Db
$T^{-6}/=T/_{+3}$		B	Eb	D	F♯	Bb	G ‖	Ab	F	E	C	Db	A
$T^{+6}/=T/_{-3}$		C	E	Eb	G	B	Ab ‖	A	F♯	F	Db	D	Bb
$T^{4}/=T/_5$		Ab	C	B	Eb	G	E ‖	F	D	Db	A	Bb	F♯
$T^{-2}/=T/_{+7}$		E	Ab	G	B	Eb	C ‖	Db	Bb	A	F	F♯	D
$T^{-3}/=T/_{-6}$		G	B	Bb	D	F♯	Eb ‖	E	Db	C	Ab	A	F
$T^{-3}/=T/_{+6}$		F♯	Bb	A	Db	F	D ‖	Eb	C	B	G	Ab	E
$T+4$		A	Db	C	E	Ab	F ‖	F♯	Eb	D	Bb	B	G
$T^{5}/=T/_4$		Bb	D	Db	F	A	F♯ ‖	G	E	Eb	B	C	Ab
$T^{+7}/=T/_{-2}$		D	F♯	F	A	Db	Bb ‖	B	Ab	G	Eb	E	C
$T^{-7}/=T/_{+2}$		Db	F	E	Ab	C	A ‖	Bb	G	F♯	D	Eb	B
$T^{+2}/=T/_{-7}$		F	A	Ab	C	E	Db ‖	D	B	Bb	F♯	G	Eb

2 (interval vector (303630)). It also contains the maximum possible number of interval-class 4, a characteristic only shared with the otherwise very different whole-tone hexachord. The limited number of intervals available within this hexachord is further reduced in the linear ordering of the set, which does not include interval-class 5:

	Eb	G	F♯	Bb	D	B	C	A	Ab	E	F	Db
interval-class		4	1	4	4	3	1	3	1	4	1	4

The source hexachord of the set can be derived by applying the customary twelve-tone operations to any of the following source trichords: [0, 1, 4], [0, 1, 5], [0, 3, 7], and [0, 4, 8]. It is a peculiarity of this hexachord that all its trichordal partitions result in two subsets which represent one of the mentioned source trichords. In the 'Ouvertüre', where trichordal partition is prominent, this results in passages which consist of successions and/or superimpositions of equivalent subsets, e.g., b. 26–27 (ex. 12), and in the case of source set [0, 3, 7] in pairs consisting of a major and minor triad.

The ordering of the set is such that under the customary twelve-tone operations the number of invariant segments is unusually high; e.g., it is possible to ascribe the segment Eb–G–F♯–Bb to four different set forms:

P₃	<u>Eb</u>	<u>G</u>	<u>F♯</u>	<u>Bb</u>	D	B	C	A	G♯	E	F	C♯
R₅	<u>Eb</u>	<u>G</u>	<u>F♯</u>	<u>Bb</u>	B	D	C♯	E	C	G♯	A	F
RI₁₀	C	G♯	A	F	E	C♯	D	B	<u>Eb</u>	<u>G</u>	<u>F♯</u>	<u>Bb</u>
I₈	G♯	E	F	C♯	A	C	B	D	<u>Eb</u>	<u>G</u>	<u>F♯</u>	<u>Bb</u>

Ex. 2.12

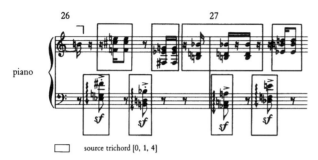

☐ source trichord [0, 1, 4]

Only in a few cases can aggregates be ascribed to a single set form unequivocally. The weakening of set-form identity in the composition, due to the large number of invariants, has far-reaching compositional consequences; for in general, the fabric of the music seems to result from the combination of invariant segments common to a large number of set forms.

In the 'Ländler' theme, the symmetries of the set are turned into a constructional feature by making formal symmetries coincide with set invariants. Its two phrases (b. 70–79 and b. 80–89) follow the same formal pattern: four-bar antecedent + four-bar consequent + two-bar extension. The *Hauptstimme* and the accompaniment are each based on permutations of a single hexachord.

In the *Hauptstimme* of the first phrase, the first and last tetrachord of the antecedent are retrograded in the consequent.

antecedent (b. 70–73)

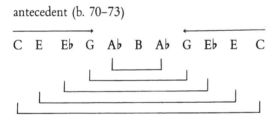

consequent (b. 74–77)

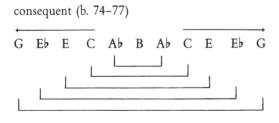

The *Hauptstimme* of both the antecedent and consequent consists of a pair of hexachords related by retrograde and consequently starts and ends on the same pitch-class. The framing pitch-classes of the consequent are in a 5:1 relation to those of the antecedent, while the two-bar extension (b. 78–79) brings the line back to its starting pitch-class, i.e. C.

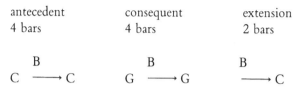

In the second phrase, the *Hauptstimme* of the antecedent starts with the same tetrachord as in the first phrase, but reverses the order of the fifth and sixth pitch-classes, i.e. G♯–B becomes B–A♭. The consequent reproduces the same sequence as b. 70–71 while the two-bar extension retrogrades the first tetrachord of its counterpart in the first phrase (ex. 13).

Ex. 2.13

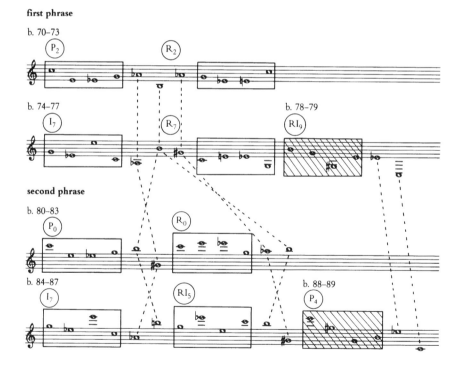

The accompaniment similarly projects set invariants. In the first phrase, the bass of the antecedent delineates *I:V* on D. This is retrograded by its consequent and the two-bar extension resulting in a *V:I* progression. The accompaniment of the first phrase consists of hexachords from different set forms: P₂ (0. . .5), RI₇ (6. . .11) and I₉ (0. . .5). Since the pitch-classes of the bass, i.e. D and A, are members of different trichords in P₂ and RI₇, the dyad which in the first instance followed D appears after A and vice-versa.

bars 70–73	D	F♯	F	A	C♯	B♭
bars 74–77	A	F	F♯	D	C♯	B♭

The accompaniment of the two-bar extension consists of the same succession of pitch-classes as the consequent, though its *Hauptstimme* represents a different set form; this is possible because of the trichordal invariants between I₉ and RI₇.

I₉ (0. . .5)   A   F   F♯ | D   B♭   C♯

RI₇ (6. . .11)   A   F   F♯ | D   C♯   B♭

In the second phrase, the accompaniment progresses in hexachordal – as opposed to the former trichordal – units, and accordingly the rate of harmonic change and number of lines are doubled. The permutations of the same source hexachords are arranged so that in every bar, one of its three semitone dyads is articulated horizontally.

The symmetries of the set and the large number of invariants between different set forms in the 'Ländler' provide the basis for the combinatorial treatment of a small number of pitch and rhythmic motifs. The symmetries in the detail of these themes have a counterpart in the overall design of the Ländler section.

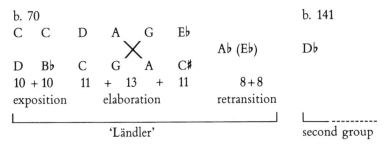

This diagram shows an outline of its formal symmetries and the main pitch-class centres which often are simultaneously active.

The compositional sketches

Preliminary drafts: composing sets and themes

(a) Sketches showing the composition of the twelve-tone set and thematic material of the first group

MS 1186, transcribed in ex. 14, is probably the first sketch of the Septet. The transcribed section contains several drafts which relate to the development of

Ex. 2.14

partial transcription of MS 1186

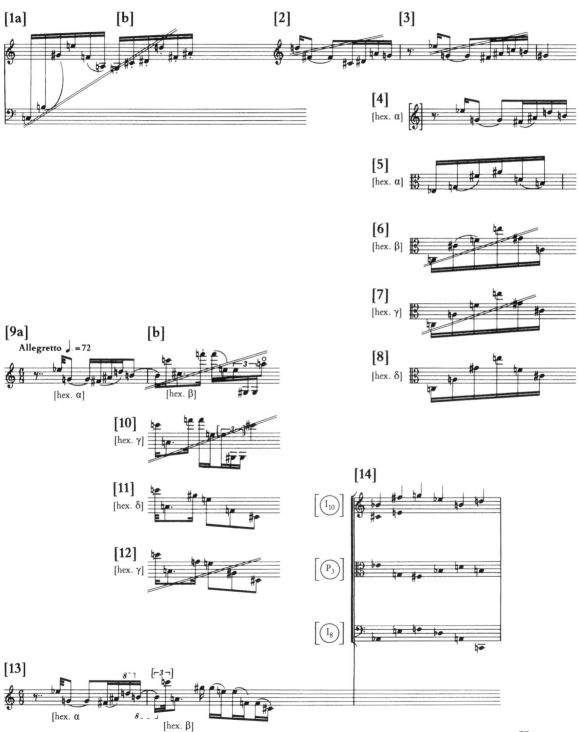

the thematic material of the 'Ouvertüre' first group and the composition of the twelve-tone set. With the exception of draft 14, all the other drafts in the group represent a totally defined musical gesture, involving melodic shape, pitch-levels, rhythm, and articulation. This material will be discussed in five sections, which I believe reflect the chronological order of composition. The suggested chronological sequence is based on analysis and the layout of the material on the page and therefore is only hypothetical.

Stage 1 (MS 1186) In draft 1, Schoenberg sketched a shape using each of the twelve pitch-classes once. He probably found the tonal implications of this shape unsatisfactory because of the rather prominent E major triad, but was still interested in hexachord *(5. . .10)*, whose pitch-classes and dyadic content were retained in draft 2 (exx. 14 and 15). From that point, the minor sixth became a motivic feature. In draft 3, the falling sixth was accommodated within segment *(8. . .2)*[25] of draft 1 by only changing one pitch-class (ex. 15).

Ex. 2.15

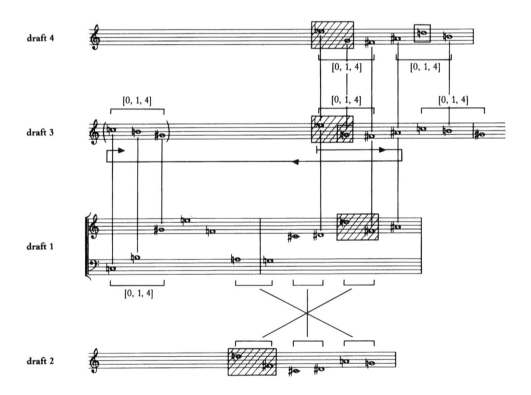

25 Segment *(8. . .2)* comprises pitch-classes with order number *8* to *11* followed by those with order number *0* to *2*.

This new arrangement uses the first trichord of draft 1 without the E major implications and retains the falling sixth without the D major colour of draft 2. Eventually, the pitch-class content of the C–B–G♯ segment was abandoned, but not its intervallic content, which is contained twice in the trichords of draft 4 (ex. 15). Schoenberg discarded the intervallic content of the first three drafts and from there on adopted the pitch-class succession of draft 4 as the definitive version of the first hexachord of the Septet set.

The rhythmic articulation in groups of six semiquavers in draft 1 and the placement of the bar-line after the sixth pitch-class in drafts 2, 3, and 4 suggest that Schoenberg was thinking in terms of hexachordal units. However, the sketches indicate that at this stage he was probably more concerned with the intervallic and motivic identity or even with the tonal implications of these hexachords rather than with their twelve-tone properties; for instance, there is no evidence in the sketches, such as set-tables, to suggest that the replacement of the C of draft 3 by the D in draft 4 responds to twelve-tone considerations, though this change radically alters the combinatorial properties of the material. Similarly, the fact that draft 4 is a representation of the third-order all-combinatorial hexachord, while none of the other hexachords exhibits any special combinatorial properties supports the interpretation that Schoenberg arrived at this hexachord by searching for promising motivic and harmonic possibilities, or at least that the motivic possibilities of the set were an important consideration.[26]

Stage 2 (MS 1186)   Once the first hexachord of the set was established, Schoenberg concentrated on defining the second half of the set, while working on a continuation for draft 4.

In draft 5, Schoenberg rewrote draft 1a using the pitch-class succession of draft 4 and subsequently sketched three different versions for the ordering of its complementary hexachord. These follow the general shape and registral limits of draft 1a (i.e. C^1 to E^3). The following step involved the sketching of four continuations to draft 4 (ex. 14: drafts 9 to 11). In draft 9, the tempo marking and general outline of what would become the first melodic statement of the 'Ouvertüre' (b. 5–7) are already present. In drafts 9b, 10, and 11, Schoenberg tried the pitch-class orderings of drafts 6, 7, and 8 for the continuation of

---

26 Drafts 1 to 4 each represent a different source hexachord, as follows:

	source hexachord	interval vector
draft 1*	[0, 1, 3, 4, 7, 8]	(313431)
draft 2	[0, 1, 2, 5, 6, 8]	(322332)
draft 3	[0, 1, 2, 5, 6, 9]	(313431)
draft 4	[0, 1, 4, 5, 8, 9]	(303630)

* The source hexachords of drafts 1 and 3 have the same intervallic vector, though they are not reducible to the same prime form. In Forte's nomenclature, these are called 'Z-related sets' (Forte, *The Structure of Atonal Music*, p. 21).

draft 9a, while modifying its contour and/or rhythm in each successive version. In drafts 10 and 12, we can observe Schoenberg's efforts to contradict the straightforward triadic arrangement of the hexachord by registrally associating pitch-classes which do not form triads. Schoenberg was probably not satisfied with the triadic arrangement of drafts 7, 10, and 12 nor with the limited intervallic content of drafts 5 and 9b (i.e. their only interval-classes are 1 and 4), all of which he crossed out. The ordering of drafts 8 and 11 was eventually adopted as the second hexachord of the set.

Stage 3 (MS 576) After deciding on the pitch-class succession for the continuation to draft 4b, Schoenberg continued working on its rhythm, as can be seen in draft 13, which was still to be revised at a later stage as a result of its interplay with the accompaniment. Example 2 shows the version which appears in the only contrapuntal draft of the first group (i.e. MS 576), which is almost identical to the final version except for the rhythm of the violin at b. 3. The rhythmic adjustments were crucial to the formation of aggregates between non-combinatorially related sets, which requires the partition of sets into unequal parts.[27]

Stage 4 (MSS 674, 1183, and 1186) The presence of a draft showing a combination of hexachords in MS 1186 (ex. 14, draft 14) denotes that at some point after defining the first half of the set, Schoenberg began to explore the possibilities of set association. In this instance, the first hexachord of the prime is combined with its inversion at the fifth above and below it. This group of associated sets is a recurring feature in the extant set-tables (e.g. see MS 1183, Plate 15).

This group of set forms is often extended to include the untransposed inversion. Such is the case in MS 674 (ex. 16), a set-table pasted on a piece of cardboard, which may indicate that it was often consulted throughout the composition of the Septet. Horizontally, it consists of the prime followed by all the inversions of the set listed in the order of the untransposed prime, and the vertical arrangement (from top to bottom) shows all the transpositions of the prime listed in the order of the untransposed inversion. The unusual disposition of this set-table indicates a preoccupation with the combination of inversionally related sets, an important feature in the 'Ouvertüre'. Certain pitch-classes are shaded using different colours on the table.[28] One colour was used to identify those pitch-classes which remain unchanged after being inverted; e.g. in both P_3 and I_3 (T and U8 in Schoenberg's notation), the pitch-classes with order number *0* and *7* are respectively Eb and A. The other colour identifies those pitch-classes in the inversions which are related by a perfect fifth to

27 See Hyde, *Schoenberg's Twelve-Tone Harmony*, p. 96.
28 Although I have only had access to black and white reproductions of the sketches, it is possible to infer that two different colours had been used from the different degrees of darkness in the reproductions. The colours in the autograph are represented by different thicknesses of line in the transcription.

Ex. 2.16

transcription of MS 674

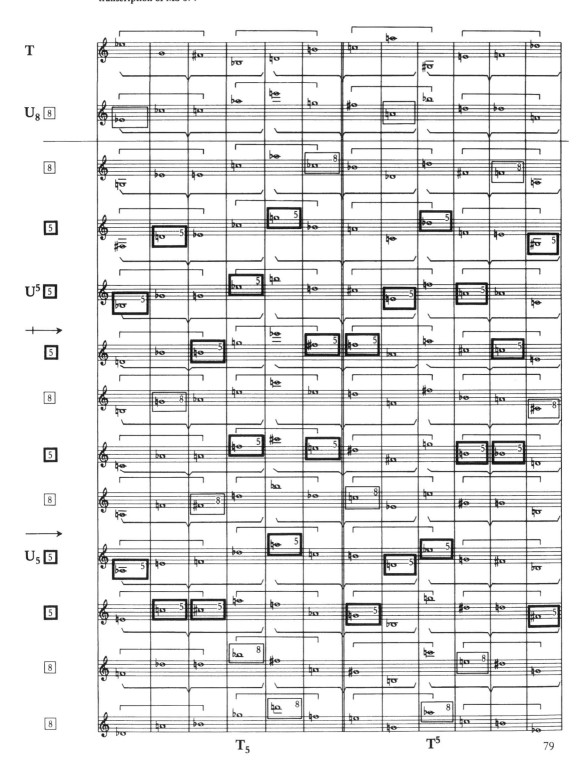

those with the same order number in the prime; e.g. in I_{10} (U^5 in Schoenberg's notation), the pitch classes with order number *0*, *3*, *7*, and *9* form a perfect fifth with those with the same order number in the prime. Schoenberg labelled all the inversions in the first category as '8' and those in the second category as '5'. He further distinguished an equivalent group formed by the prime, its untransposed inversion and the inversions starting a fifth above and below it by indicating their set names (i.e. T, U8, U^5, and U_5). The inversions starting a fifth above and below the prime are unique in having pitch-classes which are related by interval-class 5 to those with the same order number in both the prime and the untransposed inversion. A similarly related group of sets is also indicated on the table; it consists of the untransposed inversion, the prime and the transpositions at the fifth above and below it.

From the analysis of the 'Ouvertüre', it is possible to conclude that Schoenberg's concern with the relation between sets in terms of the presence of both octaves (or unisons) and perfect fifths between elements of sets with the same order number is associated with the reinforcement of pitch-class centres; e.g. most of the first group (b. 1–21) uses exclusively the described group of sets – i.e. the prime and the three inverted forms – with the purpose of establishing the predominance of E♭.

Stage 5 (MSS 576, 577, 579, and 580)   This section discusses the group of preliminary sketches related to the 'Ouvertüre' which appears in *Skizzenbuch V*.[29] In this case, it is possible to establish the chronological continuity through different sketch sheets with a greater degree of certainty than when dealing with those on loose sheets.

MS 576, the first sketch in this group (ex. 2, p. 55), already shows the basic set relations, rhythmic outline, and overall texture of the final version of b. 5–13. But there is still no indication of many details which are of great importance to the global design of the movement.

In the first section of the 'Ouvertüre' prominent events occur at either seven-bar or multiples of seven-bar intervals.[30] In MS 576 there are no signs of the

---

29 The preliminary sketches to the Septet, which appear in *Skizzenbuch V*, comprise four pages. The first four pages, of which the first page and three short fragments relate to the 'Ouvertüre', appear before the final draft of the 'Tanzschritte'. The fifth page, MS 600, which shows a draft for the 'Ländler', appears half-way through the 'Tanzschritte', on the reverse of the page ending with b. 138.

30 first group (7+7+7+7)

    introduction and first theme (b. 1–7)
    first stretto (b. 7/ii–14)
    group which includes the second stretto (b. 14–21)
    group which includes the third stretto (b. 21–28)

second group (7+14+7+7)

    subsidiary theme (b. 29–35)
    continuation (b. 36–49)
    fifth stretto (b. 50–56)
    group which includes the sixth stretto (b. 56/ii–63)

close and introduction to 'Ländler' (7)

    seventh stretto and introductory link to 'Ländler' (b. 64–70)

seven-bar units of the first section and only six instruments appear in the first four pages of sketches. The number seven became a determining factor at a later stage in the conception of the Septet. The seventh instrument, the piano, was introduced on the fifth page of the preliminary sketches in *Skizzenbuch V*, MS 580, within a fragment which was to become part of the 'Tanzschritte'. Further evidence for the emergence of a configuration based on the number seven is the presence of a small piece of paper glued to MS 580 with the proposed number and title of movements (Plate 8). One may infer from the cryptic presentation that the plan follows some private programme related to his new marriage. The sketches have numerous indications of such a programme. For instance the inscription 'Tennis-Dame'/'Frau A. S'. by an 'Adagio' passage in MS 577 is a clear allusion to the dedicatee of the Septet; these initials also appear in the title of the planned fourth movement (MS 580, Plate 8).

In MS 576, the contrapuntal continuation to the opening theme features a repeated-note pattern related to the *Hauptstimme* at b. 2, a semiquaver figure played by the viola, and a cello figure rhythmically related to the opening of the cello line at b. 1. Judging from the relatively large number of fragments related to this passage and the many modifications in the final version, it would appear that Schoenberg was not satisfied with its original rhythmic and motivic profile. Much of the material which was originally compressed in this passage was subsequently removed from its original context and used to generate new phrases, thus reducing the motivic diversity of the early version. In the final version, the repeated-note figure is reserved for the second stretto of the final version (b. 17–20), and the opening violin motif does not reappear until the end of the first section (b. 63–65).

The preliminary sketches include three fragments related to the revision of the first stretto:

A fragment in MS 577, transcribed in ex. 17a, shows the figuration which eventually replaces the quaver cello motif in MS 576 (cf. ex. 2: cello b. 5, and ex. 3: cello b. 9). This figuration first appears in MS 1186 (ex. 14: draft 5).

Two fragments in MS 579, transcribed in ex. 17b & c, represent different stages in the genesis of the first stretto. In the final version, Schoenberg retained the overall contour of the top pair of lines. The idea of overlapping entries of a motif which features in the fragment transcribed in ex. 17c prevails towards the end of the stretto in the final version (ex. 3; b. 11–13).

In MS 576, there is no indication of the violin figure at the end of the first stretto, which stands in a *V:I* relationship with its counterpart in the second stretto (ex. 4), suggesting that the final criteria for continuity were still undefined at this stage.[31]

---

31 See p. 58, *second stretto.*

Ex. 2.17

a)

transcription of an extract from MS 577

viola

b)

transcription of two extracts from MS 579

c)

In the final version, the cello motif of b. 5 in MS 576 gives way to the 'cadential motif' starting on an accented bottom D♭ (D♭⁰, B♭⁰, C1, F⁰ in b. 7), setting in motion the dynamic scheme of referential pitch centres. As explained on p. 00 of this chapter, the registral placement of this motif anticipates the bottom D♭ of the chord which introduces the second group and its retransition. Schoenberg, who claimed that the elaboration of his First String Quartet was based on the first movement of the *Eroica*,[32] might have been attracted by the connotation of the names of the first and last pitch-classes of the basic set, i.e. E♭ and D♭. The use of D♭ in the retransition as a sort of 'dominant preparation' for F♯ which is part of the main referential configuration of the recapitulation of the second group has been discussed on p. 00. In addition D♭ functions as the pitch-class centre of the *Hauptstimme* of the 'Ländler' reprise (b. 202), delaying the final F♯/E♭ resolution and cadence, b. 221–230 (ex. 18). Thus, D♭ plays a crucial role in the large-scale tonal plan of the

32 Newlin, *Schoenberg Remembered: Diaries and Recollections*, p. 185

Ex. 2.18

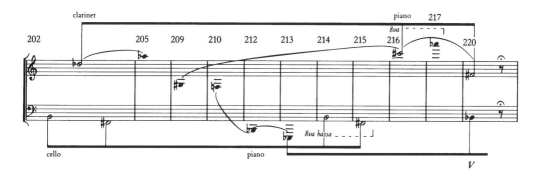

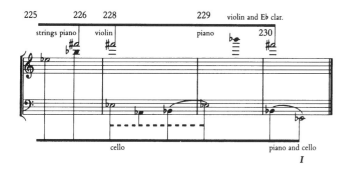

$\uparrow$ local pitch-class centre or referential configuration

$\lfloor \cdot \downarrow \cdot \rfloor$ 'cadential motif'

$\frown$ fifth support

'Ouvertüre'. The fact that in the preliminary sketches D♭ does not receive special emphasis may be indicative that in the early stages, Schoenberg did not envisage the final set of large-scale tonal relations of the 'Ouvertüre', an assumption further supported by the absence from the preliminary draft of the opening three-bar statement.

(b) Sketches related to the composition of the 'Ländler' theme

The study of the 'Ländler' sketches reveals some of the processes involved in the conception of phrase structure, in an instance where melody and harmony reflect segmental invariants determined by the structure of the set.[33] These

---

33 For a general discussion of this subject see Babbitt, 'Set Structure as a Compositional Determinant', pp. 129–48.

processes involve the enrichment of the originally symmetrical design by a multiplicity of combinatorial resources and the development of a clear-cut harmonic scheme.

The sketches on loose sheets comprise a draft, MS 1189 (ex. 19), and settable, MS 1180 (ex. 21). There is also a single in *Skizzenbuch V*, MS 600 (ex. 22), whose rhythmic refinements suggest a more advanced stage in the compositional process, although the final version draws elements from both drafts.

First layer (MS 1180 and 1189) The comparison of the *Hauptstimme* of the final version with that of drafts 1 and 2 in MS 1189 (ex. 19) shows various stages in the evolution from a somewhat static melodic and rhythmic design into a flowing melodic shape. Melodic units coincide in every case with hexachordal set segments.[34] In the first draft, all melodic units unfold from C to B/C♭ (exx. 19 and 20d), but in the alternative continuation (exx. 19, draft 2, and 20b), the third hexachordal segment is retrograded. This gives the melody a clearer sense of goal by making the final melodic unit lead back to the starting pitch-class of the phrase and causing B/C♭ to function as a pivot or common pitch-class between retrograded set segments. The exclusive deployment of pairs of retrograded segments which have C♭/B as their pivot pitch-class became an important device in the final version. C is established throughout the sketches as the pitch-class centre of the *Hauptstimme*, but in the final version this pitch-class is further supported by the interpolation of four bars before the third melodic unit given in draft 2. The first and last pitch-classes of this interpolation stand in 5:1 relation with those of the first four bars and with the last pitch-class of the two-bar extension (ex. 20f).

The 'polytonal' relation between the *Hauptstimme* and the bass, each of which projects a different pitch-class centre – the bass line D and the *Hauptstimme* C – is the more striking because each line consists of a limited number of set segments which are permutations of each other. In MS 1180, Schoenberg grouped together those sets whose segmental invariants are reflected in the combinatorial structure of the phrase (ex. 21). In this sketch, all sets have A–D as the framing dyad of either their first or last tetrachords. This dyad, which appears as the bass line of the 'Ländler' theme, is indicated by cross-marks on all the listed sets. Schoenberg tried out all these set forms when composing the 'Ländler' theme in MS 1189 (ex. 19).

Second layer (MS 600) While completing the 'Tanzschritte', Schoenberg sketched still another version of the 'Ländler' theme using the sets of the first group (ex. 22).[35] This may have been the first version, since according to

34 In the discussion of the 'Ländler' theme, 'melodic unit' designates the two-bar units of the *Hauptstimme*; and 'units' refer to groups of two bars.

35 As explained in p. 56, the only sets present in the first subject of the 'Ouvertüre' are P_3, I_3, I_8, I_{10}, and their retrogrades.

Ex. 2.19

Ex. 2.20

melodic alterations

SK 1189, draft 1

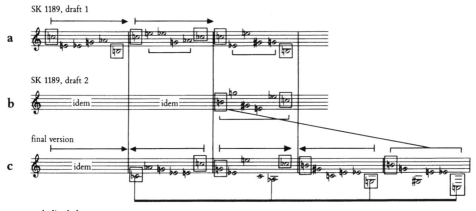

a

SK 1189, draft 2

b

final version

c

melodic skeleton

SK 1189, draft 1

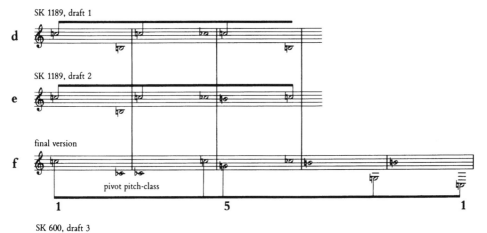

d

SK 1189, draft 2

e

final version

f

pivot pitch-class

1   5   1

SK 600, draft 3

g

1   5   1

Ex. 2.21

transcription of the bottom part of MS 1180

[*1]
T+3   −K−
          T−2

U−5   [*2]
          U+6

*1 the designation of this set as T^{+3} is incorrect; it should be T^{+7}

*2 the designation of set as U+6 is incorrect; it should be U−6

Ex. 2.22

partial transcription of MS 600

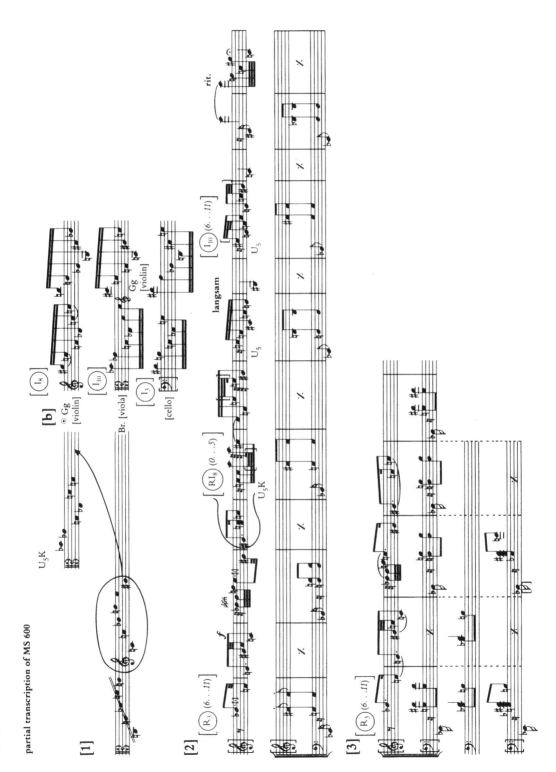

the dating in the sketches the 'Tanzschritte' was composed before all but the beginning of the 'Ouvertüre'. In draft 1, the abbreviation 'Gg' ('Geige') by the second hexachord of I$_{10}$ indicates that Schoenberg referred to this table when deciding on the pitch content of the *Hauptstimme*. Draft 3 uses all the sets of the first group with the exception of the untransposed inversion, which does not have the same invariant segments as the other sets in the group.

The *V:I* relation between the framing dyads of the antecedent and consequent gives this version a stronger sense of goal than those in MS 1189 (ex. 20; cf. d & e with g). Although the schemes of the final version and MS 600 are fundamentally the same, the former has a more strongly defined profile as a result of both the use of retrograded instead of direct repetition of segments and the breaking of its symmetry by the compression of its six units into five, as well as the branching of the *Hauptstimme* into a pair of registral lines. The bottom line of this pair, which consists of the lowest pitch-levels in each melodic unit – C♭^{1}, A♭^{1}, G^1, and C^1 (ex. 20c) – progressively becomes a foreground element bringing the *Hauptstimme* to its pitch-class goal two octaves below the C at the very beginning of the phrase.

Sketches for the second phrase (MSS 600 and 1189)   These sketches include a pair of drafts, in which complete hexachords are used for the accompaniment of each melodic unit, as in the second phrase of the final version of the *Ländler* (b. 80–89). Draft 4 in MS 1189 (ex. 19) and draft 3 in MS 600 (ex. 22) already show the disposition of each hexachord as a bass note followed by a four-note chord with one voice articulating a semitone. In these drafts, there is still no indication of the eventual extension of this pattern to include the chord progression whose bass line articulates two pairs of interval-class-five-related pitch-classes, i.e B–F and D–A.

Final draft and fair copy

(a) The music and Schoenberg's labelling of set forms

Schoenberg indicated set forms almost throughout the final draft and fair copy. Although the large number of segmental invariants between the different set forms often precludes their unequivocal identification, Schoenberg's indications enable us to understand the way he conceived the derivation of the music from the set. Without suggesting that these indications categorically represent the definitive and only correct set analysis of the music, they are relevant for the understanding of the method of composition.

In many instances, set form names show that a passage consists of the elaboration of a sequence of pairs of sets, a technique which is comparable to the reworking of a harmonic sequence. This is commonly achieved through the interchange of sets between the *Hauptstimme* and *Nebenstimme* (following

Schoenberg's practice in the sketches, these terms are used here in relation to the hierarchical function of a complete textural component and not only of a single line); e.g. b. 41–42 (MS 1117) consists of two elaborations of the same sequence of sets:

bar	41	42		43	44
$\overline{N}$	T/5	U/$_{-3}$	$\overline{H}$	T/5	U/$_{-3}$
$\overline{H}$	T/$_{-7}$	U/$_{+3}$	$\overline{N}$	T/$_{-7}$	U/$_{+3}$

The sketches show that Schoenberg almost invariably conceived six-note chords as if their bass was the first pitch-class of the hexachord, regardless of the arrangement of the other members of the hexachord. This implies that the bass of these chords defines their set-form identity; e.g. the first chord in ex. 23 can be equally ascribed to twelve different set forms, but for Schoenberg the A of the bass defines it as the first hexachord of T+4 (P_9). In the Septet Schoenberg followed this principle quite consistently when naming set forms as can be observed in the cadence towards the end of the retransition, b. 137–139 in MS 1126 (ex. 23). However, he sometimes deviated from this principle: see b. 173–175 in ex. 24.

Schoenberg's labelling of sets at the cadence near the end of the second group, b. 59–62 (MS 1119), gives us an insight into his theoretical approach. The twelve-tone chord, which is instrumentally partitioned in hexachords, was assigned to U+5K (RI_{10}). This indicates that he regarded the bass of this chord, B♭, as the first pitch-class of the set. The entry of first group material on E♭ at b. 63 implies a *V:I* resolution of the cadence and suggests that the B♭ was regarded as a kind of 'root' of the twelve-tone chord. In the recapitulation, this sustained chord is replaced by a succession of twelve-note chords whose pitch classes with order number *0*, according to Schoenberg's labelling of set forms, represent the first eleven pitch-classes of the untransposed retrograde (ex. 24). Had this section been included in the strict inverted reprise of the second group, the *V:I* on E♭ would have become *IV:I* on D. Its exclusion confirms the interpretation that the B♭ at b. 59–62 was regarded as an analogy to the 'root' of a tonal chord and therefore the cadence could not be inverted without distorting its meaning.

(b) Sketches included in the final draft

The section extending from the final phrase of the 'Ländler' to the end of the reprise of the second group is the only part of the final draft which exhibits substantial revisions. The many thematic cross-references related to the combination of the function of retransition with *Durchführung* and the convergence of several important axes of formal symmetry, added to the difficulties of composing an inverted reprise which maintains certain referential pitch levels from the exposition, make this the most intricate section of the work. It is therefore

Ex. 2.23

order numbers of the pitch-classes of the bass according to Schoenberg's labelling of set forms in the fair copy, SK 1126

Ex. 2.24

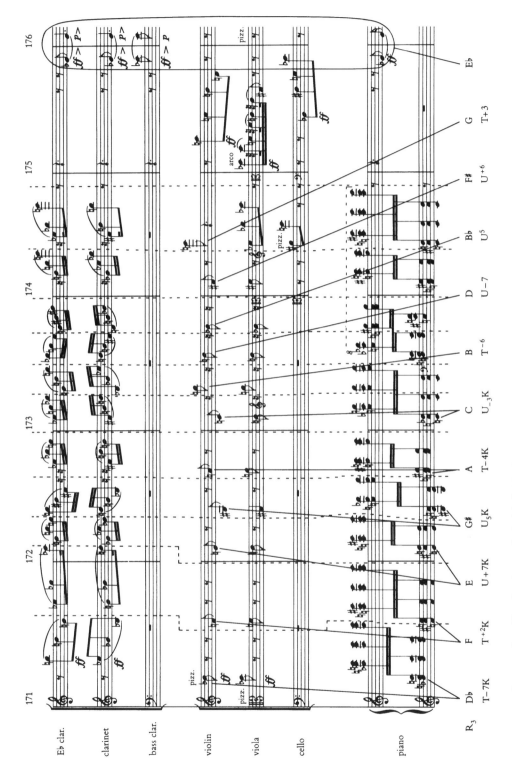

set-forms as indicated by Schoenberg in the final draft, SK 624

not surprising that its complexity is reflected in relatively considerable sketching in the final draft. For the purpose of analysis, these drafts have been
grouped according to content and chronological order.

Stage 1 (MSS 617 and 618)   The first drafts to exhibit substantial
reworking are those dealing with the last phrase of the 'Ländler' and the sec-
tional organization of the retransition. The first version of the final phrase
of the 'Ländler', b. 114–121, is an elaboration of the 'Ländler' theme which uses
the prime for the *Hauptstimme* and the untransposed retrograde for the accompaniment, MS 617 and 618 (exx. 25 and 26). The first two bars, which are the
only ones with accompaniment, already exhibit the pitch-class centres of the
final version, i.e. E♭ for the *Hauptstimme* and D♭ for the accompaniment. This
was crossed out and replaced by a version (b. 114–125 in draft b: ex. 26) which
represents a transposition of the design of the 'Ländler' theme in terms of its
pitch-class-centre scheme, pivot pitch-classes, and set relations (ex. 20f). As in
MS 617, E♭ and D♭ are retained as pitch-class centres, but the prime form of
the set does not appear until the elaboration of first group material at
b. 134–135 in the final version.

Ex. 2.25

transcription of the last three bars on MS 617

Ex. 2.26

partial transcription of MS 618

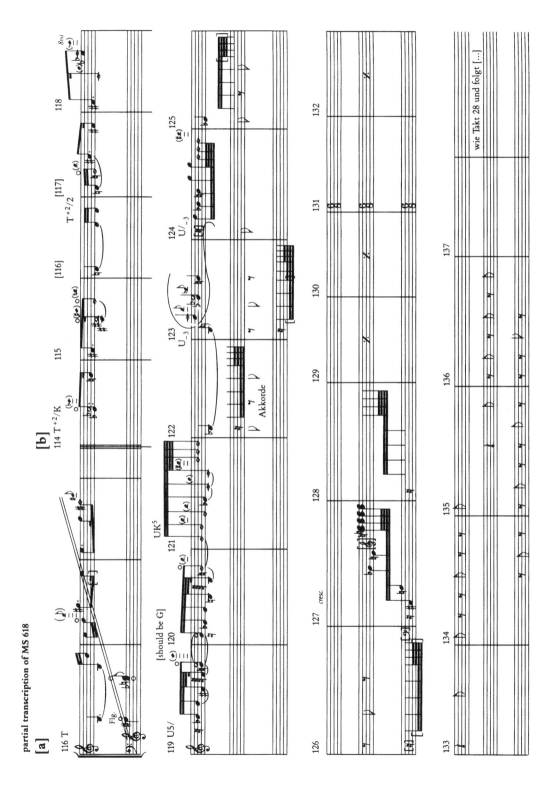

MS 618 is exceptional in that it is written in short score and only roughly specifies the devices for the construction of the section and its formal organization. After indicating the change to 6/8 metre at b. 131, the start of a new phrase is suggested by the word 'Akkorde' coupled with a texture consisting of a single component split among three instrumental groups as in the final version. The 'etc' at b. 137 followed by 'Takt 28 folge' suggests that this texture was to be continued up to elaboration of b. 28 as in the final version. The drafting of phrase lengths at this stage is indicative that the conception of the duration of sections preceded other considerations.

Stage 2 (MSS 618 and 619)   The comparison of the various drafts for the transition between 'Ländler' and retransition reveals the changes in the criteria of organization which occurred during its composition.

In the second version of the *Hauptstimme* of the last phrase of the 'Ländler', MS 618 (ex. 26 draft b), the two-bar extension brings the phrase to conclusion on E♭, the starting pitch-class of the phrase, thus following closely the organization of the 'Ländler' theme (ex. 20f). The transition-like character of the final version is already insinuated by the introduction of an imitative texture which overlaps with the last four bars of the 'Ländler' and continues into the next phrase.

There are three further drafts related to this transition, drafts a, b, and c in MS 619 (ex. 27), which differ in several aspects from the final version. These drafts show the steps involved in the construction of a sequence to extend the duration of the shape in draft a from three to six bars. First, the motif of the top line was shortened to three notes; cf. drafts a and b. In draft c, a different version of the shortened motif is used in a sequence which gradually increase the duration of the motif; cf. drafts a and c. The repeated drafting of this shape in order to extend its duration confirms the impression given by MS 618 that Schoenberg was moulding his ideas into phrases of predetermined length.

The precise shape of the two-bar extension to the *Hauptstimme* of the 'Ländler' was left undefined in MS 619. In draft c, the repeated C♯^{2} on the downbeat of b. 125 indicates its final goal, but this would be replaced in the final version by G♯^{1}. A similar change affects the pedal point of A♭$^{-1}$ (b. 127–130), which was originally conceived as C♯^{1} in MS 618 (ex. 26, draft b). This suggests that the 'interrupted cadence' on E♭ at bar 131 was only conceived at the later stages in the composition of this section, while the establishment of C♯/D♭ was an aim from the earliest stage.

Conclusion

In a review of the Septet for the Berlin periodical *Die Musik*, Adorno commented that the full mobility of the earlier works had been recaptured, which

Ex. 2.27

partial transcription of MS 619

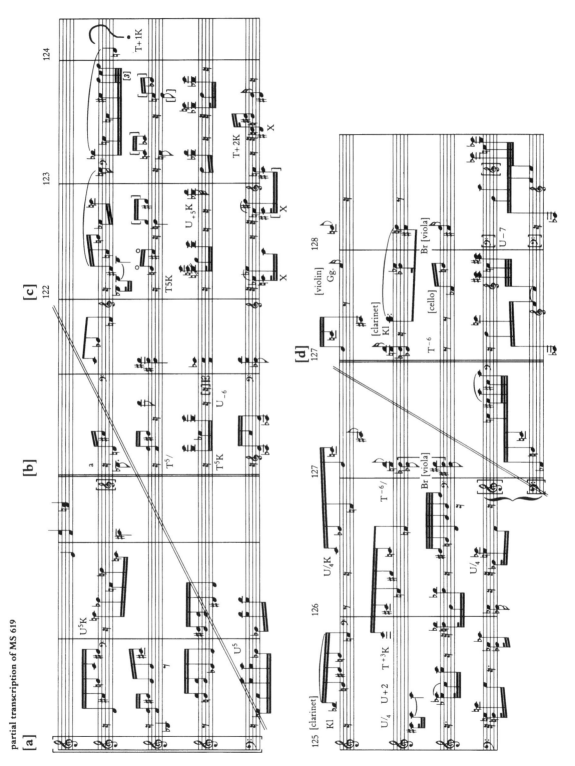

he attributed to the enrichment of the possibilities of row division, combination and transposition.[36] Adorno considered that in the Septet Schoenberg

> handled twelve-tone technique so that, with no diminution whatever in strictness, the course of the rows, and the rows themselves, are not perceptible, but disappear behind the resources of technique, thematic and compositional. The row is no longer to be thematic material, it constitutes simply the virtual thematicism, which is not manifested at all as such.[37]

Adorno's review perceptively comments on the regained thematic fluency, but incorrectly attributes it to the enrichment of twelve-tone procedures. Compared to the preceding work, the Wind Quintet, the Septet exhibits a simplification of serial technique.[38] Here, Schoenberg seems comparatively less concerned with devising complex serial schemes, such as those described in relation to the third movement of the Wind Quintet, but, on the contrary, uses simple principles of set association and thematic treatment which effortlessly contribute to the tonal directionality of the work.

Moreover, the Septet exhibits a relative simplification of texture and a decrease in linear diversity. Unlike the preceding largely polyphonic twelve-tone pieces, in which distinctly articulated chords are generally reserved for the main formal landmarks, the 'Ouvertüre' features a profusion of chordal and homophonic textures. As in the Wind Quintet, these chordal passages generally involve a limited number of different pitch collections. In the 'Ouvertüre', tonal directionality not only plays an important part in determining set association and linear cadence, but affects the very nature of the material. In those instances where the hexachords of the set tend to be partitioned into their constituent triads, the mode of progression bears striking affinities to that observed in 'Valse de Chopin'.

The type of difficulties encountered by theoreticians when tackling the question of tonality in twelve-tone music are evident in the following statement by Dahlhaus:

> 12-note harmony moves between two extremes: at one extreme, the principle of 'combinatoriality' (Babbitt), the bringing together of fragments from the different forms of a row that make up the material of the 12-note system, so that any undue predominance of individual notes (which might suggest tonality) is avoided; at the other overt or latent association with tonal chord structures and progressions, such as is found in Berg's Violin Concerto and

36 Quoted in Reich, *Schoenberg. A Critical Biography*, p. 158, Originally published in *Die Musik* (Berlin, May 1928)

37 Reich, ibid.

38 The first sketches for the 'Ouvertüre' are dated 28 August 1924, the date of Schoenberg's marriage to his second wife, but the Septet was not completed until May 1926. Even though the Septet bears a later opus number much of its first two movements was completed before Opp. 27 and 28. For a detailed dating see Hyde, *Schoenberg's Twelve-Tone Harmony: The Suite Op. 29 and the Compositional Sketches*, p. 26.

the beginning of the Adagio of Schoenberg's Third String Quartet op. 30 [b. 1–3].[39]

Dahlhaus misunderstands the relationship between triadic material, combinatoriality, and tonality. In Schoenberg, neither is 'combinatoriality' necessarily associated with non-hierarchical pitch organization, nor does triadic material necessarily imply tonal centricity. Presumably Dahlhaus is not referring specifically to Schoenberg's use of combinatoriality, which is affected by tonality as much as any other aspect of the music, but to the general principle of progression by aggregates. The principle of aggregate completion is likely to have been motivated by Schoenberg's early preoccupation with avoiding emphasis on particular notes, which then became the systematic basis of the twelve-tone method itself. Despite Schoenberg's claims to the contrary, tonal motivation, though in certain cases in a highly attenuated form, was never totally absent.

Moreover, the Roman numerals used by Dahlhaus in his example from the Third String Quartet imply tonal functions dependent on root progressions. On this matter Schoenberg commented that

> evaluation of (quasi-) harmonic progressions in such music [twelve-tone music] is obviously a necessity, though more for the teacher than for the composer. But as such progressions do not derive from roots, harmony is not under discussion and evaluation of structural functions cannot be considered.[40]

The analysis of the Septet suggests that in Schoenberg, tonal orientation is not bound to triadic material, and conversely triads do not necessarily imply tonal functionality. We have observed that Schoenberg often concentrates the implications formerly pertaining to keys or tonal regions on single pitch-classes or pitch-levels projected at prominent points and that the music exhibits a large variety of procedures for creating hierarchies.

39 Dahlhaus, 'Harmony', in *The New Grove Dictionary*, p. 183
40 Schoenberg, *Structural Functions*, p. 194

3

Tonal thought as a compositional determinant in the third movement of the Fourth String Quartet, Op. 37

Introduction

Schoenberg's programme notes to the third movement of the Fourth String Quartet read:

> The form is an A–B–A–B with a modulatory elaboration inserted before the recurrence of the B section. It begins with a recitative played in unison of the same pitch of all the four strings. The rhapsodic character of the recitative is continued, when the instruments part with the unison and contribute their individual comments. A very extended calando leads to the subordinate theme. . .[b. 630–635] a cantabile melody formulated very simple and regular, comprising six measures.
>
> A varied repetition in the cello puts more significance to the figure of 32nd notes [b. 638–639].[1]

In the context of a general introduction, the avoidance of a technical discussion of twelve-tone procedures is to be expected, but Schoenberg's reluctance to engage in such explanations was a matter of principle. A letter written one year after the completion of the Fourth String Quartet unambiguously expresses his position:

> Now one word about your intention to analyze these pieces [the Third and Fourth String Quartets] as regards to the use of the basic set of twelve tones. I have to tell you frankly: I could not do this. It would mean that I myself had to work days to find out, how the twelve tones have been used and there are enough places where it will be almost impossible to find the solution. I can show you a great number of examples, which explain the *idea* of this manner of composition, but instead of the merely mechanical application I can inform you about the compositional and aesthetic advantage of it.

---

1 Schoenberg, 'Notes on the Four String Quartets', in Rauchhaupt, *Schoenberg, Berg, Webern: The String Quartets, a Documentary Study*, p. 61

You will accordingly realise why I call it a 'method' and why I consider the term 'system' as incorrect.[2]

Babbitt's analysis of the initial bars of this movement, showing the set as a determinant of register, timbre, phrase structure, and form, exposes Schoenberg's concerns with strict twelve-tone logic.[3] Yet Schoenberg's consistent refusal to discuss the twelve-tone structure of the music, which he even admits to forgetting to some extent, implies that for him twelve-tone relations need not be conceptualized in either the listening experience or the analytical study. The analysis of the Largo will explore the interdependence of set association and tonal motivation as determinants of large-scale motivic and thematic processes.

The only allusion in Schoenberg's preface to the question of tonal directionality in the Largo is the reference to b. 671–676 as 'the modulatory elaboration inserted before the recurrence of the B section'.[4] The characterization of this passage as 'modulatory' could just refer to its *Durchführung*-like texture, but as will be shown in the discussion of the recapitulation, Schoenberg seems to be referring to the movement away from and the return to a 'home' area both in terms of set forms and tonal priorities.

Certain aspects of the tonal directionality of the Largo suggest that Schoenberg aimed at recreating many of the intervallic functions characteristic of minor-mode sonata. Moreover, aspects of detail and large-scale processes invite a comparison with the third movement of the First *Rasumovsky* Quartet, which, analysis suggests, may have served as an archetypal model. The comparison of tonal processes in these two works is not intended to provide a hypothesis on the question of modelling, but rather to draw possible analogies between a tonal and a dodecaphonic composition. The discussion adopts many of the concepts and terminology used in *Structural Functions*, a work almost contemporary to the composition of the Fourth String Quartet.

Effecting tonal functions in a non-triadic context

The expository section of the third movement of Schoenberg's quartet, b. 614–635, exhibits many similarities of detail with that of the *Rasumovsky*. The melodic design of the opening theme, b. 614–623, strikingly resembles the first theme of the Beethoven quartet. As indicated in ex. 1, a similar sequence of pitch classes is emphasized in both themes. The recitative, which involves a linear statement of the set, gives prominence to certain notes mainly by their duration, dynamic level, placement in the metric structure, and by their positioning as extreme notes of groupings, phrase structure, and cadence. The artic-

2 In Rauchhaupt, *Schoenberg, Berg, Webern: The String Quartets, a Documentary Study*, p. 66
3 Babbitt, 'Set Structure as a Compositional Determinant', pp. 139–47
4 Schoenberg, 'Notes on the Four String Quartets', p. 61

Ex. 3.1

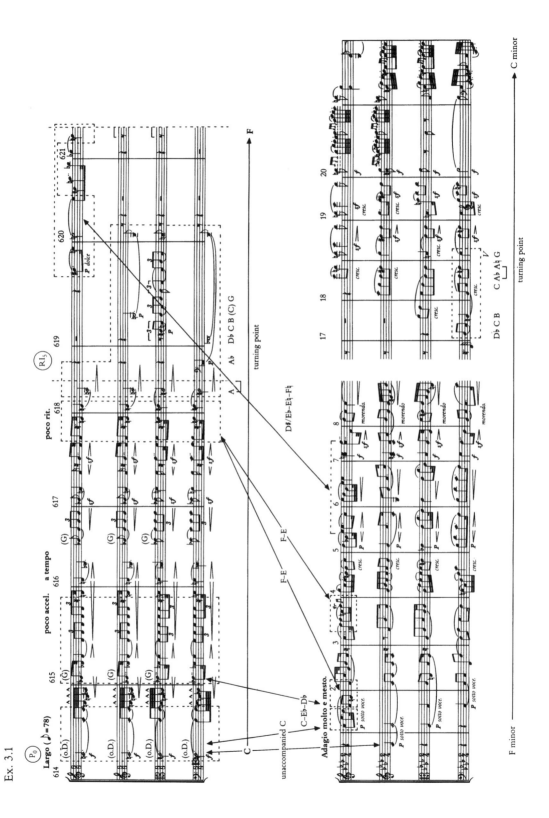

ulation of certain notes as ornamental figuration, such as appoggiaturas and turns, and more fundamentally the use of leading-note semitonal functions, help to create a hierarchy within the elements of the theme; e.g.:

The presentation of B–G–A♭ in the first bar as an upbeat turn-like figure, whose subordinate function is reinforced by the crescendo marking and its relatively short duration, renders the opening C and the E♭–D♭ (b. 614–615) as the most important pitch-levels of the first two bars. This C–E♭–D♭ succession is identical to the opening pitch-classes of Beethoven's theme (ex. 1).

The crescendo on the G♭ followed by the diminuendo on the F suggests an 'appoggiatura' resolving on the F, which is followed by a further semitonal descent (b. 616–618). While in the case of Beethoven's theme, the leading-note repeatedly resolves onto F, Schoenberg postpones its resolution until b. 621 (ex. 2a). Here the final seven pitch-classes of RI$_5$ are shaped so that the succession D♯–E–F is prominently articulated, D♯^{3} being the first pitch-level in the treble, E^3 the downbeat of the following bar, and F^3 the cadencing point of the phrase (b. 619–621). Thus Schoenberg emphasizes the same pitch-level succession that marks the cadence in Beethoven's theme (first violin b. 6–7 (ex. 1) and cello b. 14–15).

Since F and C function as the main pitch-class centres of the Largo and the key of Beethoven's piece is F minor, the most revealing coincidences between the two works are often those in which the same pitch-classes are involved in analogous processes and/or functions. For example, the pervasive B–C–D♭ segment of the Beethoven theme (e.g., b. 4–5 first violin: ex. 1), which is also a segment of I$_5$, appears in the Largo as the first three pitch-classes of b. 619. Together with the A♭–A of the previous bar and the second-violin G, this produces the same chromatic hexachord as the cello at b. 17–18 in the *Rasumovsky*, though in a different order (ex. 1):

Beethoven,	b. 17–18,	D♭–C–B–(C)–A♭–A–G
Schoenberg,	b. 618–619,	A–A♭–D♭–C–B–(C)–G

In both cases A♭ and A function as a turning-point; Beethoven uses them in a passage which modulates from F minor to the 'five-minor' (i.e. C minor) while Schoenberg employs them (in reverse order) for the passage that connects the theme, which starts on C, with its continuation, which closes on F (exx. 1 and 2a).

A comparison of the cadential scheme of the transition and second group of subjects of the *Rasumovsky* with those in Schoenberg's work also reveals many parallel processes:

In the *Rasumovsky*, the modulation to the 'five-minor', the first move away from the tonic region, involves the neutralization of D♭ and A♭. D is introduced melodically in the treble as a lower neighbour-note, which is sus-

Ex. 3.2

Ex. 3.2 (*cont.*)

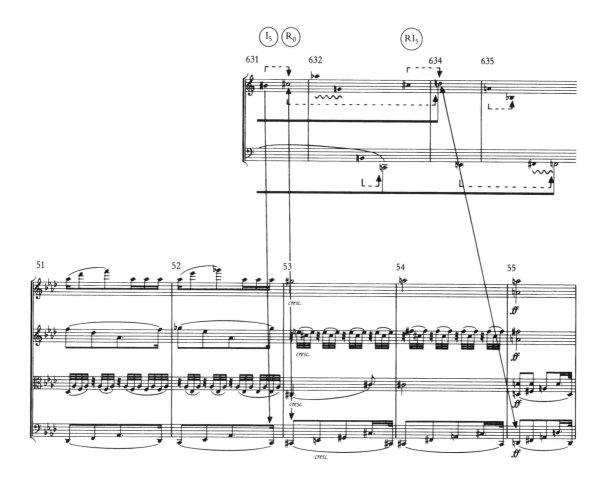

pended over the bar, and resolves upwards onto Eb (b. 18–20), while A is introduced as part of the upbeat harmony at b. 18 (ex. 1). In this conventional melodic formula the second D would ordinarily be treated as the non-harmonic note, but Beethoven treats the D as a consonance while the cello and first violin progress in parallel fifths. In the second half of the A section, Schoenberg gives prominence to the same pitch-classes by projecting them as extreme points of groupings between b. 624 and 627 (ex. 2a). The first change of hexachordal area occurs at b. 623 with the introduction of the pair of combinatorial sets which start on A and D (i.e. P_9 and I_2), and this is followed by the inversion ending on D (i.e. I_{11}) at b. 627 (ex. 2a). Here the dyad Eb–D also features melodically by virtue of its presence in both P_9 and I_2:

P_9 A   G#   E   F   C   Bb   B   G   Eb   D   C#   F#
I_2 D   Eb   G   F#   B   C#   C   E   G#   A   Bb   F

As in the Beethoven piece, the D in the treble first leads to E♭ (b. 623–624, first violin), reversing the opening C–E♭–D♭ into C–D–E♭, a common procedure for moving away from an established tonal centre. Subsequently the D becomes the cadencing pitch-class supported by A (b. 625–626 first and second violins: ex. 2a). In the sense that the opening statement gives prominence to D♭ at b. 615 and to D♭–A♭ at b. 618–619 (cello), and that the introduction of D and A as prominent pitch-classes coincides with the first change of hexachordal area, this seems a comparable situation to that described in the *Rasumovsky*.

The second close on D in the Largo (b. 627: ex. 2) is analogous to two cadences in the transition section and first subject of the second group of the *Rasumovsky*. The cadences on the 'five-minor' at b. 22–24 and b. 36–39 involve their dominant as part of a cycle of 'artificial dominants' (b. 19–23 and 31–32: ex. 2b). As in the final chord of b. 627 (ex. 2a & b), both cadences include D in the treble, F♯ in an inner part and G in the bass.

The second of these cadential passages on the five-minor reaches a climactic diminished seventh on F♯, immediately progressing to an augmented-sixth chord, A♭–C–E♭–F♯, which eventually resolves onto the dominant of the five-minor region. The augmented octave (A–A♭) between first violin and cello initiates a series of events which result in the modulation to the relative major (A♭). Subsequently A♭ features melodically as part of a prominent appoggiatura figure, appearing alternately in the treble and bass, b. 37–40; and eventually the 'five-minor' material of b. 24–27 is stated in A♭, the mediant or relative major, starting at b. 46. The quasi-sequential passage extending from b. 48 to b. 52 reintroduces the previously neutralized D♭ as the fundamental of D♭ major, which in turn is reinterpreted enharmonically as the leading-note of D at b. 53–54 (ex. 2b). In the *Largo* the establishment of G♯/A♭ as a local pitch-class centre, and the consequent change in hierarchical position between A and A♭/G♯, is effected by pausing first on the A^4 and then on the $G\sharp^4$ at b. 629, these being the penultimate and final members of RI_8 respectively (ex. 2a). This G♯ gives fifth support to the $C\sharp^3$ of the *Hauptstimme* on the downbeat of b. 631, which in turn becomes the leading-note to the D on the downbeat of b. 634 (ex. 2a). Though b. 630 returns to the initial hexachordal area, i.e. P_0/I_5, and though the first pitch-classes of these sets, C and F, appear in the treble, $C\sharp^3$ and D^3 are the focal points of b. 630–635, being emphasized as the downbeat of anacrusis turn-like figures.

The tonal meaning of the solo C which starts the third movement of the *Rasumovsky* is only gradually elucidated (ex. 1). The viola downbeat at b. 1 suggests an F triad, but due to the absence of the third of the chord, the question of mode remains undefined until the E♭ and D♭ of the first violin melody are heard, hinting at F minor. Had the first bar of the movement not been harmonized, the first violin melody alone would have been sufficient to indicate the F minor tonality. Schoenberg takes Beethoven's idea a step further by presenting the theme of the Largo as a unison statement. Tonal cadence is insinuated by melodic means – such as contour, duration, rhythm, mode of attack and/or dynamic level – while semitonal leading-note functions, and progression through the cycle of fifths, provide a counterpart to tonal function without recourse to triadic harmony. In Schoenberg's theme, the opening C–E♭–D♭ and the appoggiatura on G♭ at b. 617 suggest F minor, though this is soon contradicted by the descent of the leading note E to the A at b. 618 (ex. 1). The leading-note function of the pitch-class E, which is only tenuously implied in the unison statement, is soon confirmed by the first violin cadence at b. 620–621 (exx. 1 and 2a). The shift to C as a pitch-class centre is also effected by a solo melody (b. 622–623), which may be interpreted tonally as starting in F minor and 'modulating' to C. This first violin melody consists of the retrograde of the first hexachord of the Largo; but, unlike the opening, where C is the point of departure of a line which eventually cadences on F, C becomes the linear goal through being presented as the downbeat resolution of the B at b. 623 (ex. 2a).

Although minor-mode tonality is never explicit in the Largo, the shift to the pitch-class centre C introduces several relations commonly associated with the modulation to the 'five-minor', such as the sharpening of the third and sixth degrees of the scale, so that D♭ and A♭ are changed respectively to D and A. Beethoven effects this by introducing a seventh chord on D as an artificial dominant at b. 19–20 (ex. 1). Schoenberg introduces the pair of combinatorial sets starting on D and A, i.e. P_9 and I_2, as a prominent textural event at b. 623, overlapping the D and A with the final pitch-class of the previous set (ex. 2). This creates a situation analogous to that of a tonal seventh chord, the seventh (i.e. C) being a 'foreign' note in the regular progression of twelve-element aggregates. Moreover, the vertical configuration A–D–C is a transposition of the initial 'thirdless' harmony of the Beethoven movement, F–C–E♭.[5]

The first cadence on D (b. 625–626, first violin) is also achieved through melodic means; and in the second cadence on D, this note becomes part of another 'thirdless' seventh chord, G–D–F♯, but this time a major seventh is involved (b. 627: ex. 2a). The next step in the progression of 'thirdless' seventh harmonies through the cycle of fifths is reached at b. 636 (ex. 3). Here C–B–G is arpeggiated by the viola, first as a segment of P_0 and then as one of I_5 (b. 636–637: ex. 3). Unlike the minor-seventh trichord of b. 623, A–D–C, which can only occur through the combination of sets, this major-seventh trichord [0, 1, 5] is embedded twice in the basic set of the Fourth String Quartet and is an invariant between the members of the combinatorial pair (see p. 108).

---

5 A 'thirdless' seventh harmony is also prominent at the opening of the first movement of the *Rasumovsky*, b. 8.

Ex. 3.3

Ex. 3.3 (cont.)

P₀   *C*   *B*   *G*   A♭   E♭   D♭   D   B♭   G♭   F   E   A

I₅   F   G♭   B♭   A   D   E   D♯   *G*   *B*   *C*   D♭   A♭

Schoenberg was evidently attracted by the possibilities of extending Beethoven's idea of suggesting tonal function by 'thirdless' seventh harmonies and implying mode by fundamentally melodic means.

Large-scale developing variation

The Largo features a profusion of pairs of fifths a major third apart, both as a motif and as an important intervallic configuration in the overall voice-leading scheme of the movement. The following discussion examines the interaction between set association and the manner in which this motif is developed.

This intervallic configuration, source set [0, 1, 5, 8], is embedded in the succession of hexachords (*6. . .11*) of either the P and RI, or I and R of a combinatorial pair of sets:

b. 615–619

P₀ (*6. . .11*)   RI₅ (*6. . .11*)
D   B♭   G♭   F   E   A   A♭   D♭   C   B♭   G   D♯

and b. 624

I₂ (*6. . .11*)   R₉ (*6. . .11*)
C   A   E   G♯   B♭   F   F♯   C♯   D   E♭   G   B

The first instance of a tonal shift brought about by this configuration or motif occurs between the end of the recitative and the beginning of its continuation. The recitative ends with an unresolved leading-note, E, which momentarily gives tonal support to the pitch level a fifth below it, A (ex. 2). The following A♭–D♭ initiates a phrase which leads back to F, thus dissipating any sense of a stable close on the previous A. The cello D♭ provides tonal support to the cello G♭ at b. 621; and at b. 623–625, the enharmonic form of this dyad descends chromatically to C–F (ex. 2a). The upper line progresses by fifths from the initial C of the recitative to F–B♭, b. 621–622, before reaching A–D at b. 625–626 (ex. 2a). The cadence on G♯ at b. 629 provides fifth support to C♯ at b. 631, which eventually leads back to D (ex. 2a).

The double bar-line at the beginning of the subordinate theme marks the return to the initial hexachordal area, i.e. P₀ and I₅; yet, as explained on p. 104, the pitch hierarchy of this section is highly dissimilar to that of the opening eight bars. References to the first subject include the retention of both C–B–G

(b. 636–637), an invariant segment between P_0 and I_5, and Db/C# and Ab/G# (b. 637, cello) at their original pitch levels (ex. 3). In addition, the lower lines of the subordinate theme involve essentially the same progression: at b. 636–637, the cello plays the same dyad which closed the recitative, E–A, followed by the first dyad of the polyphonic continuation, C#–G# (Db–Ab at 618–619). As in the first subject, C#–G# progresses through the cycle of fifths to C#–F# (b. 640, cello and second violin), but before reaching F–C at b. 644–645, it moves by contrary motion to D–G (cello and viola b. 643):

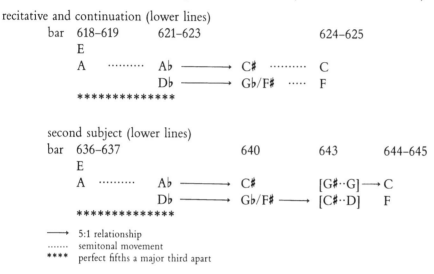

recitative and continuation (lower lines)

second subject (lower lines)

An extended sequence of events determined by this configuration occurs in the *Durchführung* section at b. 645–649, following a cello cadence on F, as in the previous presentation of this configuration in the second subject (cf. b. 635–644). While at b. 630–635, C is the final bass-line note of the three-bar antecedent and F the final note of the three-bar consequent (these being the final pitch-classes of R_0 and RI_5 respectively (b. 630–635, bass)), at b. 644–645 C–F is the final dyad of P_8. At b. 645 the invariant trichord between P_8 and I_1 is first heard as a viola ostinato, as was also the case at b. 636, and is subsequently transferred to the *Hauptstimme* at b. 646 (ex. 3). These features render b. 645–649 an elaboration of b. 635–637, as well as a further step in the development of b. 618–619, from which b. 636–637 originally derived.

The next stage in the developing variation of b. 618–619 takes place in the re-elaboration of the aforementioned *Durchführung* passage at b. 681–682 (ex. 3). Once again this material appears after a cadence on F (cf. b. 644–645 and 681). At b. 681 the cello plays F–C (the final dyad of I_9) and the invariant trichord occurs first in the accompaniment (viola and cello, b. 681) and is then transferred, as before, to the *Hauptstimme* (second violin, b. 682). The motif (F–C from I_9 and A♭–D♭ from P_4) is articulated by viola and cello at b. 681. As before, the F–C dyad initiates the progression (cf. b. 645–646 and 681–682), but whereas previously it moved to E–A, in this instance it is followed by A♭–D♭:

retransition (cello, b. 644–645)	P_8		R_8	RI_1	E A
		cadence on F	C F		
recapitulation (cello and viola, b. 680–681)	RI_5		I_9	P_4	A♭ D♭

These three dyads, which are common to the various processes involving this configuration, are the same ones which feature as points of tonal arrival in the first eight bars of the Largo (b. 614–619), namely C $\rightarrow$ F (i.e. C giving fifth support to F), E–A, and A♭–D♭. In this sense, one could interpret these passages as a large-scale 'composing-out' of the tonal relations of the first eight bars of the movement.

The fact that C–F, E–A, and A♭–D♭ remain constant elements in several contexts, despite the changes of set form, is intimately linked to the structure of the set. Between two pairs of hexachordally combinatorial sets related by transposition at the major third, certain dyads which appear as vertical inversional dyads in one pair become horizontal dyads in the other pair, and vice versa. The following diagram shows this relation between the pairs of sets of the exposition and recapitulation of the second subject and beginning of the *Durchführung*:

exposition of the second subject (b. 630–637)

P_0	C	B	G	G♯	E♭	D♭	D	B♭	F♯	F	E A
I_5	F	F♯	B♭	A	D	E	E♭	G	B	C	D♭ A♭

Durchführung (b. 638–645)

P_8	A♭	G	E♭	E	B	A	B♭	F♯	D	D♭	C F
I_1	D♭	D	F♯	F	B♭	C	B	E♭	G	A♭	A E

re-elaboration of the second subject (b. 679–680)

P_0	C	B	G	G♯	E♭	D♭	D	B♭	F♯	F	E A
I_5	F	F♯	B♭	A	D	E	E♭	G	B	C	D♭ A♭

re-elaboration of *Durchführung* material (b. 681–682)

P_4	E	E♭	B	C	G	F	F♯	D	B♭	A	A♭ D♭
I_9	A	B♭	D	C♯	F♯	G♯	G	B	E♭	E	F C

The three dyads from the 'home' hexachordal area (C–F, E–A, and D♭–A♭), which participate in the developing variation of this motif, are present as either vertical or horizontal dyads in the hexachordal areas a major third above and below it.

Babbitt described a similar type of relation between the group of sets of the first subject and transition section. He explained that 'most immediately, there is the identification of the last note of the prime with the first of the following transposition, which combines cyclically through a circuit of pitch classes by successive transpositions of the set defining a progression through the "diminished" seventh',[6] as summarized in the following diagram:

bar	614–623	623–626	626–627	628–629	630
	P_0	P_9	P_6	P_3	P_0
	I_5	I_2	I_{11}	I_8	I_5

The initial and final pitch-classes of the prime forms are as follows:

$$C/A \ \rightarrow \ A/F\sharp \ \rightarrow \ F\sharp/E\flat \ \rightarrow \ E\flat/C \ \rightarrow \ C/A$$

According to Babbitt, from a theoretical angle the choice of transposition at b. 623 also 'effects more complete and fundamental associations, if sonically less immediate ones': the presence of the 'verticals' resulting from the one-to-one combination of sets as 'horizontals' in another form of the set,[7] as illustrated in the following diagram:

opening theme (b. 614–623)

P_0	C	B	G	G♯	E♭	D♭	D	B♭	F♯	F	E	A
	|	|		|	|		|		|	|		|
I_5	F	F♯	B♭	A	D	E	E♭	G	B	C	D♭	A♭

b. 623–626

P_9	A	G♯	E	F	C	B♭	B	G	E♭	D	G♯	F♯
I_2	D	E♭	G	F♯	B	C♯	C	E	G♯	A	B♭	F

In the first subject and transition the process of transferring horizontal dyads into vertical inversional dyads, is, as Babbitt puts it, a 'sonically less immediate' feature than the identification of the last note of the prime with the first of the following transposition. But in the case of the re-elaborations of the motif from b. 618–619 the interchange between vertical and horizontal dyads involves the first pitch classes of pairs of sets and their final dyads, and since Schoenberg treats these as important cadential points and motifs the process is clearly manifested in the music.

Completion and resolution: the recapitulation

Schoenberg's twelve-tone compositions often exhibit a major recapitulatory section. As in most music written since the mid eighteenth century, recapitula-

---

6 Babbitt, 'Set Structure as a Compositional Determinant', pp. 143–4
7 Ibid., p. 144

tion generally implies 'resolution' and the restated material is often modified in order to comply with functional requirements.[8] These modifications often entail transposition or pitch-class and contour inversion of material from the exposition. The beginning of the recapitulation generally coincides with the return of the sets used at the opening of the exposition, and, in the case of the hexachordal compositions, the return to the opening hexachordal area. In general, the return to the 'home' hexachordal area tends to be associated with major thematic restatements and/or marks the boundaries of formal divisions; e.g.:

In the first movement of the Fourth String Quartet, where the first thirty and a half bars exclusively unfold the sets of a single hexachordal area, P_2/I_7, the return to the 'home' hexachordal area only occurs towards the end of the movement at b. 239–257 and in the closing coda (b. 281).

In the String Trio, where the entire Part I consists exclusively of P_2/I_7, the beginning of the recapitulation at Part III is also marked by the return to the 'home' hexachordal area.

The most systematic approach to thematic restatement is represented by those instances where formal sections or thematic restatements are related by the customary operations of the twelve-tone method; e.g.:

In the second movement of the Fourth String Quartet, the restatements of the four-bar opening theme of the Trio (b. 430–433) are related by transposition (b. 481–484), inversion (b. 442–445), and retrograde of the pattern of set partition.[9]

In Part III of the String Trio, the reprise comprises extensive axial inversion of material from previous sections. The hexachordal area, type of partitioning, and overall rhythmic profile are maintained, while the registral placement of each textural strand and the set forms attached to it change, resulting in the untransposed axial inversion of the passage concerned. For example, the *quasi recitativo* passage in the First Episode (b. 105–111) which unfolds P_8/I_1, is recapitulated in Part III in the same hexachordal area, but what originally consisted of P_8 or R_8, consists of I_1 or R_1, and vice versa, in the recapitulation.

A notable exception is the *Phantasy* for violin and piano, where Schoenberg relinquished this approach in favour of an unfolding of sets which is not directly parallel with other aspects of formal differentiation. In the *Phantasy*, changes of texture, tempi, and thematic material only occasionally coincide with change of hexachordal area, or with the completion of groups of cyclically associated set forms. For instance, the recapitulation of the group of sets associated with the opening section of the work (b. 1–32) which starts at

---

8 See Rosen, *Sonata Forms*, p. 272
9 This means that the original mode of partitioning the prime is applied to the retrograde, which is not the same relation as these sections being a retrograde of each other.

b. 110, makes no immediate reference to the thematic material of the opening section.

In the case of material which relies on the use of the perfect fifth to give support to pitch-class centres, the operations of inversion and retrograde cannot be strictly applied without the nature of such material being distorted. As was observed in the case of the 'Ouvertüre' of the Septet, where the whole of the second subject is inverted in the recapitulation, Schoenberg only treats in this way material which does not rely on cadential formulae involving perfect fifths.

In the Largo, the recapitulation involves two instances of inversional restatement of material from the exposition. The inversion takes place around the same axis of symmetry as that of the 'home' hexachordal area:[10]

P_0	C	B	G	G#	Eb	Db	D	Bb	F#	F	E	A
I_5	F	F#	Bb	A	D	E	Eb	G	B	C	Db	Ab

inversional dyads

			D	C#	C	B	Bb	A			

interval-classes

		1	3	5	5	3	1		

		Eb	E	F	F#	G	G#		

The restatement of the opening theme, which formerly consisted of P_0 followed by RI_5, as I_5 followed by R_0, is the most immediate instance of the inversional process (cf. b. 664–671 and 614–621). Since C–F inverts into F–C (see diagram above), P_0/RI_5 becomes I_5/R_0. In the exposition the invariant trichord C–B–G between P_0 and I_5 recurs at the same pitch level as in the opening theme at various points, such as the second phrase of the first subject (b. 619–621), and the second phrase of the second group of subjects, (b. 636–637). In the reprise of the recitative this trichord appears once more at its original registral placement (b. 666–667). A further reference to the exposition of this sort is the presentation of the first seven pitch levels of the movement in retrograde in the *Hauptstimme* at b. 669–670.

The other instance of inversional restatement in the Largo is the non-literal recapitulation of b. 645–649 at b. 681–684, replacing the figure at b. 636–637 from which b. 645–649 originally derive (ex. 3). Although the hexachordal area involved is an inversion of the original one with respect to the aforementioned axis of symmetry (P_8/I_1 becomes I_9/P_4), the sets are disposed so that the two passages are a transposition, as opposed to an inversion, of each other. This results in the emphasis of Db/C# as a pitch-class centre in the *Hauptstimme* (ex. 4), whilst a strict inversion would have resulted in the prolongation of E. The following comparative analysis of the retransition section of the Largo

10 These are the same inversional dyads as those used for the inverted reprise of the second subject in the Septet; see p. 64.

Ex. 3.4

with that of the *Rasumovsky* suggests that Schoenberg did not invert this material because of tonal considerations.

In the exposition of the Largo the establishment of D as a secondary pitch-class centre was seen as analogous to certain tonal processes in the *Rasumovsky*, where the modulation to the 'five-minor' involves the sharpening of the third and sixth degree of the F minor scale, as well as the introduction of B as a leading-note to C. In order to prepare for the return to F minor Beethoven neutralizes D and B by introducing a section in the submediant-major region, D♭ major, as well as repeatedly touching the subdominant-minor region, B♭ minor.

Schoenberg introduces pitch processes analogous to those in Beethoven's retransition in the passage which initiates the retransition section of the Largo (b. 645–649). In the *Rasumovsky* the preparation for the return to the tonic commences with the quasi-sequential passage which begins at b. 56 in the five-minor region. The cadencing figure, which reaches a half close in the tonic at b. 67, briefly touches the tonic major as the artificial dominant of B♭ major (b. 61 and b. 64). In the Largo, the cello cadences on F (as the final element of R_8) at b. 644–645, and the first violin reaches F^4 (as the first element of P_5) on the downbeat of b. 647, preceded by a turn-like figure including the leading-note E (ex. 4). The B♭ which closes the phrase preceded by its leading-note is given fifth support by this F. The F–B♭ dyad is further projected in the *Hauptstimme* of the cadential figure that follows (b. 650–652: ex. 4).

Beethoven postpones a full close in F minor until the restatement of the opening theme, starting at b. 84, in order to interpolate an extended section in D♭ major, starting at b. 72. The preparation of the submediant major follows the same process as that of A♭ at the beginning of the *Durchführung* (b. 37–52), the D♭ being given melodic prominence as part of the appoggiatura-like figure before it becomes a secondary tonic. Schoenberg also postpones the return of the 'home' hexachordal area until the recapitulation of the opening theme, beginning at b. 664, the prominent F in the *Hauptstimme* at b. 647 being the first pitch-class of P_5 as opposed to I_5 (ex. 4). In the passage which starts the retransition section of the Largo, Schoenberg introduces D♭/C♯ as a secondary pitch-class centre. $C♯^4$ occupies a prominent position as the downbeat of the first and third bar (b. 646–648), and is also the first note of the next phrase (D♭, b. 652). Set transposition in the *Durchführung* and beginning of the re-transition seems determined by the presence of D♭/C♯ as either the first or the final element of one set in each of the set pairs which unfolds between b. 638 and 654:

b. 638–646

P_8	G♯	G	E♭	E	B	A	B♭	F♯	D	C♯	C	F
I_1	<u>C♯</u>	D	F♯	F	B♭	C	B	E♭	G	A♭	A	E

b. 647–651

P_5	F	E	C	C#	G#	F#	G	Eb	B	Bb	A	D
I_{10}	Bb	B	Eb	D	G	A	G#	C	E	F	F#	<u>C#</u>

b. 652–654

P_1	<u>C#</u>	C	G#	A	E	D	Eb	B	G	F#	F	Bb
I_6	F#	G	B	Bb	Eb	F	E	G#	C	C#	D	A

A similar criterion applies to the recapitulation of the second group of subjects, where Db features as the first element or is involved in the final dyad of the sets which appear in the *Hauptstimme*:

recapitulation of the second group of subjects (b. 679–685)

P_0	C	B	G	G#	Eb	Db	D	Bb	F#	F	E	A
I_5	F	F#	Bb	A	D	E	Eb	G	B	C	<u>Db</u>	Ab

P_4	E	Eb	B	C	G	F	F#	D	Bb	A	Ab	<u>Db</u>
I_9	A	Bb	D	C#	F#	G#	G	B	Eb	E	F	C

P_1	<u>Db</u>	C	G#	A	E	D	Eb	B	G	F#	F	Bb
I_6	F#	G	B	Bb	Eb	F	E	G#	C	Db	D	A

Towards the end of the Db major section in the *Rasumovsky*, Gb features as an appoggiatura at b. 78, before being sharpened to G♮ in the following bar in order to prepare the return to the tonic. In the *Largo* the aforementioned Db/C# section in the retransition eventually closes on F# at b. 653 (ex. 4). The threefold repetition of the last three pitch-levels of the *Hauptstimme* (b. 653–654) neutralizes the 'tonal' obligations of the three-note shape by changing its rhythm and dynamics, preparing for the articulation of G as a pitch-class centre on the downbeat of b. 656 (ex. 4). Beethoven neutralizes the Gb in a similar way by presenting the G as a non-harmonic note (first violin turn at b. 78), and subsequently slowing down the Ab–G of the turn and treating both of them as harmonic notes in the following bar.

In the cadential figure which closes the retransition of the *Rasumovsky* the first violin plays C–B–C–D–C–B–C–D, twice reaching an *sf* on the supertonic chord (b. 80–81). Similarly towards the end of the retransition section of the *Largo* (b. 659–661), the *Hauptstimme* delineates a C–B–B–C shape, which combines the second motif of the opening phrase of the second subject (b. 631–632 & 634–635) with the *Hauptstimme* of the second phrase (b. 636–637). The hexachordal area involved, P_6/I_{11}, reverses the order and position of the C–B and F–F# dyads of the hexachordal area at the opening of the second subject, so that they become respectively F#–F and B–C, and vice versa:

P_0	<u>C</u>	<u>B</u>	G	G#	Eb	Db	D	Bb	<u>F#</u>	<u>F</u>	E	A
I_5	<u>F</u>	<u>F#</u>	Bb	A	D	E	Eb	G	<u>B</u>	<u>C</u>	Db	Ab

P_6	F♯	F	D♭	D	A	G	A♭	E	C	B	B♭	E♭
I_{11}	B	C	E	E♭	A♭	B♭	A	D♭	F	F♯	G	D

These invariant dyads between the two hexachordal areas are used to reverse the tonal direction of the second-subject material in order to return to the original pitch-class centres, i.e. F supported by C, in the 'home' area. The process of completion is reinforced by the varied restatement of thematic material from the exposition originally associated with the returning hexachordal area and its associated pitch-class centres.

D♭ and B♭, which have been established as secondary pitch-class centres in the retransition, continue to be prominent in the recapitulation. In the restatement of the second phrase of the opening theme the material is redistributed so that the long note, the B♭ at b. 669, is given prominence as the first high-register note in the recapitulation. At b. 676, B♭⁴ is the registral goal of what Schoenberg referred to as the 'modulatory elaboration',[11] which in turn gives fifth support to the *Hauptstimme* cadence on E♭ at b. 679 (ex. 4). The E♭ cadence which closes the recapitulation of first-subject material is the next step in the process of linear cadencing through the cycle of fifths, subsequently offering fifth support to the downbeat resolution of the first violin upbeat figure, the A♭ at b. 679. At b. 679–680, the second violin restates the opening figure of the second subject in its original form, but its combination with the first violin material, with its emphasis on A♭, results in the reaffirmation of C♯ as a secondary pitch-class centre (ex. 4). In the exposition the C♯ of the antecedent performs a leading-note function, but in the recapitulation D♭/C♯ is further prolonged by the *Hauptstimme* cadence at b. 683 (ex. 4).

Conclusion

Despite the remarkable similarities between the Largo of the Fourth String Quartet and the third movement of the *Rasumovsky*, there is no conclusive evidence that Schoenberg used the Beethoven as a specific model. The importance of such a comparison lies not so much in suggesting a direct link between these two compositions, but in the possibility of drawing meaningful analogies between music which has been widely regarded as belonging to totally separate musical systems.

On one side Schoenberg creates an analogy to a 'home' key by making the initial hexachordal area, and the first element of its prime and inversion, C and F, perform a referential function analogous to that of a tonic key. These mark out the main formal divisions of the movement from a thematic viewpoint. On the other hand true tonal functions play an important part in giving direction to individual lines and polyphonic complexes.

11 See pp. 98 and 99

An important criterion for associating hexachordal areas in the Largo is the presence of some vertical dyads of one area as horizontals in another one, and vice versa. Since these dyads intervene in an important motif (the pairs of fifths a major third apart) the criterion for associating sets has a tangible effect on the thematic processes. Furthermore, these perfect fifths have been shown to perform an important role in the tonal unfolding of the movement through their presence in linear cadences. Thus this movement exhibits a remarkable integration of motivic processes, the association of sets according to twelve-tone principles, and tonal thought as a determinant of detail and large-scale structure.

4

Musical continuity and prolongational procedures in the Ode to Napoleon Buonaparte

The fact is that every writer *creates* his own precursors. His work modifies our conception of the past, as it will modify the future   Borges[1]

Introduction

Comparing the *Ode* with its immediately preceding work, the *Variations on a Recitative*, Neighbour observed:

> Each is rooted in a special harmonic procedure that gives it a peculiarly individual sound. The D minor work borrows from serialism; the dodecaphonic *Ode* ends in E♭. The *Variations* respect the integrity of their melodic theme, the series of the *Ode* is freely permutated.[2]

Leibowitz commented on the *Ode* in similar terms:

> In contrast to Op. 40, which shows a principal tonality, the *Ode to Napoleon* seems to oscillate perpetually among all possible tonalities, and, though it ends in E flat major, it is impossible to say that this tonality plays a preponderant part in the entire composition. Here, then is revealed a new tonal principle, which surely fulfils Schoenberg's plan.
>
> The work is entirely free in its use of the twelve-tone system. In fact, there is not a single place where the row appears as such, but its functional action is felt in every measure because of the functional role assigned to certain melodic and harmonic intervals (which produces coherence according to tone-row principles) and also because of the use of the total resources of chromaticism.[3]

Leibowitz correctly characterizes the most puzzling features of the *Ode*, but his readiness to regard the *Ode* as a twelve-tone work while declaring it free from any systematic constraints is problematic and ultimately precludes an understanding of the type of musical thought involved.

---

1 Borges, quoted in Foucault, *Language, Counter-Memory, Practice*, p. 5
2 Neighbour, 'Schoenberg', in *The New Grove Dictionary*, p. 718
3 Leibowitz, *Schoenberg and His School*, p. 128

The sketches for the *Ode* give us some information about the technique of composition. An extensive set-table, MS 766 transcribed in ex. 1, indicates that Schoenberg was working with systematic permutations of various orderings of a hexachord. Yet an evaluation of the syntactical relevance of these hexachords cannot be based on set-tables alone, but requires an understanding of the structure of the music. For, as Babbitt explained,

> [in twelve-tone music,] the normative factor is determined without any reference to means of its being so recognized other than by internal structure, which is not true in tonal music, and by priority, which is not necessary in tonal music.[4]

Accordingly, for a set to have a normative function, this should be evident from its position of priority within the internal structure of the work.

Leibowitz accepts the idea of the 'free use of the twelve-tone system' without inquiring into the implication of 'licence' in this context. In this respect Babbitt commented that

> in the past, idiomatic change has usually been the surface manifestation of a systematic extension, demanded, or at least motivated, by the relations of the individual work. But much twelve-tone music has indulged in 'licences' which make it impossible to infer what stable properties the composer associates with the principles of the system. Often licences appear to be motivated by the desire to secure certain idiomatic events that do not imply a twelve-tone context at all. Thus, the work originates and eventuates outside the domain of the system, which seems to function merely as the source of sonic details, and as the basis for analytical rationalization after the fact.[5]

My discussion of the *Ode* deals with this matter in its attempt to characterize the dynamic interaction between systematically derived and independently conceived detail, indicating areas of synthesis and contradiction.

The *Ode* continuously modulates between serial and extended tonal logic, creating a profusion of intricate syntactical situations. The nature of tonal thought in Schoenberg's works written after his formulation of the twelve-tone method remains largely unexplained. Goehr has commented that as early as the *Harmonielehre*, Schoenberg's writings about tonality approach a permutational view of chord structure, and that there is a parallel between Schoenberg's definition of 'weak' and 'strong' chord progressions in terms of 'repetition of notes and the formulation of the twelve-tone method, which is similarly formulated in terms of repetition and non-repetition'.[6] The question of 'multiple meaning' in chord progressions is a central issue both in the *Harmonielehre*

4 Babbitt, review of *Quatrième Cahier (n.d.) Le Système dodécaphonique*, p. 265
5 Ibid., pp. 266–7
6 Goehr, 'The Theoretical Writings of Arnold Schoenberg', p. 89

Ex. 4.1

partial transcription of MS 766

overwritten on the first two
staves of 'antecedent *c*'

121

and in *Structural Functions*. A section of the latter dealing with harmonic progression in the *Durchführung* closes with the following evaluation of the compass of modulation in the Prelude to *Tristan*:

> Analysis of the Prelude to *Tristan* proves that on the basis of the interchangeability of t and T, ♭M and ♭SM (of T) comprise the furthest compass of modulation – if one recognizes that those sections which seem to go further are only roving on the basis of the multiple meaning of a vagrant harmony.[7]

This passage indicates a concern with the identification of an all-embracing configuration, which in this case is a group of tonal regions accounting for the compass of modulation of the entire piece. The *Ode* involves a strikingly similar configuration both at the local and large-scale level. The progression C♯ Mm – A Mm – E Mm[8] underlies the piano part of the opening theme (ex. 2), which according to the nomenclature used in *Structural Functions* are the combinations of T and t, ♭SM and ♭sm followed by ♭M and ♭m.[9] The relationship between

Ex. 4.2

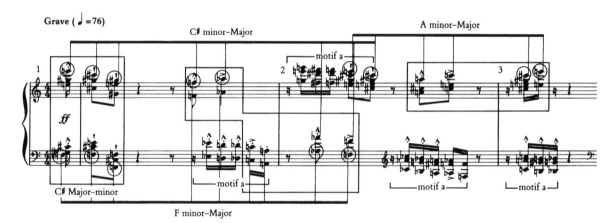

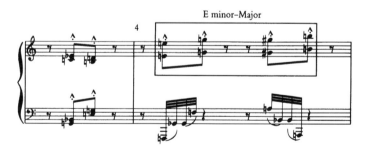

7 Schoenberg, *Structural Functions*, p. 164

8 'M' stands for major and 'm' for minor.

9 T: tonic, t: tonic minor, ♭M: flat mediant major, ♭m: flat mediant minor, ♭SM: flat submediant major.
  Schoenberg, *Structural Functions*, p. 20

certain sections of the *Ode* can also be understood in terms of this harmonic configuration; e.g. the introduction establishes E^4–$C\sharp^4$–$G\sharp^3$–F^3 as the main referential configuration and E^4–$C\sharp^4$ as the 'home' pitch-level centres, the first stanza prolongs an A Mm tetrachord, and $G\sharp$–E forms the core of the second stanza.[10]

These observations, which in this specific instance may be referring to no more than a fortuitous coincidence, point towards a largely unexplored area of Schoenberg's preoccupations. Schoenberg's moulding of compositional ideas on his analytical understanding of the structure of the musical monuments of the past may be the key to the understanding of his use of tonality after the formulation of the twelve-tone method. Thus, it seems more appropriate to regard the *Ode* as a dodecaphonic work *about* tonality, rather than as a 'disrupted' dodecaphonic work having 'occasional tonal tendencies'.[11]

This study examines the different modes of thought involved at local and large-scale levels taking as its starting-point the theoretical notions implicit in the sketches to the *Ode*. The aforementioned set-table lists systematic permutations of four orderings of the third-order all-combinatorial hexachord (MS 766, transcribed in ex. 1), which account for the majority of events in the *Ode*.[12] Schoenberg designated them as 'ant[ecedent] a, b, and c and con[sequent]'.[13] The empty spaces between the vertical strokes on the right side of MS 766 indicate that Schoenberg originally intended to include two other forms of the 'consequent', but in the *Ode* the basic units of progression are individual hexachords as opposed to twelve-tone sets comprising an 'antecedent'–'consequent' pair. The four forms of this source hexachord which function as the 'home' forms are included within the group of eight hexachords on the top pair of staves. They are as follows:

'antecedent a'	E	C♯	G♯	F	C	A
'antecedent b' (inverted)	D	E♭	G	B♭	G♭	C♭
'antecedent c'	E	F	D♭	C	G♯	A
'consequent'	B	F♯	G	E♭	B♭	D

Since each of these hexachords determines a distinct thematic and textural context associated with certain particular means of prolongation and development, it is convenient to deal with each of them individually in the context where they first appear before attempting to outline the global design of the *Ode*.

Throughout this study, I refer to the configurations involving triads by their tonal names. However, this does not imply any a priori hierarchy within the

---

10 Discussed on pp. 134–9
11 Whittall, *Schoenberg's Chamber Music*, pp. 57–8
12 Schoenberg's earlier E♭ twelve-tone work, the Septet, also uses this source hexachord.
13 In order to differentiate between the terms 'antecedent' and 'consequent' used in relation to these hexachords from their use in relation to phrase structure, the former are indicated by the use of quotation marks.

elements of the configuration; accordingly, the expression 'C♯ Mm tetrachord' does not imply that C♯ is the root or fundamental of the chord. On the contrary a feature of the *Ode* is that often pitch-class centres of referential configurations do not coincide with their tonal roots. Moreover, the naming of these configurations by analogy with their tonal counterparts does not imply that the evaluation of the structural function of these chord progressions can be considered in the way described by Schoenberg in *Structural Functions*.

Checked against Schoenberg's autograph, the G. Schirmer score contains many mistakes and inaccuracies, some of which are indicated in the examples.[14]

'Antecedent a' – the introduction

From the very opening gesture, 'antecedent a' accounts for the major linear and vertical events in the introduction, b. 1–24. Schoenberg almost consistently partitions this hexachord into two overlapping major-minor tetrachords, i.e. two representations of the source tetrachord [0, 3, 4, 7]. The ambivalence created by the overlap of the pair of major-minor tetrachords embedded in 'antecedent a' results in 'roving' or 'vagrant' harmonies which invite multiple interpretations. For instance, the first complete statement of these tetrachordal relations occurs at b. 1 between the top line of the piano, which articulates C♯ Mm and the last two notes of the piano left hand, which when combined with the last two notes of the top line results in F mM (ex. 2). The pivot dyad between these tetrachords, i.e. A♭ and F, is subsequently retrograded in the piano left hand and becomes part of C♯ Mm, the starting tetrachord:

```
E   C♯   G♯   F
          A♭   F    C    A
                    C    A    A♭   F
                              A♭   F    E    C♯
```

Moreover, often different Mm tetrachords are simultaneously unfolded by the top and bottom lines; e.g., at b. 1–2 C♯ mM is articulated by the top line of the piano and F Mm by the bass line (ex. 2).

The dynamic potential of these harmonies becomes further extended as they are shaped into structural hierarchies by a variety of often conflicting means. Local hierarchies result from the emphasis given to particular pitch-classes or pitch-levels achieved by the following means:

Pitch-class and pitch-level centres are placed at the boundaries of groupings. For instance, E^4 is the first and final note of the piano top line which extends from the opening gesture to b. 3 (exx. 2 and 3).

---

14 The autograph material is kept at the Arnold Schoenberg Institute. It comprises a fair copy (MS 730–65) and a blueprint of the work (MS 768–800).

Ex. 4.3

introduction

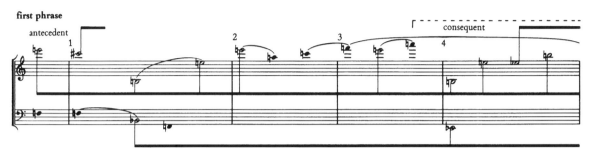

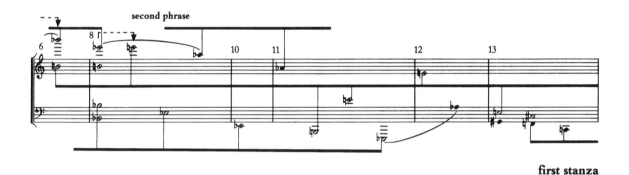

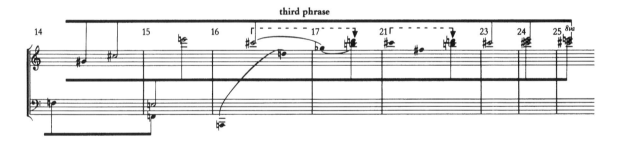

Registral disposition: the predominant lines of chordal sequences and generally of most textures are the highest and lowest.

The bass supporting and participating in the overall harmonic movement in a manner analogous to that of tonality; e.g. in the first phrase, b. 1–8, the bass line anticipates the general progression of the top line by reaching $E\flat^0$ at b. 4 (ex. 3).

The functional deployment of an implied 5:1 or *V:I* linear relation to support pitch-class centres. For instance, at the beginning of the first phrase (b. 1–8)

E⁴, which first appears as the top note of the first piano chord, is supported by the B² of the first string chord before being repeated an octave lower by the second string chord (ex. 3).

The use of the leading-note relation to support the predominance of a pitch-class or pitch-level and to give a sense of linear goal. For instance, in the antecedent of the first phrase, b. 1–3, the highest registral point on the beat is the A⁴ played by the second violin in b. 3, which performs a leading-note function in relation to the sustained Bb⁴ at b. 5/iii–7, the highest note of the consequent. This leading-note relation is important in terms of the overall design of the phrase. The main pitch-level centre of the top line of the introduction, E⁴, is temporarily displaced in the consequent by the subsidiary Eb, which in turn performs a leading-note function in relation to the beginning of the second phrase. The link between the elements supporting the two pitch-level centres is the described leading-note relation between the highest points of the antecedent and consequent. The overall sequence is shown in the following diagram, which must be read in conjunction with ex. 3:

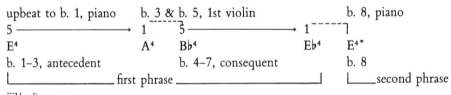

```
upbeat to b. 1, piano      b. 3 & b. 5, 1st violin                    b. 8, piano
5 ─────────────────────→ 1      5 ──────────────────────→ 1
E⁴                          A⁴     Bb⁴                    Eb⁴     E⁴*
b. 1–3, antecedent                 b. 4–7, consequent             b. 8
└──────────────────── first phrase ──────────────────────┘   └────second phrase
```

⌐ leading-note
→ fifth support

* In the second phrase the piano plays in octaves for reasons of balance. E⁴ is the continuation of the top line of the previous phrase.

Further ambivalence is created by the fact that often the hierarchical structure of textural components and/or of a particular instrumental line contradicts that of the overall design or total ensemble. For instance, in b. 1–4, the piano bass line projects F as its pitch-class centre by repeating and placing it at the extreme of groupings (ex. 3). But understood in terms of the overall design of b. 1–4, F is subordinated to the Bb–Eb progression in the bass of the string chords to which it gives support by being V of Bb. While the strings and the top part of the piano establish E⁴, the piano bass line articulates F¹–Bb⁰–Eb⁰.

In the sections of the *Ode* determined by 'antecedent a', this hexachord and/or, its Mm tetrachordal segments account for the majority of the main events, but often not for detail. 'Antecedent a' provides a linear and vertical framework to which not only conventionalized formulae, such as neighbour-notes or 'nota cambiata' figures, are attached, but also motifs which are completely independent of the intervallic identity of the hexachord. The differentiation between fundamental and ornamental or motivically independent events is supported by the metric structure, so that the events determined by the hexachord tend to be accented and fall on the beat while the structurally subsidiary or ornamental ones normally do not: e.g. the first three notes of 'motif a' (indicated in ex. 2), the unaccented notes of the string chords in b. 1–4 (ex. 4a) and the double neighbour-note ornament of the piano A♭ at b. 9 (ex. 4b). Another instance of the combination of the Mm tetrachord with conventionalized formulae occurs at b. 8–18: the prominent incomplete 'nota cambiata' figures of the piano at b. 8 are repeated by the viola and cello at b. 12 and sequentially extended by the piano at b. 13–14 before being taken by the first violin at b. 15 to link the E^4 of b. 15 to the D^4 of b. 18 (ex. 4b & c).

In the introduction to the *Ode*, we can identify various prolongational procedures and a variety of means for achieving continuity which, in combination with the functional ambiguity implicit in the unit of progression, result in a syntax of great subtlety and plasticity.

Often the prominence given to particular pitch-levels create thematic connections between events which are otherwise unrelated. For instance, the beginning of the second phrase, b. 8–9, and the chord which introduces the first stanza of the poem, b. 25–26, refer to the opening piano statement despite the very different contexts (ex. 5). The connection results from the fact that in these three instances the pitch-levels of the first tetrachord of the 'home' form of 'antecedent a' are fixed as E^4, $C\sharp^4$, $G\sharp^3$, and F^3.[15]

E^4 and $C\sharp^4$ are the main pitch-level centres of the introduction; but while E^4 is predominant right from the opening gesture, the process of establishing $C\sharp^4$ involves the whole of the introduction (ex. 3). $C\sharp^4$ emerges as the final goal of a succession of hierarchically predominant pitches related by perfect fifths. This cycle starts on $B\flat^4$, the highest note of the first phrase (b. 5–6), which supports the $E\flat^4$ at b. 8. The chain of pitch-level centres related by perfect fifths is interrupted in the third phrase where after progressing to $G\flat^2$ (b. 17, first violin), $C\sharp^4$ performs a leading-note function (second violin, b. 21). The D^4 has been repeatedly superimposed on $F\sharp^3$–B^3, the next step in the sequence. The emphasis on D serves the double purpose of neutralizing the tendency to continue the sequence of fifths, which would have resulted in a quick return to E, and of giving $C\sharp^4$ particular emphasis.

As explained above, the sequence of fifths which underlies the pitch-level centres of the top line of the first phrase starts on $B\flat^4$–$E\flat^4$ in the consequent. From the onset of the introduction this dyad is predominant in the bass line, which at b. 4 centres on $E\flat^0$ (ex. 3). At the beginning of the consequent of the first phrase, b. 4, a new branch of the E♭ line appears at the top of the texture determining its cadence (ex. 3). Since both the antecedent and consequent start with a pair of string chords which have B^2 as their top note, the change of the top note in the second string chord, from E^3 in the antecedent to $E\flat^3$ in the consequent, is a deviation from the model and hints at a change

---

15 As explained above, in the second phrase, these pitch-levels are doubled in octaves for reasons of balance. I regard the lower line as predominant, since it is the continuation of the top line of the previous phrase.

Ex. 4.4

a)

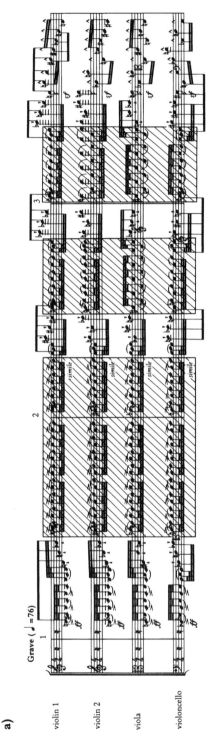

only some of the instances of the Mm tetrachord are indicated

▱ Mm tetrachords

▨ Mm tetrachords with neighbour-notes

b)

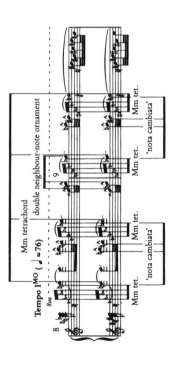

Ex. 4.4 (*cont.*)

c)

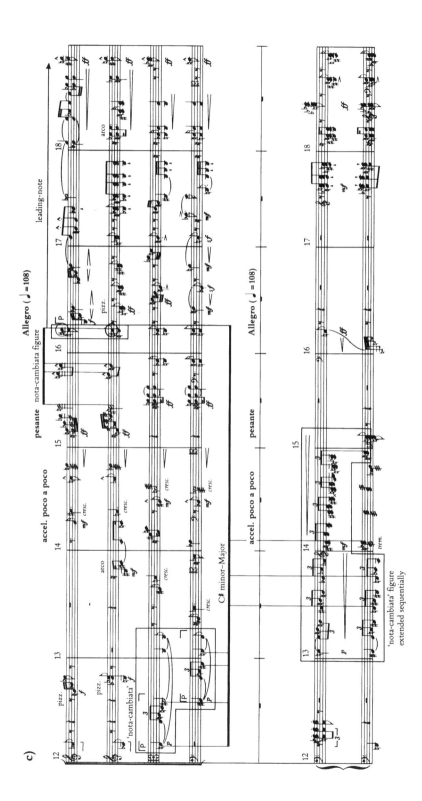

Ex. 4.5

Ex. 4.5 (*cont.*)

opening of the second phrase

opening of the first stanza

Ex. 4.6

introduction

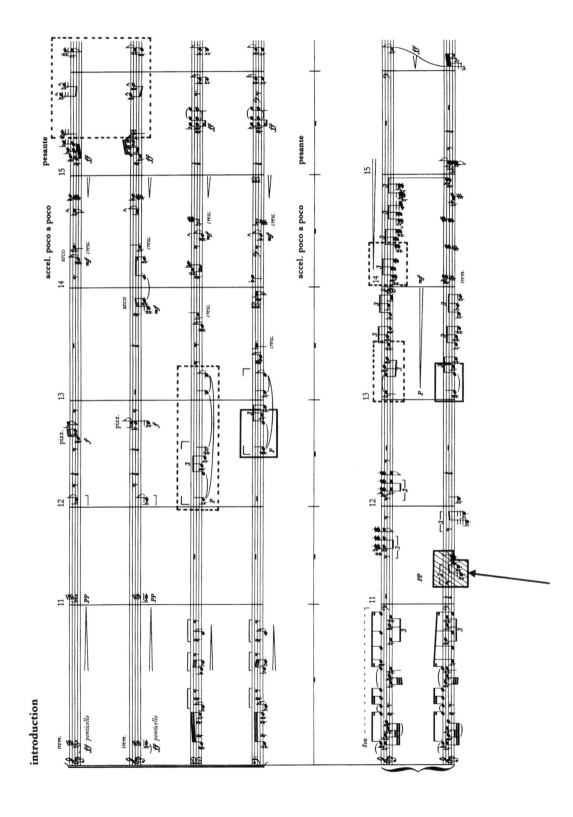

Ex. 4.6 (*cont.*)

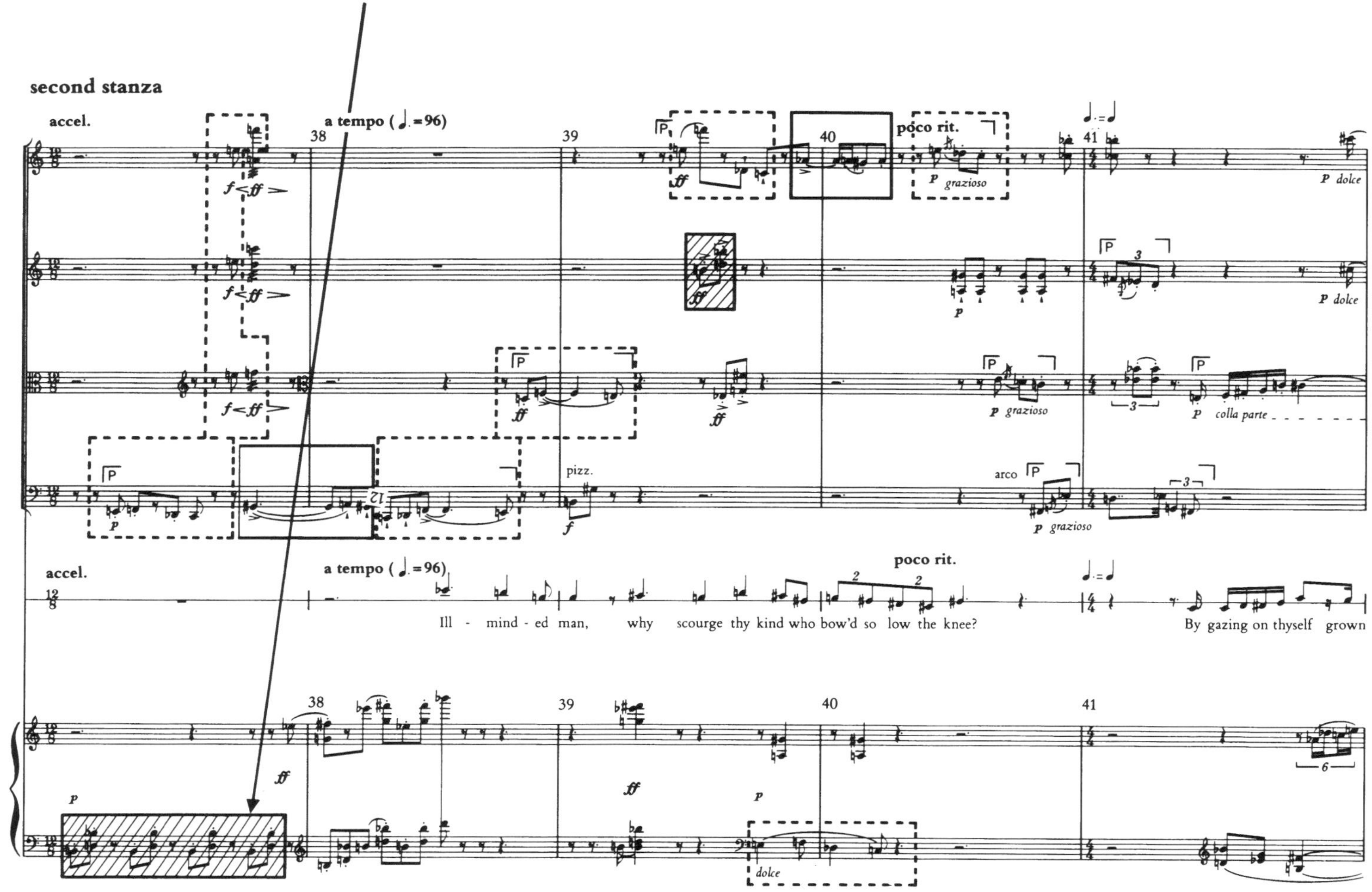

second stanza
accel.
a tempo (♩. = 96)
poco rit.
♩. = ♩
38
39
40
41
f < ff >
ff
p grazioso
p dolce
p
p colla parte
pizz.
arco
f
12
Ill - mind - ed man, why scourge thy kind who bow'd so low the knee?
By gazing on thyself grown
dolce
6
3
2

of local pitch-class predominance. Yet Eb^3 is only a subordinated event at b. 4. The Eb line establishes its priority only at b. 5 with the Bb of the last chord of the string progression. This consists of the same pitch-classes as the first string chord of the antecedent but their registral distribution is reversed, indicating the crossing of the E and Eb lines:

b. 1   b. 5

B^1 Bb^4
G^1 D^4
D^1 G^3
Bb^0 B^2

At b. 5, the E line recedes giving way to the sequence of local pitch-class centres related by fifths (ex. 3). This sequence is however a local event: E^4 remains predominant throughout the introduction, appearing at the top of the texture at important points such as the beginning of the second phrase (b. 8) and the opening of the first stanza (b. 25: ex. 3).

A three-note chromatic figure descending from Eb to Db permeates b. 27–28 (ex. 7). This figure, which uses the same sequence of pitch-classes as the ending of the *Eroica* theme – henceforth the '*Eroica* motif' – first appears as part of 'motif a' in ex. 7. The '*Eroica* motif' is repeated many times until it is finally played $f\!f$ in octaves by violins and piano at b. 28. The first violin Eb^4–D^4–Db^4 at b. 28 chromatically fills the minor third formed by the E^4–$C\sharp^4$ at b. 25. The descending gesture depicting Napoleon's fall, which closes the stanza, b. 34–36, also starts on E^4–$C\sharp^4$ and ends on a piano ostinato using Db–C–A, the same pitch-classes as the second half of the untransposed form of 'motif a'. Thus, the first stanza is framed by an AMm tetrachord containing the '*Eroica* motif' in its first half:[16]

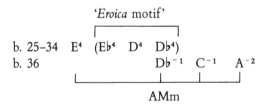

'*Eroica* motif'

b. 25–34 E^4 (Eb^4 D^4 Db^4)
b. 36 Db^{-1} C^{-1} A^{-2}

AMm

'Antecedent c' – second to fifth stanzas

Although the second stanza introduces a new ordering of the source hexachord, 'antecedent c', it exhibits strong thematic and motivic links with the preceding sections, and in a broader sense could be interpreted as a synthesis of important pitch relations in the introduction and first stanza.

16 According to Schoenberg's autograph, at b. 36 the third note of each piano triplet is A^{-2} and not B^{-2} as in the Schirmer edition.

'Antecedent c' incorporates a modified version of the incomplete '*nota cambiata*' figure which features in the introduction at b. 8–16 (E–F–D–C♯ and G♯–A–F♯–F: ex. 4b & c). But unlike the original figure, the modified version, E–F–D♭–C, is a subset of the source hexachord. The modified '*nota cambiata*' figure first appears starting on the same pitch-class as in b. 12 and it is followed by the first two pitch-classes of the second figure at b. 12, G♯–A:

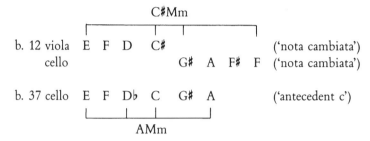

Ex. 4.7 (*cont. on pp. 136–7*)

second stanza (opening)

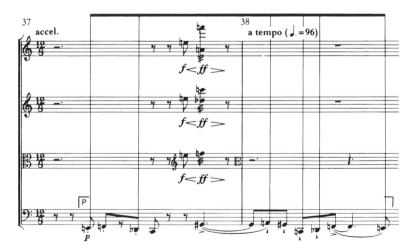

Ex. 4.7 (*cont.*)

first stanza (opening)

Ex. 4.7 (*cont.*)

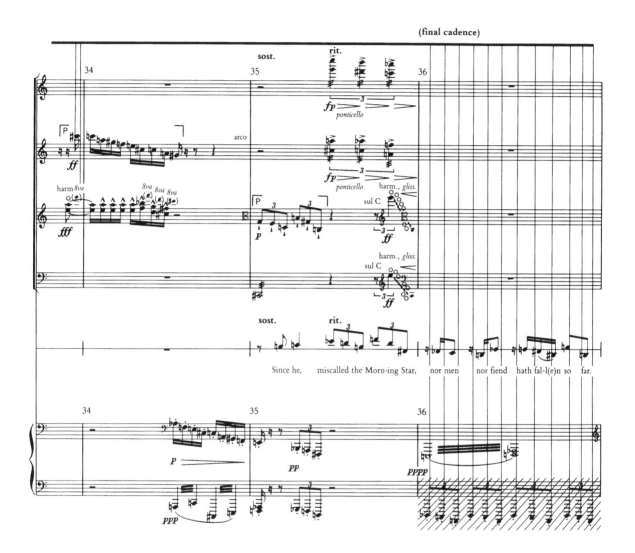

In addition to retaining some intervallic characteristics and pitch-classes of the original figures in the 'home' form of the new ordering of the hexachord, other features of the second stanza contribute to articulate the connection, such as the use in the accompaniment of a similar piano figuration and same metre as in b. 11–16. Furthermore, the texture of these two passages is similar in that they both display free imitative treatment and fragmentation of motivic material (ex. 6).

The continuous unfolding of twelve-tone aggregates generally results in a very active pitch discourse. In the *Ode*, Schoenberg devised many procedures for counteracting this tendency. In general, while the twelve pitch-classes appear in continuous permutation at the level of detail, the overall design of each section is restricted to simple intervallic configurations, such as those described in relation to the introduction and first stanza. Several important thematic events of the second stanza involve a melodic shape delimiting E–G♯. This dyad frames the 'principal part' at the beginning of the second stanza, b. 37–38, and provides the core of its closing phrase, where the cello, initially doubled by the second violin, plays a melody which after dwelling upon G♯ reaches E, b. 45–49. In addition, the thematic procedures used in the section extending from the beginning of the second stanza to the first extended instrumental interlude, b. 37–85, contribute to a slower rate of unfolding of hierarchically significant pitch events than in the preceding section.

The section extending from the beginning of the second stanza to the first extended instrumental interlude includes the transposed restatement of the opening theme of the second stanza at t 2,[17] b. 70–71, which is followed by the first major cadence of the section at b. 77 closing on C♯ (viola). At the beginning of the second stanza the predominant pitch-class centre is E but this is gradually displaced by F♯. Initially, E is associated with B (e.g. cello b. 45/iii–49/i) and later on C♯ with F♯ (e.g. first violin b. 51/iii–53). Since E and C♯ are also the main referential pitch-classes of the introduction and first stanza, these pitch-classes play a central role in the overall tonal plan from the introduction to the end of the fifth stanza:

first stanza | second stanza | fourth and fifth stanzas

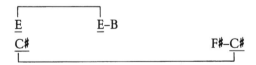

This tonal shift involves a variety of processes some of which are determined by the characteristic of 'antecedent c', while others relate to developmental processes:

17 t 2: transposition level 2

The opening theme of the second stanza, b. 37–39, comprises a pair of retro-graded hexachords. The second hexachord of the pair is both the retrograde of the first and its inversion at t 5:

theme (b. 37–38)

prime						inversion at t 5
						and retrograde

E   F   Db   C   G#   A   G#   C   Db   F   E

This relates to the fact that 'antecedent c' is intervallically symmetrical, so that under retrograde inversion at t 5 it maps into itself:

```
   1      4      1      4      1
E      F      Db      C      G#      A
```

The combinatorial properties of this hexachord determine the treatment of this theme and its accompaniment at t 2 (b. 70), which results in the unordered hexachordal content of the theme becoming that of the accompaniment and vice versa:

prime	E	F	Db	C	G#	A	theme
t 7 inversion/	B	Bb	D	Eb	G	F#	accompaniment
t 2 retrograde							

t 2 prime/	F#	G	Eb	D	Bb	B	theme
t 7 retrograde inversion							
t 7 inversion*/	C#	C	E	F	A	G#	accompaniment
t 4 retrograde*							

*this hexachord appears in various orderings

The reinterpretation of function of referential pitch-classes is an important means for achieving continuity. We have observed that the first theme of the second stanza associates G#[1] with E[1], which appear respectively as a strongly articulated note and the cadencing point of the melodic curve. The phrase which closes on C# at b. 77 starts at b. 74 with the transposition of part of the viola and cello material at b. 45–48 and is followed by a viola melody starting on G#[2] at b. 76. While at b. 45–49 G# is part of the melodic arch G#[1]–E[1], at b. 76 it gives fifth support to the final C#[2]. The reinterpretation of the function of G# is clearly presented by means of the thematic interconnection.

The cadence on C# at b. 77 is preceded by the establishment of F# and B as secondary pitch-class centres. Two cadential passages involving ostinati are interpolated before the restatements of the opening theme of the second stanza

(b. 54–57 and 66–69). The first of these cadences leads to the elaboration of the first theme of the introduction: at b. 58, the first violin plays the same pitch-levels as at b. 4, prominently projecting B in the treble. The presence of F♯ at the extreme of groupings is already evident at b. 49–53, and the restatement of the opening theme of the second stanza starts on F♯ and its accompaniment on C♯:

b. 37	52	58	70	77
E	(F♯)	B	F♯	C♯
B			C♯	

While the preparation for the transposed reprise of the opening theme of the second stanza accounts for the main thematic processes of the section, this overlaps with development treatment of material from other sections of the work. As mentioned above, a reference to material from the introduction occurs at b. 58, and a transposed version of the opening bars of the first stanza appears at b. 73/iv–74. At b. 76, each of the two textural components played by strings refers to different previous events: the string harmonics are a reference to b. 25–26 and the viola and cello play a transposition of the viola and cello material at b. 45. The C♯ cadence at b. 77 gains its intensity partly from the expressive viola line, marked 'very pathetic', which is left to cadence alone, and partly from the thematic overlap. The following diagram shows the processes in the pitch domain which correspond to the described overlapping of thematic processes.

stanza	1	2	3		4		5
b.		25	37	50	58	70	74	77
			E	(D♭)	B	F♯		C♯
			B	F♯	C	C♯		
		E					A	
		C♯					F♯	

└──────── 5:1 ────────┘

'Consequent' and 'antecedent b' – first instrumental interlude and sixth stanza

The 'consequent' accounts for certain melodic aspects of the opening theme of the first extended instrumental interlude, b. 86–90. Although the complete 'consequent' has not been present until then, two dyads from its 'home' form, F♯–B and B♭–E♭, are prominently articulated throughout the movement. The 'consequent' is the only hexachord of the *Ode* which contains both dyads. The F♯–B/B♭–E♭ configuration appears in many contexts where it acquires a motivic function. Manifold repetitions of this configuration often feature in the 'principal part' at cadences: e.g. in the final cadence of the introduction,

b. 19–24, and in the passage leading to the final cadence of the second stanza, viola and cello b. 44–45. F♯–B doubled by B♭–E♭ also appears at the opening of several phrases: e.g. the viola and cello at the beginning of the first stanza, b. 27–29. Generally, this configuration is prominently articulated in melodic statements: e.g. the first violin melody doubled by second violin at b. 30–31. Moreover, it often appears in contexts where some or all of the other textural components also consist of interval-class five: e.g. at b. 19–21 the 'principal part', played by the second violin, consists of repetitions of F♯–B doubled by the viola B♭–E♭, which together with the first violin and cello G–D form a representation of the source hexachord of the *Ode*, and in conjunction with the piano part, also entirely consisting of fifths, form a twelve-tone aggregate.

The 'principal part' at the opening of the interlude (b. 86–90) consists of the 'consequent' in combination with 'antecedent a' (ex. 8). Segment (*1. . .3*) of the 'consequent' is the same trichord which is twice contained in 'antecedent c':

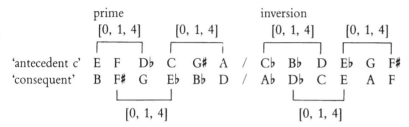

These hexachords are also interrelated in that two consecutive statements of the 'home' form of 'antecedent c' embed a tetrachord equivalent to the first one of the 'consequent'. The 'principal part' at b. 88–89 is an instance of two successive statements of 'antecedent c', where, by adding an F after the first A♭, the prime form of 'antecedent b' is also created (ex. 8):

'principal part' at b. 88–89

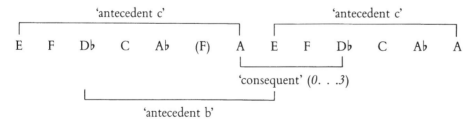

The piano theme at b. 86 starts with the first three pitch-classes of this tetrachord (i.e. consequent (*0. . .3*), A–E–F), and its restatement at b. 178 starts with the statement of the complete 'consequent' starting with these pitch-classes, i.e. A–E–F–D♭–A♭–C. Since the first trichord of 'antecedent b' is also a subset of 'antecedent c', their combination tends to create ambiguous situations with respect to the serial unit of progression.

Ex. 4.8

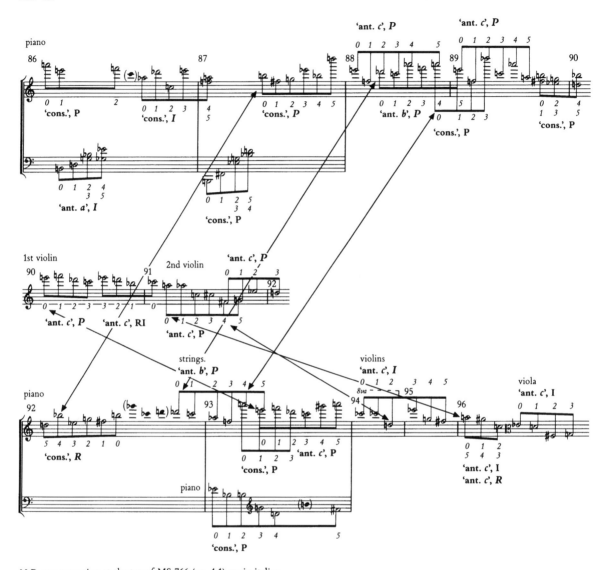

N.B. sets appearing at the top of MS 766 (ex. 4.1) are in italics

The presentation of the 'consequent' starting with A–E is not only determined by the derivation of the first tetrachord from the union of the last pitch-
class of the 'home' form of 'antecedent c' with its first trichord (as explained
above), but it is also related to other thematic processes. The F♯–B/B♭–E♭
configuration appears at the opening of a phrase for the first time at b. 26/iv–27
played by the viola and cello. When this material reappears at b. 74/iv–75, this
configuration is transposed one step in the cycle of fifths. The 'principal part'
at b. 86 represent a step further in the cycle of fifths:

$$
\begin{array}{ccc}
\text{F\#–B} & \text{B–E} & \text{A–E} \\
\text{B\flat–E\flat} & \text{D\#–G\#} & \text{C\#–G\#} \\
\text{b. 26–27} & \text{74–75} & \text{86}
\end{array}
$$

→ V:I

The first instrumental interlude elaborates material both from the second stanza, which in turn derives from b. 11–24 of the introduction, and from the fourth stanza. Generally, the interlude draws its material from the second stanza, but in some cases it refers directly to the model (i.e. b. 11–24). For instance, the '*nota cambiata*' figuration of the 'principal part' at b. 90–91 derives from the second stanza (b. 37–41) where the same pitch-class succession appears in various parts, while the left hand of the piano at b. 86 resembles more closely b. 11 than b. 37. Its final cadence, b. 93–95, incorporates material from the cadential passage consisting of a succession of fifths, b. 59–62, which leads to the '*Victory* motif' at b. 63–64.[18]

The theme of the sixth stanza, viola b. 96/iii–100, consists of the combination of 'antecedent b and c'. The criteria for continuity and set association in this instance fall into two categories. On one side, phrase construction involves the use of leading-note and 5:1 relations. The opening theme of the sixth stanza starts on E$\flat^2$ and closes a semitone higher (ex. 9). In the antecedent of

Ex. 4.9

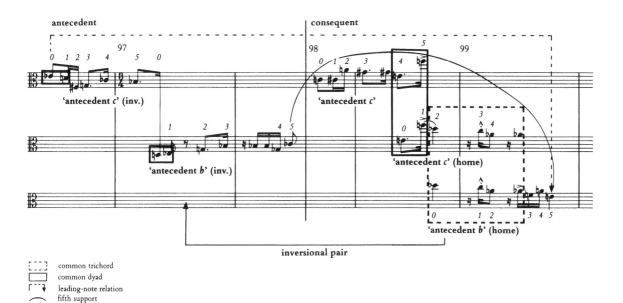

18 This reference to Beethoven's Fifth Symphony has been pointed out by Whittall, *Schoenberg's Chamber Music*, p. 56

this phrase, the first E♭ is supported as a pitch-class centre by the D–E♭ from 'antecedent b', which is separated from the rest of the hexachord by a quaver rest (b. 97: ex. 9). The final note of the phrase, E, receives fifth support from the last note of the antecedent, C♭. On the other side, a criterion for association is to limit hexachords used in main themes to their 'home' form and the inversional pair as listed at the top of MS 766. The first three pairs of inversionally related hexachords on this set-table share the same vertical dyads:

C	C♯	E	F	G♯	A
|	|	|	|	|	|
E♭	D	B	B♭	G	F♯

Therefore, each of the reorderings of the 'antecedents' is also a permutation of these inversional dyads. The choice of form of hexachord used in the theme of the sixth stanza maximizes segmental intersection between these hexachords while using the 'home' forms of the hexachords and their inversional pairs. The second half of the antecedent and consequent of this phrase consist of the inverted and 'home' forms of 'antecedent b' respectively. The consequent begins with the form of 'antecedent c' which ends on the first two pitch-classes of its 'home' form, from which only the first five pitch-classes are stated, and it is followed by the 'home' form, form of 'antecedent b' with which it shares a common trichord (ex. 9).

A similar criterion for association applies in the instrumental interlude, where the second phrase (b. 92–96) is an elaboration of its first phrase (b. 86–92: ex. 8). The 'principal part' of its first two bars consists of a succession of hexachords similar to those of the 'principal part' at b. 87–89 (see arrows in ex. 8). At the opening of the first phrase, the 'principal part' revolves around E^4 and A^4/A^3, which consistently appear on the first beat of the bar until b. 90 where $B♭^3$ is reached. This is followed by an elaboration of the imitative passage based on the 'nota cambiata' figure of the second stanza: cf. 90–92 and 40–41 (ex. 9). At the beginning of this passage the 'principal part' contains the 'nota cambiata' motif using the same pitch-classes as the first violin and viola at b. 40/iii– 41/i, and at b. 91 the viola and cello play F♯–G–E♭–D, the same pitch-classes as the cello in b. 40–41/i. The 'principal part' at b. 90–91 also comprises the inversion of this motif starting first on $E♭^4$ and then on A^3. The complete progression contains two overlapping 5:1 relations: the first one involves the last note of the piano 'principal part' at b. 90 and the first note of the second statement of the motif by the first violin, and the second one involves the first note of the first violin 'principal part' and that of the second violin:

	'principal part'	piano	1st violin	2nd violin
b. 90–91		——————→		
		B♭	E	E♭	A
			——————————→	

→ fifth support

E–E♭ acquires great significance in terms of the overall design of the work. For it prepares the temporary displacement of the pitch-class centre E by E♭ at b. 97–125 – the section which leads to the recapitulation – and, moreover, this tonal displacement is also manifested in the final E♭ cadence of the work.

The 'principal part' at b. 92 (piano) starts with a retrograde of the left-hand semiquaver figuration at b. 87, and is followed by a canonic restatement of the 'principal part' at b. 88–90 (ex. 8), leading to the incomplete statement of the second violin 'principal part' at b. 91 (first violin b. 96). The viola theme, which follows after a caesura, further prolongs the E♭–E relation. The new theme commences with a reordering of the tetrachord that should have completed the restatement of b. 91 by the first violin at b. 96 (E♭–D– F♯–G at b. 96 and F♯–G–E♭–D♭ at b. 91).

The beginning of the viola theme on E♭ has also been anticipated in the immediately preceding bars by the piano, b. 94–95, consisting of a canon which alludes to the cadence appearing before the presentation of the '*Victory* motif', b. 59–64 (ex. 9). This progression, which in its original context reaches E♭² at the word 'victory', is in this instance followed by the viola theme starting on the same pitch level.

Large-scale design

Composing with numbers

In the *Ode*, the duration in bars of phrases and sections and the disposition of many themes seem to follow a numerological scheme. Phrase duration in bars and the relative position of certain thematic or motivic cross-references seem to be determined by a complex grid arising from the combination of eight-, twelve-, and twenty-five-bar units and their multiples. Although in the majority of cases the proposed formal grid coincides with the duration and disposition of events counted in bars, these are not necessarily complete bars. Moreover alterations of tempo, metre, and changes from anacrusis to on-the-beat rhythms suggest that we are dealing with a rather abstract scheme. The following description of the main formal symmetries and prolongational processes summarizes the previous discussion while outlining the general design of the work.

The introduction, b. 1–24, consists of three eight-bar phrases.[19] However, any sense of regularity is avoided by the fact that each of these phrases starts and finishes on different beats of the bar (first phrase, upbeat to b. 1 to b. 8/i; second phrase, upbeat to second beat of b. 8 to b. 16/i; and third phrase, upbeat to second beat of b. 16 to the end of b. 24). The opening of the first phrase

---

19 A 'unit' may comprise several phrases, but in the case of the eight-bar-long unit it always comprises one phrase, thus I refer to it as the 'eight-bar phrase'.

Ex. 4.10

motivic restatements involving pitch-class retention

Ex. 4.10 (*cont.*)

establishes E⁴ as the main pitch-level centre of the top line, which is gradually displaced by Eb⁴ – supported by Bb⁴ – towards the end of the phrase. The 'principal part' of the second phrase starts on E⁴ thus subordinating the Eb⁴ by giving it a leading-note function (b. 8–9). This phrase emphasizes G#–C#, while the third phrase repeatedly leans on Gb/F#. The next step in the cycle of fifths would lead directly to E but the return is delayed by making C#⁴ perform a leading-note function – i.e. C#⁴–D⁴ at b. 21 – which also serves the purpose of giving special emphasis to C#. By the beginning of the first stanza C# shares with E the function of principal pitch-class centre, and E⁴ and C#⁴ function as the main referential pitch-levels. The second stanza, which prolongs a configuration formed by the A Mm tetrachord containing the '*Eroica*' motif starting of Eb, extends for twelve bars. So while the introduction contains three eight-bar phrases (12×2), the section extending from the beginning of the *Ode* to the end of the first stanza comprises thirty-six bars (12×3). The second stanza introduces 'antecedent c', which is the main hexachord from b. 37 to the beginning of the first extended instrumental interlude (b. 86). The first sixty-bar unit (12×5) extending from the beginning of the first stanza to the instrumental interlude contains an important cadence on C# at b. 77, which is reached by a sequence of secondary pitch-class centres arranged in ascending order according to the circle of fifths.

From b. 50, several thematic processes overlap, resulting in the simultaneous or overlapping development of different material. For instance, the cadence which is abruptly interrupted at b. 57 is followed by an elaboration of material from b. 3 leading to the statement of the 'Victory motif' at b. 63. An elaboration of the previous cadence, cf. b. 54–57 with 66–69, leads to the transposed restatement of the opening theme of the second stanza, which is included in a twelve-bar-long unit leading to the first extended instrumental interlude. An analysis of the disposition of thematic material and phrase duration shows that a new layer of phrase durations, which follows an identical pattern to that starting at the beginning of the *Ode*, commences at b. 50, overlapping with the first layer. For instance, the beginning of the instrumental interlude at b. 86 is determined by the multiples of the twelve-bar unit of the second layer, but its ending at b. 96 marks the end of the sixty-bar unit of the first layer (b. 37–96 (96=8×12), exx. 11 and 12). The fact that b. 86 (the beginning of the interlude), which is the thirty-seventh bar of the second layer, is an elaboration of the thirty-seventh bar of the first layer, supports the interpretation that Schoenberg was thinking in such terms. Other instances of the greater thematic intricacy resulting from the introduction of the second layer are as follows:

The twenty-fifth bar of the second layer, i.e. b. 74, which transposes b. 25 a step down in the cycle of fifths, overlaps with the process of cadencing on C# at b. 77, which is an event of the first layer.

Ex. 4.11

N.B. Only downbeats are counted. Anacrustic beginnings are seen as belonging to the following bar.

The coincidence of two layers in the grid is marked by important thematic events. For instance, the sixty-bar-long unit of the first layer comprises three units of almost equal duration. In order to compensate for the change from anacrusis to downbeat gestures at b. 37, the first unit is twenty-one bars long and the last one nineteen. The C♯ cadence at b. 77 marks the end of the second of these units, which starts at b. 58. Bar 58, which is the beginning of the twenty-bar unit of the first layer and of the second eight-bar phrase of the second layer, is marked by the first interpolation of material from the opening of the introduction.

Important events are often the origin of new *axes* of symmetry based on the number twenty-five; e.g.:

The second layer starts twenty-five bars after the first stanza.

The second extended instrumental interlude commences at b. 178, a hundred bars after the elaboration of material from b. 4 at b. 78.

The beginning of the fifteenth stanza at b. 203 uses the same pitch-class material as the 'secco recitative' passage at b. 103.

The section extending from the opening of the work to the beginning of the full recapitulation (b. 1–126) includes the setting of the first eight stanzas of the poem. From the entrance of the speaker (b. 26) to the recapitulation, there are a hundred bars, and from the latter to the entrance of the speaker in the seventeenth stanza there is the same number of bars. Therefore the first sixteen stanzas of the poem are disposed within two hundred bars, separated into two groups of equal duration in bars by the beginning of the recapitulation at b. 126.

From the entrance of the speaker to the last word in the poem there are two hundred and forty bars ($240 = 8 \times 30 = 12 \times 20$).

The establishment of E♭ as a secondary pitch-class centre in the sixth and seventh stanzas precedes the full recapitulation, whose pattern of phrase duration is almost identical to that of the exposition, with the exception of the first phrase which consists of ten instead of the original eight bars. A reduced version of the second layer commences with the elaboration of the second phrase of the exposition at b. 142 (cf. b. 8–16/i with 142).

Formal symmetries and thematic processes

The material of the first and second phrase of the introduction, and that of the first stanza, are manifestations of a common thematic idea. This idea involves 'antecedent a' in combination with the following motifs and referential pitch-levels: the E^4–$C\sharp^4$–$G\sharp^3$–F^3 tetrachord, followed by the retrograde of its second dyad spelt as F^3–$A\flat^3$ combined with either 'motif a' starting on E♭, or only the *'Eroica* motif'. These features are common to the different forms of the theme,

Ex. 4.12

first phrase (b. 1–8) second phrase (b. 9–16) third phrase (b. 17–24) first stanza (b. 25 . . .)

b. 1   6   8   11   16   17   25

E♮⁴

Bb⁴ Eb⁴   Ab² C♯⁴ D³ (Gb/F♯³ B²)   E♮⁴   E♮⁴

C♯⁴   D³   C♯⁴

'Eroica motif'
E⁴ (Eb⁴ D⁴ Db⁴)
b. 25–34
b. 36
C♯⁻¹C⁻¹ A⁻²
A Mm

first stanza   stanza 1   second stanza   third stanza   fourth stanza   fifth stanza
b. 25   b. 37   52   58   70   77   78

E♮⁴   E♮⁴

C♯⁴   C♯⁴

                              ←── 1:5 ──→ ←── 1:5 ──→
                      ─1:5─   1:5

E⁰   E⁰   B   F♯¹
B   (F♯)   B   C♯   C♯¹

2   3   4   5
37   50   58   70   74   77
E⁰   (Db)   C   C♯   F♯   C♯¹
B   F♯   A
theme   theme   A
4 bars   4 bars   F♯
           5:1   5:1

'principal part' b. 90–91   2nd violin
1st violin

Eⱼ⁴

A–E
G♯–C♯⁴   86

B–E
D♯–G♯   74–75

C♯ cadence   5:1

elaboration b. 4

(elaboration of b. 3
leading to 'Victory' motif)

'principal
piano   Bb   Eⱼ⁴   Eⱼ⁴
instrumental
interlude   A

instrumental interlude
(beginning of the recapitulation)

Eⱼ⁴ Eⱼ⁴   Bb Eb Eⱼ⁴
                    C♯⁴
            Eⱼ⁴   b. 107
            b. 96   b. 126
seventh and eighth stanzas
sixth stanza

introduction   first phrase   second phrase   third phrase   first stanza   second stanza   first stanza   third stanza   fourth stanza   fifth stanza   sixth stanza   seventh and eighth stanzas

E♮⁴

stanza 1
b. 25
E⁴
C♯⁴
F♯–B
Bb–Eb   5:1

                      26–27

b. 66
cadence

       8   8   8   8
       24   12   20   36
       8   12
       20 + 1   20 + 1   60   20 – 1   20 – 1
       36   20 + 1

8   8   8   36   24   12

prolonged pitch-class centre or referential configuration

first layer
second layer

prolonged pitch-level

leading-note relation

fifth support

while the elements which individualize each of its manifestations are as follows:

The first phrase of the introduction features a sequence of string chords using neighbour-note figuration, and interconnected by arpeggiations of Mm tetrachords.

The second phrase (b. 8–16) features a canon at the major third, in which the frame of the *dux* is the C♯ Mm tetrachord and that of the *comes* F Mm; thus in this instance the retrograde of the second dyad of the C♯ Mm tetrachord is the beginning of the *comes*. The canonic component is characterized by its open texture, which includes conventionalized formulae such as *nota cambiata* and double-neighbouring-note figuration. The other component is played by the cello and viola and consists of the '*Eroica* motif', giving rise to a descending chromatic scale.

The use of chords in harmonics, as in b. 25–26, is the distinctive characteristic of the theme of the first stanza.

This thematic idea, which will be referred to as the 'main theme', pervades the *Ode*. While the themes of the second phrase and first stanza appear in various transpositions throughout the work, the pitch-classes and often even the pitch-levels of the 'principal part' of the first phrase remain constant in each appearance. For instance:

At b. 58–60, the 'principal part' is almost identical to that at b. 4 and 5.

At b. 78, the 'principal part' is moulded on the first arpeggio at b. 58.

The almost literal recapitulation of the first four bars of the theme occurs at b. 126–129, the only significant difference between b. 1–4 and 126–129 being the change in instrumentation.

Bars 154–155 are also a reorganization of the material of b. 1–2, the chords being played by the piano, second violin, and cello, and the F–A♭ followed by the sequential treatment of 'motif a' by first violin and viola.

The last appearance of this theme occurs at b. 212 and consists of a sequence of Mm tetrachords starting with the same pitch classes as the connective arpeggios at b. 1–2.

Since the theme of b. 1–8 is varied but never transposed, its function is similar to that of a 'refrain' in Classical sonata rondo. The appearances of this 'refrain' are disposed almost symmetrically with respect to the opening of the work and the beginning of the sixteenth stanza (b. 212). In its last appearance the 'refrain' is extended to comprise the whole of the sixteenth stanza (b. 212–223). The second and the penultimate occurrences are at fifty-seven and fifty-eight bars respectively from the opening of the *Ode* and the beginning of the sixteenth stanza. The other appearances of the 'refrain' are also disposed equidistantly from these points.

The numerological plan, which seems to underlie the simultaneous and/or overlapping unfolding of several thematic processes, the overlapping of phrases, and the disposition of the main cadences, may indicate Schoenberg's concern for systematizing procedures which he very much admired in the music of such composers as Beethoven and Brahms.

Conclusion

In order to assess the scope of twelve-tone thought in the *Ode*, let us assume for a moment that each of the presentations of its four hexachords functions only as a theme from which the total material of the *Ode* is derived, rather than also being the presentation of the serial unit of progression. Were this to be a correct analytical judgement, the *Ode* might then be regarded as an instance of that procedure which Schoenberg termed 'composing with tones' and/or 'working (composing) with the tones of a motif'. [20] Examining the *Ode* under this assumption leads to the following conclusions:

The work is generated from the motivic material of the three main themes (i.e. the opening theme, b. 1–8; the theme of the second stanza, b. 37–38; and the theme of the first extended instrumental interlude, b. 86–90). Two successive statements of the first six pitch-classes of the theme of the second stanza produce a segment which is the first tetrachord of the theme of the instrumental interlude. Several motifs and figurations are connected with the third-order all-combinatorial hexachord and the Mm tetrachord, which are the regulating units of progression. The theme of the second stanza (b. 37–88) involves a twofold statement of a 'nota cambiata' figure which is independent of the units of progression and first appears as linking successions of Mm tetrachords. From an analytical point of view, the first striking feature is that the modification of the 'nota cambiata' figure from b. 12 is such that it becomes incorporated into a unit equivalent to the first hexachord in the top line of the piano. As at b. 37, where a non-thematic conventionalized formula is altered to fit into the first hexachord of the theme, this is a remarkable example of the same motif acting as an ornamental and a structural element in the piece.

Often the combination of the 'principal part' of these themes with their accompaniment results in aggregates, and their restatement involves transposition in such a way that the pitch-class content of the accompaniment becomes that of the theme and vice versa: e.g. cf. b. 37–38 with 70–71.

In the cases in which the 'principal part' and its accompaniment consist of a single hexachord, restatements often involve one of the transpositions which results in the complementary hexachord: cf. b. 8–9 with b. 141–142.

20 In a letter written in English to Nicholas Slonimsky, Schoenberg wrote:

> I may mention the pieces Op. 23. Here I arrived at a technique which I called (for myself) 'composing with tones', a very vague term, but it meant something to me. Namely: in contrast to the ordinary way of using a motive, I used it already almost in the manner of a 'basic set of twelve tones'. I built other motives and themes from it, and also accompaniments and other chords – but the theme did not consist of twelve tones.   (Quoted in Reich, *Schoenberg*, pp. 130–1)

The constructional use of the motifs within these themes depends on interval-class content. Therefore these motifs are themselves pitch-class sets and/or collections, which are often transposed, inverted and retrograded: e.g. the consequent of the viola theme at b. 96–100 begins with a transposition of the theme of the second stanza (b. 37–38), but while in the latter the motif starts with a minor second up followed by the major third down, in the former the motif appears as a minor second down followed by the minor sixth up.

A further feature is that the music generally progresses in representations of the third-order all-combinatorial hexachord comprising the above motifs, although this is not a consistent feature of the work: e.g. at b. 26 the viola and cello play F♯–B and B♭–E♭, while the D and G which would complete the hexachord are not present. Often non-complementary hexachords are unfolded simultaneously, resulting in repetitions of pitch-class: e.g. the consequent of the opening theme (b. 4–8) combines hexachords which intersect on E♭, G, and B.

From this the following generalizations may be made:

The transformations of motifs obey the customary operations of transposition, inversion, retrograde and retrograde-inversion. In some cases these transformations result in permutations of the pitch-classes of the motif, and in others in different collections in respect of pitch-class content.

Motivic identity depends on interval-class content.

There is a general tendency to incorporate elements which originally were independent of the hexachord, or which originated from various types of combination into the intervallic structure of the hexachord.

Babbitt has observed that the first two points were already features of the method of 'working with the tones of a motive',[21] and therefore are not exclusively twelve-tone procedures. He has also explained that Schoenberg was particularly attracted by one feature of the twelve-tone method: namely, that each note occupies a unique position within the set, therefore the unit of progression is stable and ambiguity of motivic function can be compositionally exploited without compromising the unit of progression. In 'composition with the tones of motifs', a single pitch-class may often have more than one function, since it may belong to more than one motif at the same time (e.g. the same note may be simultaneously the first pitch-class of one motif and the third of another), and since the motif functions in this case as the unit of progression, this duplication of functions creates undesirable constructional ambiguity.

In the majority of Schoenberg's twelve-tone works, linear statements of the set are reserved for structurally and/or dramatically significant points of the work: e.g. the opening theme of the Fourth String Quartet and the theme of the *Orchestral Variations*, Op. 31. Motifs are more often derived sequences or

---

21 Babbitt, 'Since Schoenberg', pp. 6–7

segments which result from the partition of the set, so that motifs and set are kept as two related but separate entities: whereas the set assures a stable unit of progression, the motif may always be interpreted ambivalently. But against this, we have observed that in the *Ode* each ordering of the hexachord is turned into a theme and for this reason serial unit and pitch motif are inseparable. Since different orderings of the hexachord are often combined in the same context and/or unfold simultaneously (e.g., the sixth stanza), the identity of the set, the distinctive feature of the twelve-tone method, is highly compromised. The String Trio, Op. 45, on the other hand, involves reorderings of the hexachords which are never unfolded simultaneously. In this respect the *Ode* should be regarded as being technically akin to the works composed immediately before the formulation of the twelve-tone method. But in other respects the *Ode* reflects certain tendencies generally associated with, though not exclusive to, Schoenberg's American twelve-tone works:

The combination of complementary hexachords from different set forms, and a prevalence of the hexachordal partition of aggregates.

The use of fixed inversional dyads, i.e. the inversional dyads formed between the prime and inversion of 'antecedent a, b, and c' which appear at the top of MS 766, are in each case the same.

Thematic restatements related by the customary twelve-tone operations: cf. b. 8–9 with 141–142.

Certain features of the sets of the *Ode* are uncharacteristic of the type of sets normally favoured by Schoenberg. He generally preferred sets containing inversionally related hexachords which do not produce disjunctive hexachords under transposition.[22] 'Antecedent c' is a set which Hugh Wood described to a radio audience as assuring 'comparatively simplified harmony, or at least one with a lot of the same sort of chords'.[23] It is interesting that when Schoenberg sketched the set for the Septet, which uses the same source hexachord, he rejected those orderings which resulted in arpeggiation of tonal chords.

This leads to the issue of tonality in the *Ode*. We have observed that the ambivalence created by the Mm tetrachords embedded in 'antecedent a' results in harmonies which invite continuous reinterpretation. The combination of these with often conflicting leading-note relations, and lines supporting different pitch-class centres, results in a syntax of great subtlety and complexity. The ideas involved in the treatment of the material can be traced to the type of harmonic thought in the *Harmonielehre* and *Structural Functions*, where there is great emphasis on the compositional potential of harmonic progressions based on the reinterpretation of chords.

---

22 See Babbitt, 'Since Schoenberg', p. 7.
23 Wood, 'Introduction for Round House concert', unpublished

Often, relations which appear at the local level become expanded into relations between whole sections of the work: e.g. the establishment of the secondary pitch-class centre Eb towards the end of the antecedent of the opening theme, resolving as a leading-note onto E at the beginning of the second phrase, is at the local level the same relation as exists between the settings of stanzas six to eight and the recapitulation of the opening theme. Another example is the unfolding at the large-scale level of the '*Tristan* configuration'. Although Schoenberg indulged in some simple musical word painting, he gave the *Ode* an intricate symmetrical plan which gives thematic processes a certain degree of independence from the text.

In the *Ode* we have observed references not only to elements of the music of the past, but to Schoenberg's analytical view of these works, and to the way in which he caused all these elements to interplay. Elements independent of the hexachords are modified in order to be treated systematically and motifs originally related to the hexachords sometimes 'go independent', often to be reincorporated later into the serial unit of structure. The method used for controlling irregular phrase construction and the unfolding of simultaneous thematic processes while creating intricate formal symmetries suggests an attempt to systematize the formal aspects of the work. Yet no analysis can exhaust the wealth of cross-relations and references in the *Ode*; it can at most point to the fusion of modes of thought involved. In the radio broadcast mentioned above, Wood observed that the lack of a classical education precludes the majority of people from understanding the references to classical antiquity in Byron's *Ode*, without which the poem cannot be fully appreciated, and continued:

> By analogy, can't we foresee a similar danger threatening Schoenberg's music? Doesn't it, too, depend upon reference – not factual, but references of sensibility – and not to a single issue like tonality, but to the whole of the music of the past, all of the tradition in which it was so securely grounded?[24]

24 Ibid.

5

Towards a general theoretical framework (2)

Epochs in which the venture of experimentation enriched the vocabulary of musical expression have always alternated with their counterparts, epochs in which the experiences of the predecessors were either ignored or else abstracted into strict rules which were applied by the following generations.[1]

Introduction

This chapter examines Schoenberg's compositional practice in relation to various areas of twelve-tone theory. It proposes ways of approaching the subject of twelve-tone relations in conjunction with Schoenberg's notions of musical logic. The discussion centres around the String Trio.

The String Trio represents a synthesis of various trends in Schoenberg's development. On one hand, Schoenberg described the Trio as a 'kind of fruit' of the illness he suffered in 1946.[2] Through the account of some of his friends, we know about the precise stimuli behind various passages[3] and the symbolism of many of its 'impossible' but 'rewarding' tonal effects, as Schoenberg described them to Thomas Mann.[4] In this respect the Trio exhibits strong affinities with the works of the Expressionist period. On the other hand, the jagged imagery of the work unfolds according to a type of logic comparable to that of his most 'abstract' compositions. The abandonment of classical phrase-construction in the Trio and its replacement by a kind of 'musical prose', reminiscent of that of the Expressionist period, have been viewed as the counterpart of a more autonomous type of twelve-tone syntax.

The Trio is generally regarded as exhibiting rather attenuated tonal motivation. As with the Wind Quintet discussed in the first chapter, it is interesting to assess whether in an instance of this kind Schoenberg is applying a set of preferences in his handling of the twelve-tone method similar to that observed in the more overtly tonal twelve-tone compositions. Since the Trio represents both a consolidation and a further extension of Schoenberg's use of the twelve-tone method, it provides an appropriate conclusion to this study.

---

1 Schoenberg, 'Apollonian evaluation of a Dionysian epoch', *Structural Functions*, p. 192
2 Quoted in Mann, *The Genesis of a Novel*, p. 172
3 See Bailey, *Programmatic Elements in the Works of Schoenberg*, pp. 151–7
4 Quoted in Mann, *The Genesis of a Novel*, p. 172

Composing with a 'harmonic source-set'

The fragmentary textures of the String Trio are reminiscent of the continuous variation and juxtaposition of elements in *Erwartung*. But instead of the loose arch encountered in *Erwartung*, Schoenberg provides a clearly defined arch-form with a substantial recapitulatory ending and a strong sense of direction. In the Trio Schoenberg abandons the type of balancing phrase-construction and triadic material of previous twelve-tone works. Yet its harmony conveys a sense of inevitability, possibly due not only to the pervasive octave repetitions, but to the fact that 'harmonic' considerations (the vertical dimension) determine the structure in a more comprehensive manner than in the works of the twenties and thirties.

In the early twelve-tone works, Schoenberg conceived the set as an ordered arrangement of the twelve pitch-classes, whose elements can appear as simultaneities (vertical harmonies), in the composition, but whose identity is primarily defined by linear ordering. This emphasis on the linear dimension represents a radical change of direction from the structural basis of 'the style of the freedom of the dissonance', in which the linear and vertical forms of motifs are interchangeable and have no structural priority over each other. In the Trio, Schoenberg is particularly concerned with harmonies which involve the vertical dyads of the combinatorial pair of sets. The combinatorial pair acquires the function of a two-dimensional set (with a linear and a vertical dimension), whose role in determining not only the vertical but also the horizontal dimensions of the music is almost as pervasive as that of the linear set. In order to differentiate a set defined exclusively by succession from one which is defined by both simultaneity and succession, I shall refer to the latter as a 'harmonic source-set'.

The first bar of the String Trio cannot be described as a set in relation to other aggregates in the composition. The inversional dyads of the combinatorial pair in Part I are symmetrically disposed in terms of register, but what later emerges as the set or its source hexachord is not defined temporally or registrally at this point (ex. 1a).[5] Similarly the first two aggregates of Part II (b. 133–144: ex. 1b) and the chordal passage towards the end of Part I (b. 37–40: ex. 1c) cannot be described as sets. Although the chords at b. 37–40 can be ascribed to the one-to-one combination of the first four trichords of P_2 and I_7 of the eighteen-element set which appears in MS 1055, this is not explicit from the registral disposition of the trichords (exx. 1c and 2). The presence of aggregates, which can be ascribed to the 'harmonic source-set' but not to the basic set, indicate the relative independence of the inversional dyads. Other aggregates in the Trio which combine elements from two set forms in the same textural line stand in a less equivocal relation to the set. For instance,

---

5 See Babbitt, 'Since Schoenberg', p. 7, and Lewin, 'Inversional Balance as an Organizing Force in Schoenberg's Music and Thought', p. 144.

Ex. 5.1

a)

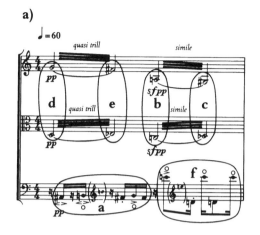

basic inversional dyads

b)

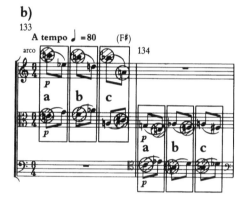

tetrachords of the 'harmonic source-set'

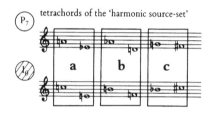

c)

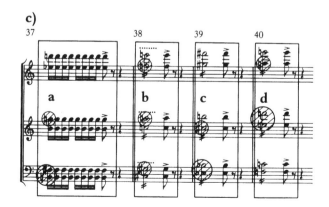

hexachords of the 'harmonic source-set'

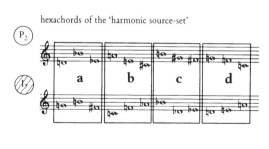

Ex. 5.2

a)

partial transcription of MS 1055

b)

partial transcription of MS 1057

the passage extending from b. 148 to b. 153 consists of three textural lines, two of which articulate tetrachords *7–10* of a pair of combinatorially related sets, while the third one articulates elements *6* and *11* of both pairs (chapter 1, ex. 15). Since Schoenberg assigns *6* and *11* of the prime and inversion to the same instrument and does not treat register in any systematic manner, there is no contextual evidence to suggest which elements belong to which set form. This implies that Schoenberg is treating the combinatorial pair as a structural unit.

In the Trio, the verticalization of elements of sets is paralleled by the derivation of linear elements from the 'harmonic source-set' (i.e. verticals becoming horizontals). Such a process takes place in the closing bars of the first half of the First Episode and its altered reprise in Part III. The principal part at b. 107/ii–109/ii and 253/ii–255/ii consists of a linear statement of the inversional dyads of the 'harmonic source-set', which does not differentiate by means of register or ordering between the elements of the two set forms constituting the combinatorial group.

Any pair of inversionally combinatorial sets results in aggregates which permute the invariant vertical dyads formed by pitch-classes with the same order numbers.[6] In Schoenberg's aggregate-forming works, invariant vertical dyads are different for every transposition of the pair of combinatorial set forms, with the exception of t 6. This property is exploited, for instance, in the first movement of the Fourth String Quartet, whose restatement of its opening theme (starting at b. 165) involves the tritone transposition of the original hexachordal area and thus retains the original inversional dyads (P_2/I_9 and P_8/I_1):

	0	1	2	3	4	5	6	7	8	9	10	11
P_2	D	C♯	A	B♭	F	E♭	E	C	A♭	G	F♯	B
	|	|	|	|	|	|	|	|	|	|	|	|
I_7	G	A♭	C	B	E	F♯	F	A	C♯	D	E♭	B♭
P_8	A♭	G	E♭	E	B	A	B♭	G♭	D	C♯	C	F
	|	|	|	|	|	|	|	|	|	|	|	|
I_1	C♯	D	F♯	F	B♭	C	B	E♭	G	A♭	A	E

In the Fourth String Quartet, these dyads appear consistently in textures which articulate separately the elements of each set-form involved. In the Trio, on the contrary, the 'harmonic source-set' occasionally functions independently of the set.

In Schoenberg's later music, set association is often determined by the presence of vertical inversional dyads of one hexachordal area as horizontal

---

6 See Babbitt, 'Twelve-Tone Invariants as Compositional Determinants'.

adjacencies in another area and vice versa. In the Largo of the Fourth String Quartet, this type of association was shown to underlie certain developmental processes. In the String Trio, a similar criterion determines the transposition level of the first change of hexachordal area, which takes place at the beginning of the First Episode. The following diagram shows that, in addition to both hexachordal areas having six dyads in common, the hexachords formed by the combination of the trichords of the first hexachord of each set-form remain invariant:

Part I

P_2/I_7, hex. *(0. . .6)*

D	Bb	Eb		A	E	C#
|						|
G	B	F#		C	F	Ab

First Episode

P_{10}/I_3, hex. *(0. . .6)*

Bb	F#	B		F	C	A
|						|
Eb	G	D		Ab	C#	E

In the set-table showing the twelve-element set, MS 1057, Schoenberg grouped the trichords of the combinatorial pair, which may be taken as an indication of a concern with the association of sets through invariance between combinatorial pairs (ex. 2b). Whereas in the Largo of the String Quartet this type of association determines important developmental and tonal processes, in the String Trio it only seems to determine the first change of hexachordal area, and in this sense it has a less tangible effect. The presence of a similar principle of association in the *Phantasy*,[7] which was originally conceived for solo violin (the violin part consisting of elements belonging only to one set at a time), indicates that Schoenberg was concerned with highly abstract relations between sets. The use of the inversional combinatorial pair as determinant of set association and tonal processes is to be observed in Schoenberg's music from the Orchestral Variations on, but it is not until the Trio that the vertical dimension acquires a paramount structural importance.

Combinatoriality and tonal thought

Schoenberg frequently employs more than one set in the same work (e.g *Von Heute auf Morgen* and the String Trio), but almost invariably the sets used in a composition are generated from a single source hexachord, and he generally avoids stating different orderings of the set simultaneously. In the *Ode*, however, we have observed the simultaneous unfolding of various orderings of the source hexachord, which often results in pitch-class repetitions. In several later dodecaphonic works, different orderings of a source hexachord, as opposed to a complete twelve-tone set, determine different sections of the work, while one or more twelve-tone sets eventually emerge in the composition as the predominant ordering of such hexachords. For instance, the first nine bars of the

---

7 Babbitt, 'Set Structure as a Compositional Determinant', pp. 144–5

Phantasy are based on a single hexachord, and the complete twelve-tone set is stated for the first time at b. 9/ii–11 (violin). In the second movement of the Fourth String Quartet, the secondary sets of the opening theme, which have the same source hexachord as the basic set for the entire work, account for the majority of events in its first and last sections, and in this sense function locally as basic sets.

In the String Trio, Schoenberg devised new ways of dealing with various orderings of a single source hexachord in a systematic manner. Parts I and II of the String Trio present an eighteen-element set, which is occasionally combined with its inversion at t 5.

P_2 followed by I_7

0	1	2	3	4	5	6	7	8	9	10	11	12	13	14	15	16	17
D	Bb	Eb	A	E	C#	B	G#	F#	G	F	C	E	D	Bb	A	C#	D#
G	B	F#	C	F	Ab	Bb	Db	Eb	D	E	A	F	G	B	C	Ab	Gb

The secondary set which results from the succession of the underlined pitch-classes of the prime (see above) followed by those of its RI at t 5 features prominently in the work; in Schoenberg's set table, these framing dyads are separately stemmed (ex. 2a):

secondary set

P_2						RI_7					
0	5	6	11	12	17	17	12	11	6	5	0
D	C#	B	C	E	D#	Gb	F	A	Bb	Ab	G

The intervals of transposition under which a set holds inversional combinatoriality are not a property of its source hexachord, but of its particular ordering.[8] Although Schoenberg's sets are usually constructed so that they are inversionally combinatorial under t 5, the relation only holds true between the first pitch-classes of the prime and inversion, but not necessarily for the first pitch-classes of the other two forms of the combinatorial group. In fact, there is only one instance of the use of t 5 between both P/I and R/RI: the set of the Piano Piece, Op. 33a.[9]

The contexts in which the secondary set appears in the Trio suggest that the use of inversion at t 5 is governed by tonal considerations. The secondary set (violin, b. 12–17) initiates the most extensive melodic statement in Part I (b. 12–21: ex. 3). Its final element, G (b. 17), is rendered a cadential goal by the disruption of the regular rhythmic pattern, the repetitions of the preceding Ab[4] (b. 16), and the subsequent change of texture. A more definite close follows at b. 21 on D[2]. The G–D polarity was anticipated in the previous phrase. The

8 Ibid., p. 133
9 Ibid.

principal part at b. 5–6 (viola) reaches a G on the downbeat of b. 6, and the treble of the contrapuntal continuation concludes with a descending figure which has G and D as its boundaries (violin, b. 8–9: ex. 3).

The stretto towards the end of Part I, b. 41–44, involves the same hexachords as the one at b. 6–7, and the final Ab^4 in the treble at b. 44 recalls the Ab^4 which preceded the close on G^1 at b. 16–17 (ex. 3). The preparation of the cadence on G by the written accelerando at b. 43–44 (the change to triplets) is brought to a halt by the sudden change of texture at b. 45. Although the following two bars contain the same pitch-classes as the first cadence on G^1 (b. 17, B–F#–C–F–Ab/G#–G), the manner in which the G^1 is presented (viola, b. 46–7) distracts from its original cadential function. This phrase, which serves as a transition between Part I and the First Episode (b. 45–56), involves references to various cadences in Part I (ex. 3). The first six bars are an echo-like rendering of the trichords contained in the last two bars of the previous cadence (b. 39–40). B. 45 and 48 articulate the trichords which form the chord at b. 39 (P_2 and I_7, trichord (*6. . .8*)) and b. 46–7 and 48–9 the trichords at b. 40 (P_2 and I_7, trichord (*9. . .11*). The final six bars of this transition, which articulate trichords (*12. . .14*) and (*15. . .17*) of P_2, refer both to the cadence on Eb^2 at b. 33 (violin and viola, A^3–C#^{4}–Eb^2) and to the 'interrupted phrase' at b. 36 (viola, D–Bb–A–C#), which anticipate the use of Eb and Bb as pitch-class centres at b. 57–80 (ex. 3).

The manner in which material from Part I is introduced and modified in Part III confirms the structural importance of the 'cadences' on G and D just described, and their function as the main pitch-class centres in Part I. The recapitulation of the opening bars is introduced by an unaccompanied G (b. 207), giving particular emphasis to the G of the previously hierarchically neutral aggregate. Part III omits several passages whose function was essentially to prolong tonal relations, thereby bringing the major cadences into closer contact and thus simplifying the tonal outline of the section. For instance, Part III does not include the stretto which emphasizes G–D at b. 6–7, and the *tremolando* over the sustained chord at b. 20–21, thus bringing closer together the first cadence on D^2 (b. 213) and the one on G^1 (b. 220). The second cadence on D^2 (b. 21) is not restated, and the final chord of the previous cadence is held for two bars, reinforcing the predominance of G as a pitch-classss centre. The passage (b. 222–228) which leads to the recapitulation of b. 37–40 is shorter than in the exposition. Therefore the association between the Ab^4s at b. 220–221 and b. 228 is more immediate than that between the corresponding cadences in Part I (i.e. b. 17 and b. 44).

The other prominent appearance of the 'secondary set' occurs at the beginning of Part II (viola, b. 135–41: ex. 4).[10] The intervening sets are P_7 and I_0;

---

10 The only other appearance of the secondary set occurs at b. 154 (violin, starting on F and ending on Bb). Since this is only of local significance it will not be discussed here.

Ex. 5.3

⊘ elements projecting G–D as pitch-class centres

▨ secondary set

Arnold Schoenberg: *notes, sets, forms*

Ex. 5.3 (*cont.*)

166

Ex. 5.3 (*cont.*)

model

variation

Ex. 5.4

Part 2

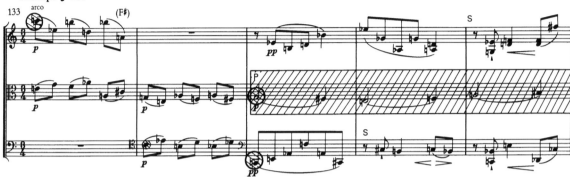

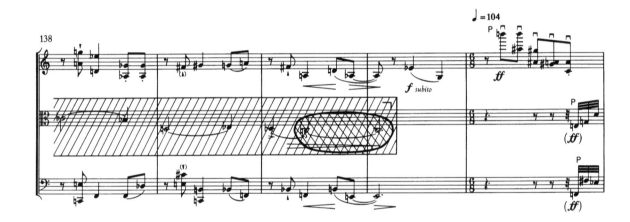

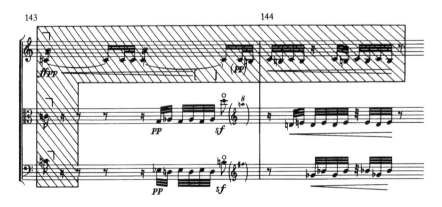

▨ secondary set
▨ elements supporting C as pitch-class centre

accordingly the melody opens on G and closes on C, a further step through the cycle of fifths from the previous appearance of the secondary set (D–G). As explained on p. 179, C – or more precisely C and B – performs an important referential function in the Trio, and particularly in Part II. Thus, the secondary set is mainly used in the context of 5:1 progressions supporting the main pitch-class centres.

In the Largo of the Fourth String Quartet we observed the use of a secondary set, which also results from the succession of prime and retrograde inversion at t 5. In the opening theme (b. 614–621), Schoenberg presents P_0 and RI_5 in such a way that the final F appears as the tonal goal of the phrase (chapter 3, exx. 1 and 2). The manner in which secondary sets are used here and in the Trio suggests that the almost exclusive use of inversional combinatoriality at t 5 in Schoenberg's compositions is linked both to the use of the perfect fifth for supporting tonal centres, and to the first element of P and t 5 I as tonal centres. Inversional combinatoriality at t 5 only makes possible, but does not determine, this type of tonal relation. In numerous other contexts no tonal opposition between the first elements of the combinatorial pair is involved, as in the first two phrases of the second movement of the Fourth String Quartet (shown in chapter 1, ex. 6, p. 26).

Without knowledge of Schoenberg set-tables, there would be insufficient evidence to establish the existence of the eighteen-element set.[11] The only complete linear statement of the eighteen-element set occurs in the final four bars of the composition (violin, b. 290–293), and even in this instance there is an ambiguity as to elements *4* and *5* (b. 291, C♯–E: ex. 5). In contrast, the many linear statements of the twelve-element set in the First Episode unambiguously establish its identity (e.g. hexachord (*6. . .11*) at b. 64 and the complete set at b. 81–2, violin: ex. 6).

Ex. 5.5

11 Rochberg views the Trio as an instance of composition with unordered hexachords ('The Harmonic Tendency of the Hexachord', p. 223–30). Neighbour thinks that the material of the Trio derives from four hexachords and their combinatorial inversions, each of which may be used with one of four other hexachords to make up an aggregate. He concludes that 'there is no regular twelve-tone series' ('Dodecaphony in Schoenberg's String Trio', p. 489). Babbitt also points towards the difficulties in determining whether there is a set at all ('Set Structure as a Compositional Determinant', p. 139). Only those analysts who have knowledge of Schoenberg set-tables have identified the eighteen-element set: Hyde ('The Root of Form in Schoenberg's Sketches', pp. 25–31) and Leibowitz (*Schoenberg*, p. 148). Leibowitz does not mention Schoenberg's set-tables, but it is obvious that he has seen them from the way he presents the set.

Ex. 5.6

Ex. 5.6 (*cont.*)

variation

(*cont. on the following page*)

Ex. 5.6 (*cont.*)

The presence of non-set aggregates at the beginning of Parts I and II, which are determined by the 'harmonic source-set' alone, and the gradual emergence of various sets in the course of the work, suggest an analogy with the type of harmonic ambiguity often encountered in late nineteenth-century music (such as the Prelude to *Tristan* or Brahms's Intermezzo Op. 119/I) in which tonally ambiguous areas coexist with others of greater tonal definition. The Largo of the Fourth String Quartet represents the very opposite compositional approach to the Trio. Not only is the set linearly stated at the opening of the movement but the main pitch-class centres of the work are established from the outset. The Trio, on the contrary, juxtaposes passages with a sense of tonal direction with others almost totally devoid of tonal orientation, and displays a gradation of sets and non-set aggregates. For instance, the opening of the Trio shows no indication initially of a tonal hierarchy. D and G are only established as tonal centres in the first stretto (b. 6–9), which is preceded by the first linear statement of the hexachords (*0. . .5*) and (*6. . .11*) of the set (viola, bar 5/iii–iv). The second cadence on D² (b. 21) is followed by a section ending on an ostinato with no clear tonal orientation, in which the dyads originally present in b. 4 (C–B, F♯–F, and A♭–G) are freely permuted (b. 26–30). Had the first aggregate started with an unaccompanied G, as in Part III, the process of tonal definition which takes place at the beginning of Part I would have lost some of its impact.

Tonal criteria seem of paramount importance in determining combinatorial preferences in Schoenberg's twelve-tone compositions. Although the Trio's expressionist style makes it stand apart from his earlier twelve-tone works, it exhibits a similar kind of tonal motivation in its use of combinatoriality. If the Trio is taken as Schoenberg's final position on this matter, it would confirm that generally his approach to combinatoriality shows remnants of tonal thinking.

Pitch-class association and developing variation

Besides combinatorial relations, Schoenberg uses segmental association as a basis for connecting the musical presentation of two or more set forms. 'Segmental association' refers to the use of segments common to two or more sets which can provide a basis for connecting the musical presentations of sets systematically.[12] In Schoenberg segmental association generally involves unordered set segments. Schoenberg's music also exhibits various other techniques for associating pitch-classes between sets which have been less often discussed; these include 'extracted sequences', which either replicate or permute a set segment from another set, and the permutation of non-contiguous pitch-classes occupying the same order position between sets. Segmental association, combinatoriality, and the use of a basic axis of inversion exploit relations among pitch-classes and not just among intervals. In this respect they fall into a fundamentally different category from the mainly intervallic harmonic association (not restricted to a specific pitch-class content) which Hyde proposes as operating in Schoenberg's music.

Even if, as Lewin and Babbitt have shown, Schoenberg's music exhibits a rich interaction between textural, rhythmic, motivic, and registral factors, and the deployment of segmental association, an analysis of the music exclusively in terms of segmental invariants, while demonstrating the procedure, could not satisfactorily account for the reason behind the compositional deployment of one specific invariant segment at any particular point in the music. To restrict oneself to general principles is as far removed from reconstructing musical thought as is the enumeration of common triads or pivot-tones among tonal regions from an analysis of a tonal composition.

A more fruitful way to relate twelve-tone association and musical thought would be to involve Schoenberg's own notion of 'developing variation'. Schoenberg viewed the twelve-tone method as a means for fortifying musical logic in the absence of tonality, and thought that 'meaningful advantage can be derived from this art of composition when it is based on knowledge and realization that comes from musical logic'.[13] The following excerpt from the *Gedanke* MS gives us some idea of what he meant:

> Now musical art consists of the production of large and small formations which are connected with each other by this motive, which are connected with it also within their own content, and which are connected with each other in such a manner that the *logic* of the total combination is equally apparent as that of its single parts and of their combination.[14]

---

12 See Lewin, 'A Theory of Segmental Association in Twelve-Tone Music', p. 96.
13 Letter of 17 April 1932 to Edgar Prinzhorn, quoted in Rufer, *The Works of Arnold Schoenberg*, p. 140
14 Quoted in Goehr, 'Schoenberg's *Gedanke* Manuscript', p. 14 (German) and p. 23 (English translation)

Goehr's comments on the concatenated terms which Schoenberg employs in his attempt to define musical *Gedanke* help to clarify the notion of 'musical logic':

> We are shown here a string of terms, one derived from another: theme leading to variations and developments, or *Grundgestalt* (basic form) leading to derived *Gestalten* (forms). But theme *Gestalten* are not the same as *Gedanken* (ideas), which are continued by means of *musikalische Logik* (musical logic). For logical thought gives rise to new combinations of theme, variation and development.[15]

Goehr points out that for Schoenberg,

> logical thought in music is not merely a transposition from logical thought in language (with its own significations), but a self-sufficient and independent system for describing the real world, where a musical idea, turning into a *Gestalt* and becoming in the act of composing a *Grundgestalt*, generates further *Gestalten* and thus expresses a musical logic.[16]

This suggests that motivic and developmental processes should be taken into account in order to understand the rationale behind Schoenberg's deployment of pitch-class association.

The following discussion of the opening section of the First Episode of the Trio, b. 57–85, and its relation to Part I attempts to give an account of such detail in terms of Schoenberg's notions of variation and developing variation. Schoenberg conceived developing variation as

> a form in which the simple juxtaposition characteristic of variation sets might be combined with through-composition, and in which, on the small scale, any variation of an idea might be seen as a development.[17]

Referring to the *Variations for Orchestra*, Op. 31, Schoenberg writes:

> I employ constant variations, hardly ever repeating anything unaltered, jump quickly to the remoter stages of development.[18]

'Varying means repeating. . .' (Schoenberg, Gedanke MS)

Part I of the Trio is based on only the untransposed eighteen-element set and its combinatorial inversion. Consequently each pitch-class is associated with only three hexachords. This enables Schoenberg to associate texturally dissimilar events simply by sounding the dyads of any of these hexachords; for instance, b. 24–30 and b. 4/ii–iv are related in this manner. The opening section of the First Episode (b. 57–85) also consists of a small number of sets: the two

15 Goehr, 'Schoenberg and Karl Kraus', p. 62
16 Ibid., p. 63
17 Griffiths, 'Variation' in *The New Grove Dictionary*
18 Quoted by Griffiths, ibid.; a talk originally reprinted in *The Score*, 1960

pairs of sets listed at the top of the right-hand column in MS 1057 (P_{10}/I_3 and P_5/I_{10}). Unlike Part I all aggregates are determined by the set, and the music gradually explores the formulations concealed within the theme and the relation between the two intervening pairs of sets according to principles of developing variation. The second half of this section (15 bars) may be construed as a variation of the first half, since it retains the overall phrase construction, the sets, and thematic material of its model (ex. 6):

model	b. 57–62	63	64	65–66	67–70
bars	6	1	1	2	4

$$P_{10}/R_{10} \qquad P_7$$

variation	71–76	77	78–80	81–85
bars	6	1	3	5

$$P_{10}/R_{10}/I_3/RI_3 \ (P_7) \qquad P_7/I_0$$

'. . . *but only partially repeating.* . . '

The developing variation of the first two bars (b. 57–58) starts at b. 65, where the original trichords are retrograded and given a new figuration. The first trichord of b. 65 reappears at b. 67 but in this instance the continuation introduces a different set, P_7 (ex. 6). The second half opens with an inverted statement of the first three bars of the theme (cello, b. 71–72) and is followed by a rhythmically altered repetition of the violin material at b. 59–60/i (ex. 6):

model	P_{10}	0	5	7	11		0	5	6	11
b. 57–60		B♭	A	C♯	G♯		B♭	A	D	G♯

variation	I_3	0	5	7	11	P_{10}	0	5	6	11
b. 71–73		E♭	E	C	F		B♭	A	D	G♯

'. . .*The repeated parts can be replaced by other material.* . . '

The presentation of the theme in its inverted form is prepared in the closing phrase of the first half (b. 67–70), which consists of a double statement of P_7, and serves as a link between P_{10} and I_3. The chord G–E♭–A♭ associates b. 65 and b. 67, and in addition to being a 'pivotal trichord' between P_{10} and P_7, is also a thematic reference in the process of continuous variation (ex. 6):

	0	1	2	3	4	5	6	7	8	9	10	11
P_{10}	B♭	G♭	C♭	F	C	A	D	C♯	E	G	E♭	A♭
P_7	G	E♭	A♭	D	A	F♯	B	A♯	C♯	E	C	F

The final trichord of P_7 (E–C–F) serves as a pivot between P_7 and the second to fourth notes of the inverted theme, but unlike the previous example the pitch-classes in common constitute a segment in one of the sets and an extracted sequence in the other (ex. 6).

ensemble, b. 67–70

P_7 G Eb Ab D A F# B A# C# E C F

ensemble, b. 71–72

I_3 Eb G D Ab Db E B C A F# Bb F

The diagram shows that these sets have a tetrachord in common, but at this point Schoenberg chooses to project only the trichord E–C–F, which is a derived sequence and not a segment in I_3. Possibly this is because Schoenberg conceives the second half of the section under discussion as a variation of the first, and for this reason it opens with a variant of the opening theme (the inversion at t 5 involves the trichord E–C–F). The invariant tetrachord between P_7 and I_3 is presented only after the opening bars of the model are varied (b. 74–75: ex. 6).[19]

'. . .or can be omitted without replacement. . .'

The first three pitch-classes of the first theme of the First Episode appear in two different contexts towards the end of Part I. At b. 35–36, the principal part ends with Bb–A–C#, and the same sequence reappears as the accompaniment at b. 42 (viola: ex. 3). The latter is restated after the theme of the First Episode, in the context of the new hexachordal area (b. 63: ex. 3). Its appearance without its original principal part at this point reinforces the establishment of P_{10}/I_3 as the local 'home' hexachordal area. Moreover, the subsequent ascending figure (b. 64), besides being reminiscent of the principal part at b. 42 and b. 44, represents a new ordering of the hexachord (ex. 3).

'. . .But it is also possible to repeat in entirety. . .'

The closing phrase of the section under discussion (b. 81–85: ex. 6) returns to the hexachordal area of the corresponding phrase in the first half (b. 67–70: ex. 6). While the principal part repeats the total pitch-class content of the model, the accompaniment (viola and cello) introduces I_0 for the first time. The accompaniment presents the same partition of the set as b. 63, which up to then had been absent from the process of developmental variation in the second

---

19 Much of the detail of this section projects set invariants. For instance, B, which is order number 6 in both I_3 and P_7, is played by the cello as a repeated note in both the model and the variation (b. 74 and 75).

half (ex. 6). The violin Bb–B–C at b. 63 becomes C–Cb–Bb at b. 81 (cello). In this case the association involves non-adjacent pitch-classes:

P₁₀	Bb	Gb	Cb	F	C	A	D	C♯	E	G	Eb	Ab
I₀	C	E	Cb	F	Bb	Db	Ab	A	F♯	Eb	G	D

'. . . and to add new characteristics. Then it is an extension. . .'

The final four bars of the model are not only considerably varied but extended from four to five bars. As in the model, the principal part twice states P_7, but the second statement is incomplete and ends on Ab–D–A, the retrograde of the ending of the second half of the opening theme (b. 59–60: ex. 6). The Bb, which would complete this part of the theme, is provided first by the ending of the cello figure at b. 83 and later, more conclusively, by the violin Bb at b. 85 (ex. 6):

	P₁₀	0	5	6	11	10	9	
b. 59–60		Bb	A	D	Ab	(G	Eb)	
		violin				accompaniment		

	P₇	0	1	2	3	4	P₀	4
b. 83–85		G	Eb	Ab	D	A		Bb
		violin						cello/violin

In this way, Schoenberg closes the section with a reference to the opening theme in the context of a different hexachordal area.

'. . .The variation does not have to take place in the melody but can be effected solely in the harmony.'[20]

The principal part of the opening theme (b. 57–62) and the inversion of the first of its phrases (b. 57–58) appear in various contexts in the second half. At b. 71–73, Eb–E–C–F is extracted from I_3 and Bb–A–D–Ab from P_{10}, but at b. 78–79, the first of these sequences is extracted from R_{10} and at b. 77 and b. 79–80 the second one from RI_3 (ex. 6). Therefore the variation is mainly harmonic:

b. 57–58 & 72–73	P₁₀	0	5	7	11
		Bb	A	C♯	G♯

b. 71–72	I₃	0	5	7	11
		Eb	E	C	F

b. 77 and 79–80	RI₃	10	8	4	3
		Bb	A	C♯	G♯

20 Quoted in Goehr, 'Schoenberg's *Gedanke* Manuscript', p. 15 (German) and p. 24 (English translation).

b. 78–79   R₁₀ *10   8   4   3*
                  Eb   E   C   F

The cases of pitch-class association discussed here represent only a small sample of the many instances in which the musical detail in the first part of the First Episode is determined by pitch-class invariance. In Schoenberg, the criteria determining which of the many such invariants amongst two or more set forms are deployed at any particular moment seem to be thematic, motivic, tonal, and formal.

'Composing with notes' (2)

We have seen that Schoenberg's use of combinatoriality and pitch-class association concerns the possibility of creating relations between the same groups of notes appearing in different contexts. Another aspect of this approach is the referential use of particular single notes or dyads at the local and large-scale level.

The Second Episode of the Trio introduces new orderings of the set. These sets are derived from the twelve-tone set of the First Episode. In this set, elements *2* and *3* (the central dyad of hexachord *0*) of the prime appear as elements *6* and *11* (the framing dyad of hexachord *6*) of the combinatorial inversion, and vice versa, e.g.:

	0	*1*	*2*	*3*	*4*	*5*	*6*	*7*	*8*	*9*	*10*	*11*
P₄	E	C	F	B	F#	Eb	G#	G	Bb	C#	A	D
I₉	A	C#	G#	D	G	Bb	F	F#	Eb	C	E	B

Schoenberg derives the new orderings of the set in a systematic and original manner. He operates separately on two sub-groups of sets. 'Sub-group I' comprises those forms of the twelve-element set which have F–B as the central dyad of their first hexachord and D–G# as the framing dyad of their second hexachord; and 'sub-group II', those which have D–G# as central dyads and F–B as framing dyads. In the reorderings of the set which take place in the Second Episode F–B and D–G# are disposed so that their position in one hexachord is different from their position in the other hexachord, while the disposition of tritones within each hexachord is symmetrical:

re-ordering of 'sub-group I':

original order numbers

	0	*2*	*3*	*1*	*4*	*5*	*6*	*8*	*9*	*7*	*10*	*11*
P₄	E	F	B	C	F#	Eb	G#	Bb	C#	G	A	D
P₁₀	Bb	B	F	F#	C	A	D	E	G	C#	Eb	G#
I₀	C	B	F	E	Bb	C#	G#	F#	Eb	A	G	D
I₆	F#	F	B	Bb	E	G	D	C	A	Eb	C#	G#

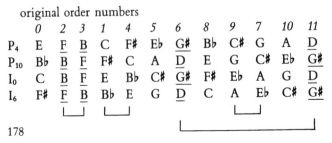

re-ordering of 'sub-group II':

ordering order numbers

	0	2	3	1	4	5	6	8	9	7	10	11
P_1	C♯	A	E♭	<u>D</u>	G♯	C	<u>F</u>	E	F♯	G	B♭	<u>B</u>
P_7	G	E♭	A	<u>G♯</u>	<u>D</u>	F♯	<u>B</u>	B♭	C	C♯	E	<u>F</u>
I_9	A	C♯	G	<u>G♯</u>	<u>D</u>	B♭	<u>F</u>	F♯	E	E♭	C	<u>B</u>
I_3	E♭	G	C♯	<u>D</u>	G♯	E	<u>B</u>	C	B♭	A	F♯	<u>F</u>

The complete group of sets associated by tritones F–B and D–G♯ is used between b. 184, and b. 194 (ex. 7). The phrase extending from b. 188 to b. 192 exhibits a very close integration of the rhythmic and pitch domains. In the first half of this phrase – suggestively instructed to be played '*sempre ppp* and without accentuation' – these tritones appear either as elements with order number *0* and *5* or as elements *1* and *2* of every hexachord. Since the sets are linearly stated, since the distance of imitation is constant, and since the rhthymic values are equal, a 'rhythm of pitch-class recurrence' is created by the periodic recurrence of tritones F–B and D–G♯ (ex. 7, p. 181). This rhythm shapes the passage: the beginning of the phrase exhibits maximum concentration of these tritones and establishes an intense rhythmic pattern, which is relaxed initially by the subsequent augmentation of this rhythmic pattern, and finally liquidated by the increasingly long distances between re-attacks.

At the level of large-scale form, Schoenberg establishes a referential dyad, which acts as a unifying device for the whole Trio. In many places through the work, C–B is projected boldly in extreme registers and dynamics with either abrupt registral changes or its extreme opposite, triple unison (ex. 8). At the very opening of the work (b. 2), this referential dyad is articulated prominently by quick repetitions in four different octaves, and halfway through the work (b. 145) it reaches its maximum possible registral span (ex. 8c).

Conclusion

The examination of the music through the categories described by Schoenberg in his philosophical, theoretical, and didactic writings indicates that the detail and logic of continuation in his music follow such categories precisely. Although many of Schoenberg's theoretical notions can be traced back to Marx, Sechter, and Riemann, they constitute an idiosyncratic abstraction and extension of late-nineteenth-century views. The published extracts from the *Gedanke* MS indicate that Schoenberg's enquiry on the subject of musical logic proceeded generally without explicit reference to tonality.[21] The techniques of developing variation and liquidation, the notion of formal prototypes, and the

21 See Dunsby and Whittall, *Music Analysis in Theory and Practice*, p. 76.

Ex. 5.7

Ex. 5.7 (*cont.*)

distances between re-attacks of tritones F–B and G#–D

Ex. 5.8

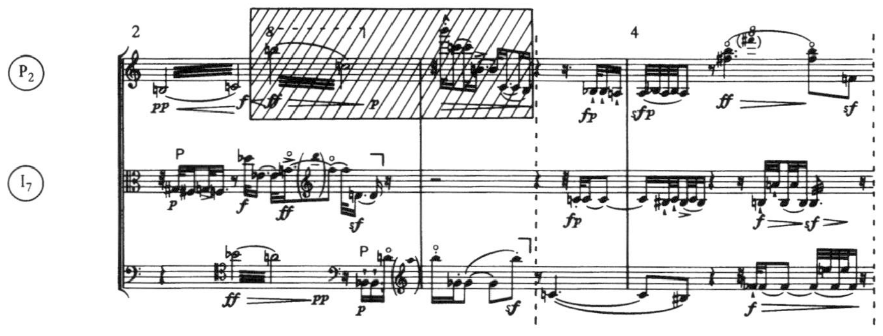

a) Part 1
2
4
P₂
I₇
P
ff
sf
fp
sfp
pp
f
p

b) Episode 1
111
112
113
114
115
a tempo ♩ = 72
P
I₇
R₈
pizz.
arco
ff
sf
p

c) Part 2
♩ =104
142
144
P₁₁
I₄
I₀
P₇
P
rit.
ff
pp
sf
f
maximum registral distance

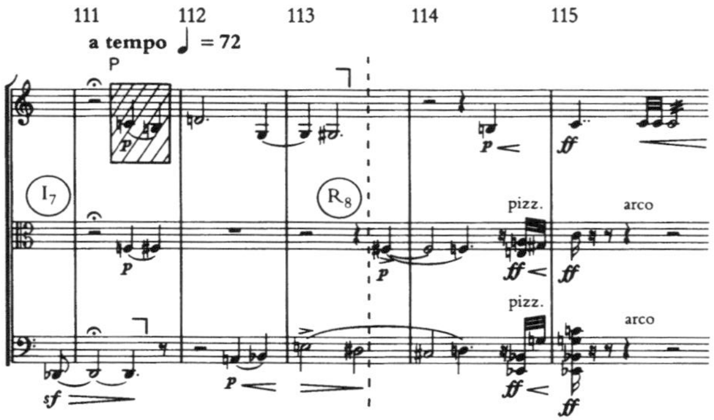

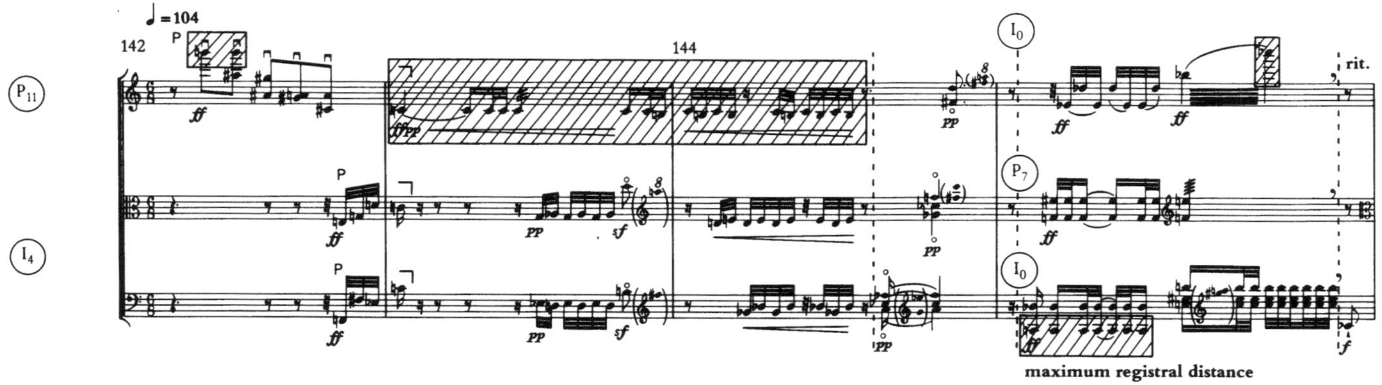

Ex. 5.8 (cont.)

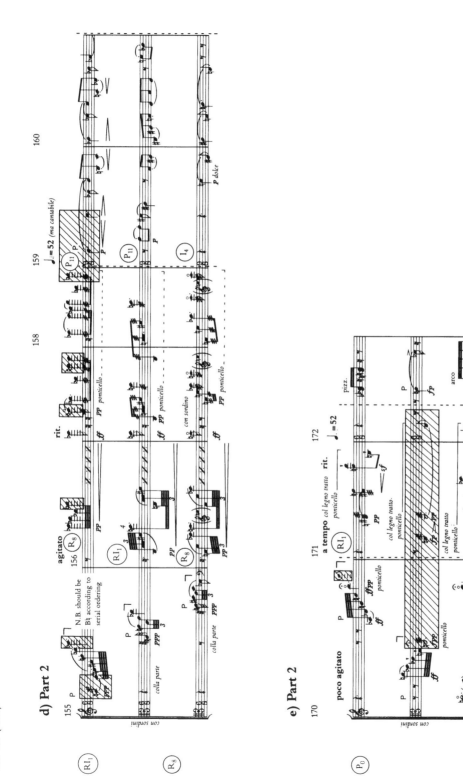

d) Part 2

e) Part 2

use of antecedent–consequent phrase construction, as described in *Fundamentals*, represent the elements of his actual compositional practice.

It is commonly thought that Schoenberg imposes tonal orientation on neutral twelve-tone structures in a rather arbitrary manner, and that the presence of tonal sonorities in his music is only a remnant of a bygone epoch, rather than a feature of structural importance. The analyses of the music and sketch material in this study indicate a rather different situation. In Schoenberg tonal orientation is not bound to triadic material, and conversely triads do not necessarily imply tonal functionality. Tonal considerations appear to be a primary concern in the composition of the set itself and an important criterion determining set association and thematic unfolding. The sketches for the Septet, which give us the rare opportunity to observe Schoenberg's method for composing a set, show him exploring tonal relations within the set. In the *Ode to Napoleon*, complex tonal relations were shown to be implicit in the tetrachordal groupings of its hexachords. The combination of these tonally ambiguous harmonies with frequently conflicting leading-note relations, and lines supporting different pitch-class centres, appear to be not just an arbitrary feature of its quasi-tonal ending, but seem central to the syntax of the whole. The Largo of the Fourth String Quartet exhibits an organic synthesis of tonal thought and the strict twelve-tone procedures of Schoenberg's aggregate-forming compositions of the thirties.

It is generally assumed that once Schoenberg gave up tonal composition and adopted the twelve-tone method, the music is to be appropriately understood in terms of this method exclusively. Is it then legitimate to read hierarchies in a context where not all elements comply with such hierarchical structuring? Can single pitch-classes or pitch-levels placed at boundaries of groupings, supported by tonal idiomatic gestures, conceivably represent tonal centres? Is it pertinent to discuss tonal functionality when dealing with triadic material which does not unfold according to the traditional rules of harmony? Is it possible to regard such relations as crucial to the aural and aesthetic understanding of the music? Each of these questions stems from situations encountered in the music, and should therefore not be overlooked if one wishes to appreciate the scope of Schoenberg's ideas.

A large number of critical studies of Schoenberg lack the historical dimension which would permit an informed and sympathetic understanding of his achievements. A purely analytical approach is bound to prove unsatisfactory when dealing with music which radically breaks with tradition, but remains deeply imbued with it. The revolutionary force of Schoenberg's music lies in the fact that its classicism is neither a matter of style nor of compositional technique, but derives from its adherence to a particular type of musical logic, while its modernism is fundamentally a matter of content.

Plate 1 Wind Quintet, Op. 26 in *Skizzenbuch V*: MS 508

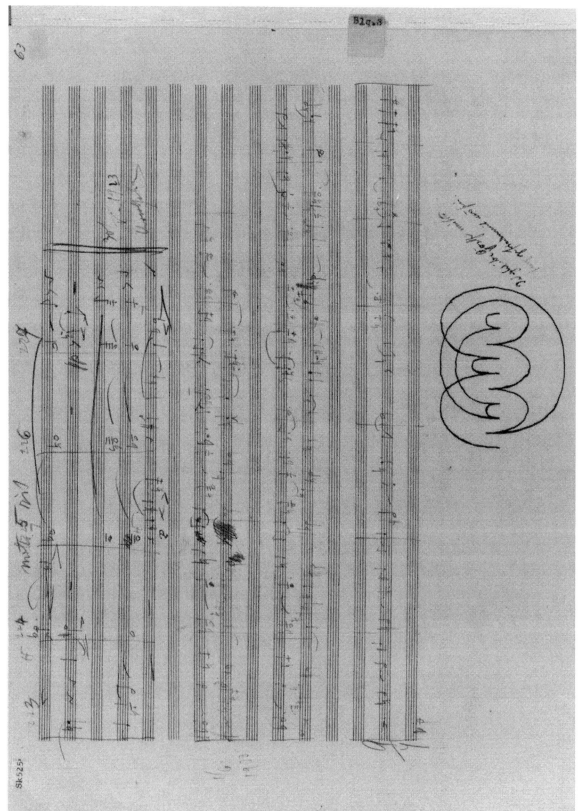

Plate 2 Wind Quintet, Op. 26 in *Skizzenbuch V*: MS 525

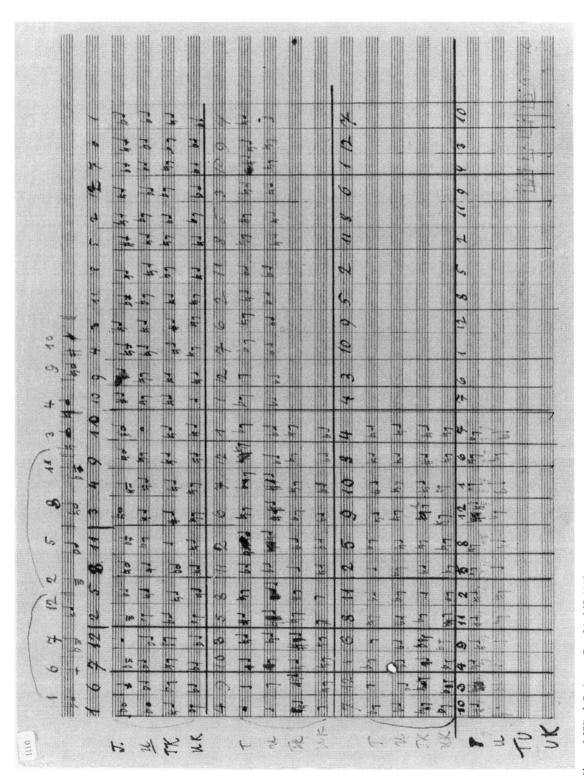

Plate 3 Wind Quintet, Op. 26: MS 1110

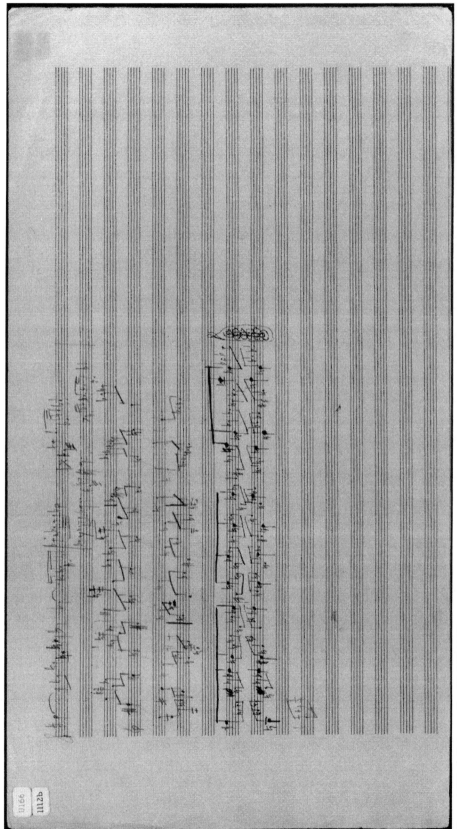

Plate 4 Wind Quintet, Op. 26: MS 1112b

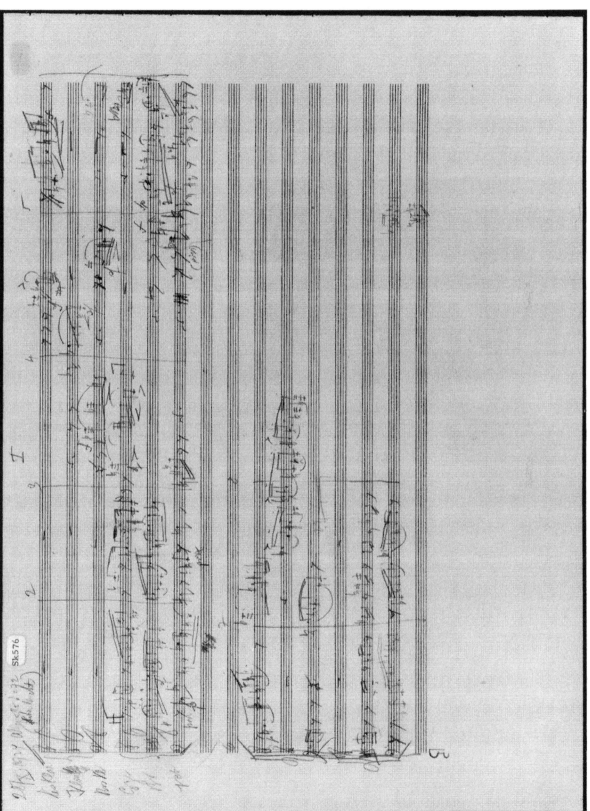

Plate 5 Septet, Op. 29 in *Skizzenbuch V*: MS 576

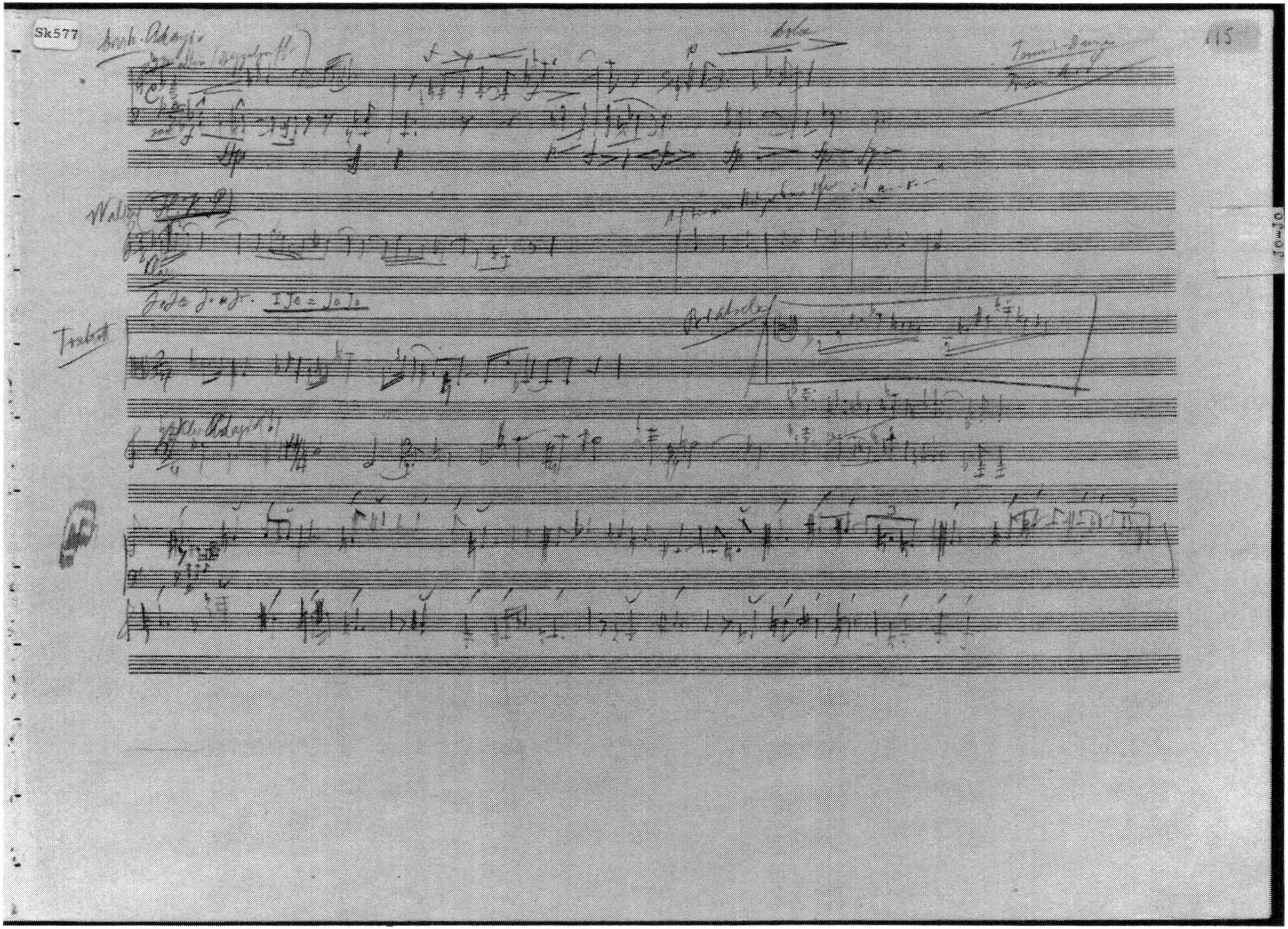

Plate 6 Septet, Op. 29 in *Skizzenbuch V*: MS 577

Plate 7 Septet, Op. 29 in *Skizzenbuch V*: MS 579

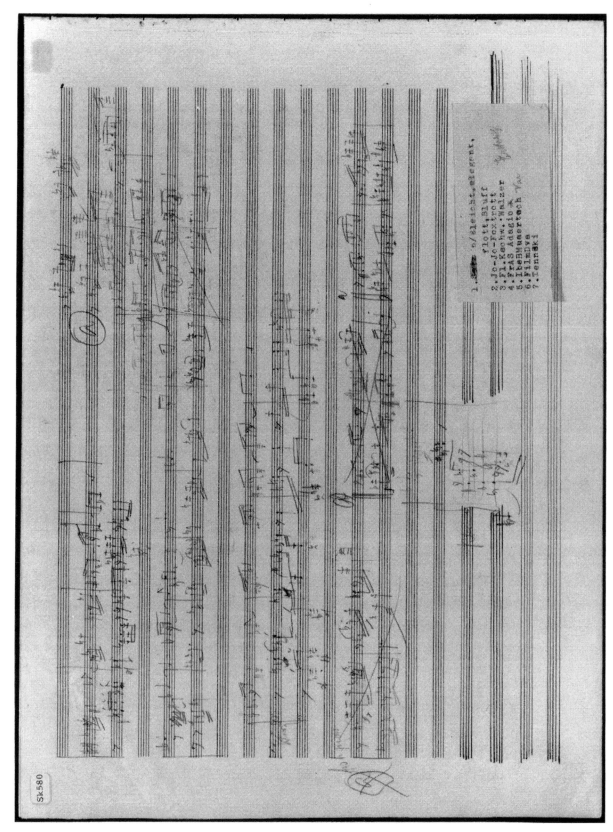

Plate 8 Septet, Op. 29 in *Skizzenbuch V:* MS 580

Plate 9 Septet, Op. 29 in *Skizzenbuch V*: MS 600

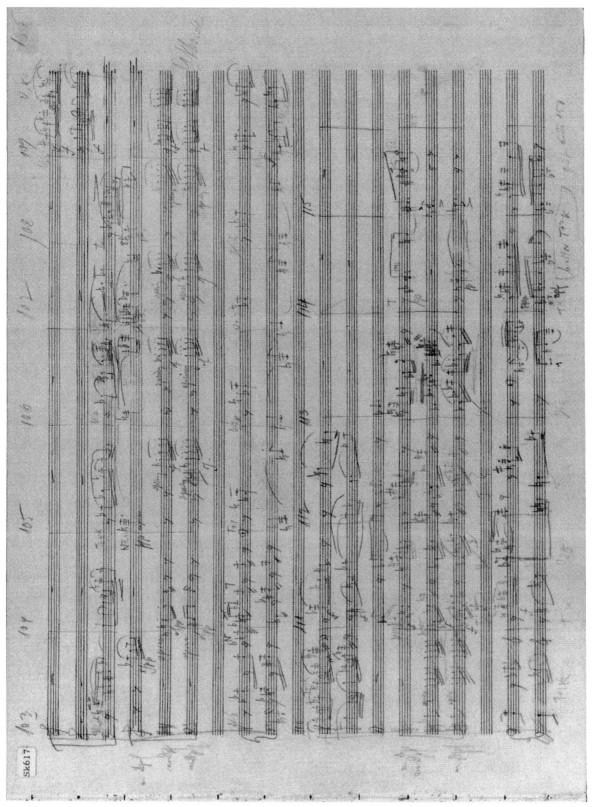

Plate 10 Septet, Op. 29 in *Skizzenbuch V*: MS 617

Plate 11 Septet, Op. 29 in *Skizzenbuch V*: MS 618

Plate 12 Septet, Op. 29 in *Skizzenbuch V*: MS 619

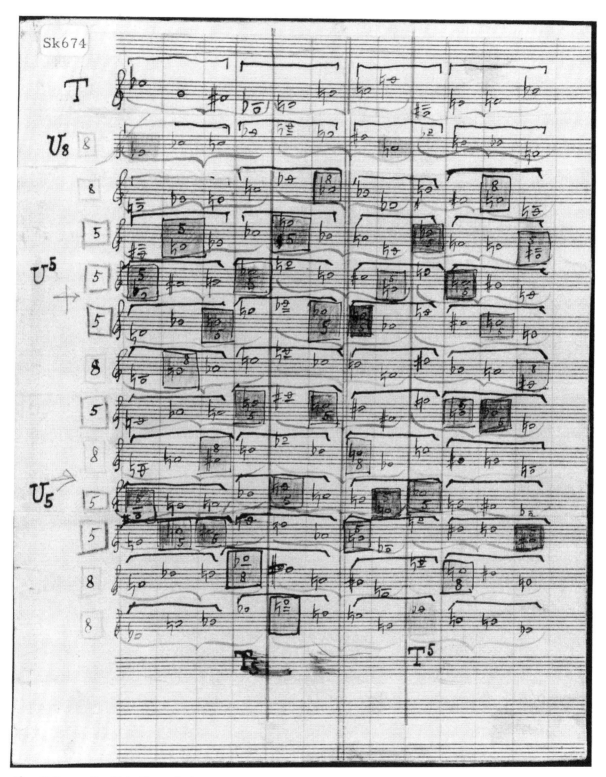

Plate 13 Septet, Op. 29 in *Skizzenbuch V*: MS 674

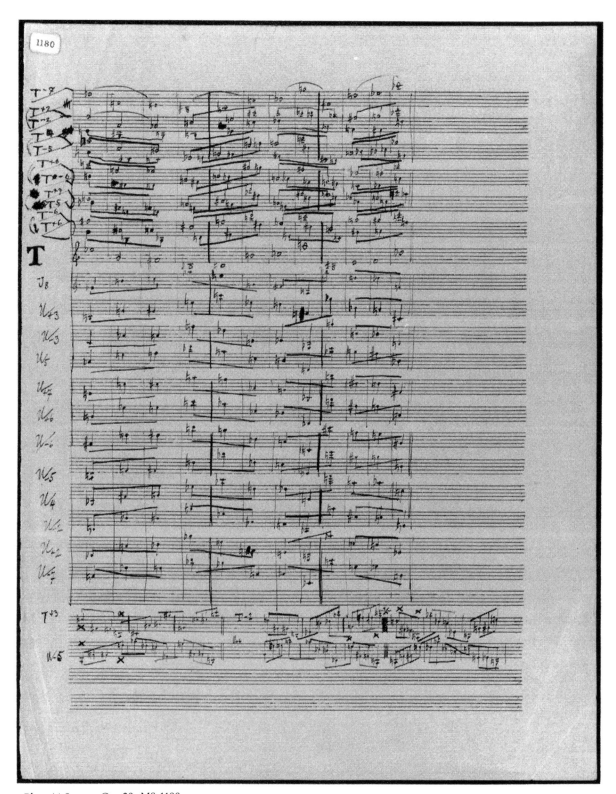

Plate 14 Septet, Op. 29: MS 1180

Plate 15 Septet, Op. 29: MS 1183

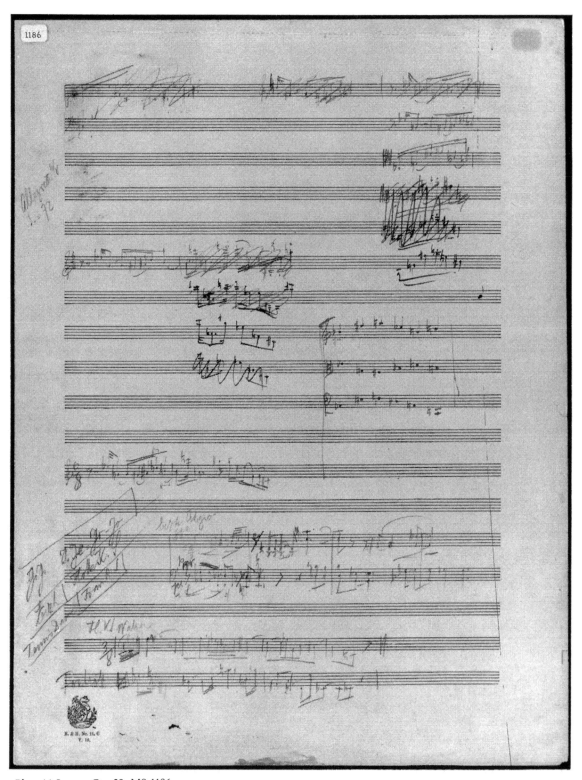

Plate 16 Septet, Op. 29: MS 1186

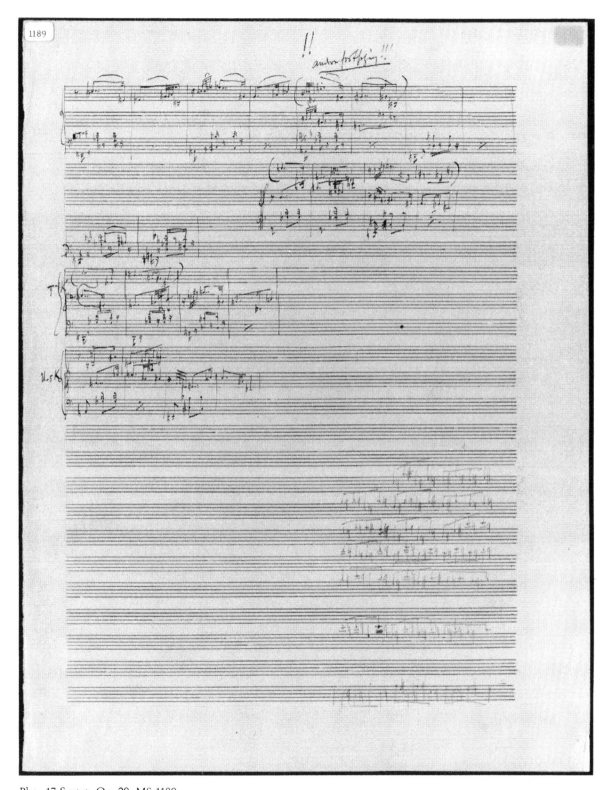

Plate 17 Septet, Op. 29: MS 1189

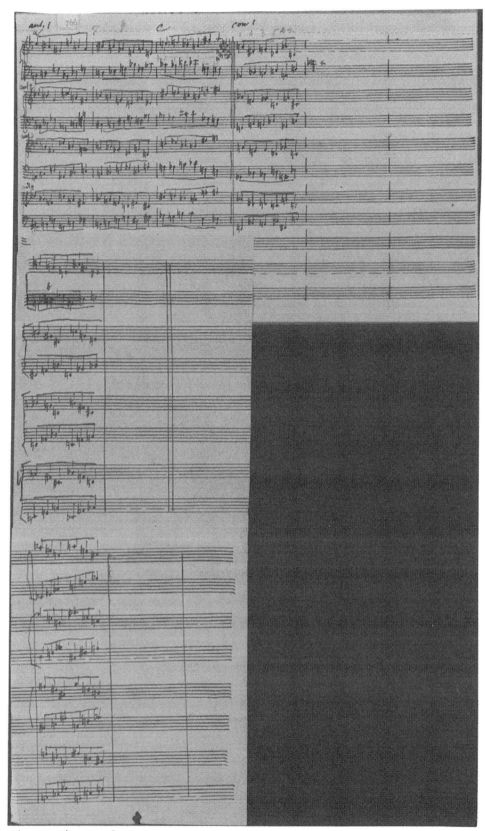

Plate 18 *Ode to Napoleon Buonaparte*, Op. 41: MS 766

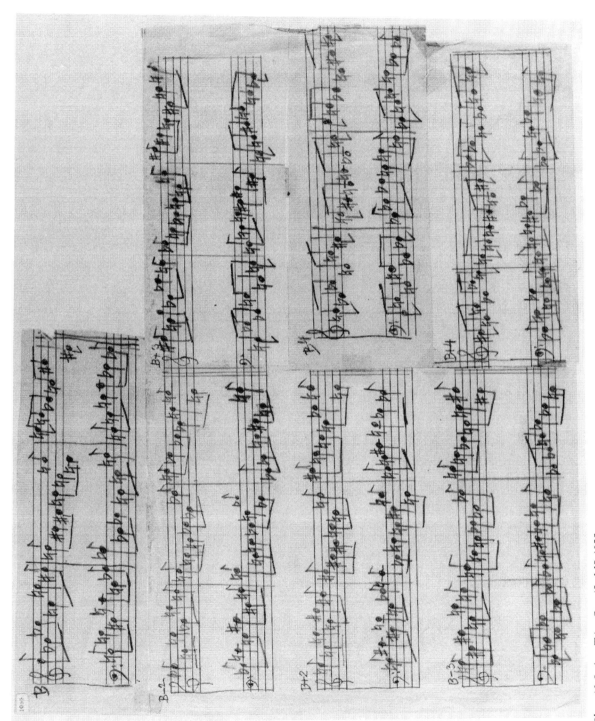

Plate 19 String Trio, Op. 45: MS 1055

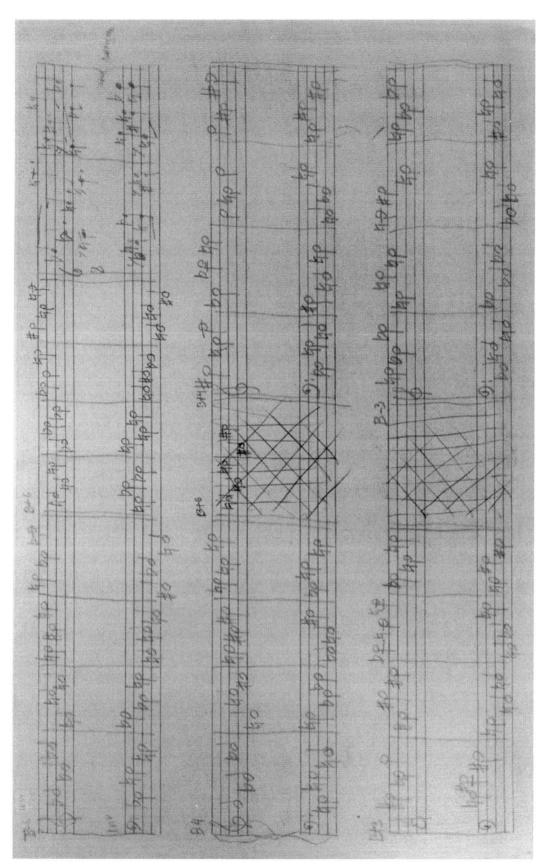

Plate 20 String Trio, Op. 45: MS 1057

Bibliography

Manuscripts

Schoenberg, Arnold. Wind Quintet, Op. 26: *Skizzen und Reihetabelle* (MSS 1106–12), *Skizzenbuch V: III. Satz Adagio* (MSS 508, 514, 525–8, 548–50, and 561–7) and *Reihe* (MS 673).

Septet (Suite), Op. 29: *Skizzenbuch V: Ouvertüre* (MSS 576, 586, 600, and 607–30) and *Reihe* (671/2), *Manuskript, Ouvertüre* (MSS 1115–32), *Reihentabellen* (MSS 1179–88), and *Skizzen* (MSS 1189–1206).

Ode to Napoleon Buonaparte, Op. 41: *Manuskript, Lichtpause* (MSS 728–65), *Reihen* (MSS 766–7), *Manuskript, Bleistift* (MSS 768–800), *Skizzen* (MSS 801–27).

All in the Arnold Schoenberg, Institute, Los Angeles

Scores

Schoenberg, Arnold, Second String Quartet, Op. 10, in *Sämtliche Werke*, ed. C. Schmidt (Mainz, 1982).

Erwartung, Universal Edition (Vienna, 1950).

Pierrot lunaire (A. Giraud), Op. 21, Universal Edition (Vienna, 1979).

Piano Suite, Op. 25, in *Sämtliche Werke*, ed. E. Steuermann and R. Brinkman (Mainz, 1968).

Bläserquintett (Quintet for Wind Instruments), Op. 26, Universal Edition (Vienna, c. 1925).

Suite (Septet), *für Kleine Klarinette, Klarinette, Bassklarinette, Geige, Bratsche, Violoncello und Klavier*, Op. 29, Universal Edition (Vienna and London, 1968).

Fourth String Quartet, Op. 37, in *Sämtliche Werke*, ed. C. Schmidt (Mainz, 1987).

Ode to Napoleon Buonaparte (Lord Byron) for string quartet, piano, and reciter, Op. 41, G. Schirmer (New York, 1944).

String Trio, Op. 45, in *Sämtliche Werke*, ed. C. Schmidt (Mainz, 1982).

Phantasy, for violin with piano accompaniment, Op. 47, Peters Corporation (London, 1952).

Books and articles

Arnold, Stephen, and Graham Hair. 'An Introduction and a Study', *Perspectives of New Music*, 14/2 (1976), pp. 155–86.

Ashford, Alden. 'Linear and Textural Aspects of Schoenberg's Cadences', *Perspectives of New Music*, 16/1 (1978), pp. 195–224.

    'Schoenberg's Cadential Devices' (doctoral dissertation, Princeton University, 1971), University Microfilms International.

Babbitt, Milton. 'Contemporary Musical Composition and Musical Theory as Contemporary Intellectual History', in *Perspectives in Musicology*, ed. B. Brooks, E. Downes, and S. Van Solkema (New York, 1971).

    (review) '*Quatrième Cahier (n.d.): Le Système dodécaphonique*', *Journal of the American Musicological Society*, 3/3 (1950), pp. 264–7.

    'Remarks on the Recent Stravinsky', in *Perspectives on Schoenberg and Stravinsky*, ed. B. Boretz and E. T. Cone (Princeton, NJ, 1968), pp. 165–85.

    (review) 'René Leibowitz. *Schoenberg et son école*' and 'René Leibowitz. *Qu'est ce que la musique de douze sons?*', *Journal of the American Musicological Society*, 3/1 (1950), pp. 57–60.

    'Set Structure as a Compositional Determinant', in *Perspectives on Contemporary Music Theory*, ed. B. Boretz and E. T. Cone (New York, 1972), pp. 129–47.

    'Since Schoenberg', *Perspective of New Music*, 12/1 (1973), p. 33.

    'Some Aspects of Twelve-Tone Composition', *The Score and IMA Magazine*, 12 (1955), pp. 53–61.

    'The String Quartets of Bartók', *Musical Quarterly*, 35 (1949), pp. 377–85.

    'Three Essays on Schoenberg; Concerto for Violin and Orchestra, *Das Buch der hängenden Gärten, Moses und Aron*', in *Perspectives on Schoenberg and Stravinsky*, ed. B. Boretz and E. T. Cone (Princeton, NJ, 1968).

    'Twelve-Tone Invariants as Compositional Determinants', *The Musical Quarterly*, 46 (1960), pp. 246–59.

    Words about Music, edited by J. Straus (Madison, WI, 1987).

Bailey, Walter. *Programmatic Elements in the Works of Schoenberg* (Ann Arbor, MI, 1984).

Bent, Ian. 'Analysis', in *The New Grove Dictionary*, 6th edn (London, 1980).

Berg, Alban. 'Why is Schoenberg's Music so Difficult to Understand?', in W. Reich, *Alban Berg: A Critical Biography* (London, 1971), pp. 189–204.

Berger, Arthur. 'Problems of Pitch Organization in Stravinsky', in *Perspectives on Schoenberg and Stravinsky*, ed. B. Boretz and E. T. Cone (Princeton, NJ, 1968), pp. 123–54.

Berry, Wallace. *Structural Functions in Music* (Princeton, NJ, 1976).

Boretz, Benjamin. 'Meta-Variations, Part IV: Analytic Fallout (1)', *Perspectives of New Music*, 11/2 (1972), pp. 146–223.

Boulez, Pierre. 'Schoenberg is Dead', *The Score*, 6 (1952), pp. 18–22.

Buccheri, John. 'An Approach to 12-Tone Music: Articulation of Serial Pitch Units in Piano Works of Schoenberg, Krenek, Dallapiccola and Rochberg' (unpublished doctoral dissertation, Rochester University, 1975), University Microfilms International.

Cone, Edward T. 'Beyond Analysis', in *Perspective on Contemporary Music Theory*, ed. B. Boretz and E. T. Cone (New York, 1972), pp. 72–90.

Dahlhaus, Carl. 'Harmony', in *The New Grove Dictionary* (London, 1980).

'Schoenberg and Schenker', *Proceedings of the Royal Musical Association*, 100 (1973/74), pp. 209–15.

'Some Models of Unity in Musical Form', *Journal of Music Theory*, 19/2 (1975), pp. 1–30.

Dunsby, Jonathan, and Arnold Whittall. *Music Analysis in Theory and Practice* (London, 1988).

Forte, Allen. *The Compositional Matrix* (New York, 1974).

The Structure of Atonal Music (New Haven, CT and London, 1973).

Friedheim, P. 'Rhythmic Structure in Schoenberg's Atonal Compositions', *Journal of the American Musicological Society*, 19 (1966), pp. 59–72.

Friedmann, Michael. 'A Methodology for the Discussion of Contour: Its Application to Schoenberg's Music', *Journal of Music Theory*, 29 (1985), pp. 223–48.

Goehr, Alexander. 'Schoenberg's *Gedanke* Manuscript', *Journal of the Arnold Schoenberg Institute*, 2/1 (1977), pp. 4–25.

'The Idea behind the Music: Schoenberg and Karl Kraus', *Music Analysis*, 4/1–2 (1985), pp. 59–71.

'The Theoretical Writings of Arnold Schoenberg', *Proceedings of the Royal Musical Association*, 100 (1973/74), pp. 85–96.

Goehr, Walter, and Alexander Goehr. 'Arnold Schoenberg's Development towards the Twelve-Tone System', in *European Music in the Twentieth Century*, ed. H. Hartog (London, 1957).

Graebner, J. 'An Analysis of Schoenberg's *Klavierstück*, Op. 33a', *Perspectives of New Music*, 12 (1973), pp. 128–40.

Gradenwitz, P. 'The Idiom and Development in Schoenberg's Quartets', *Music and Letters*, 16/3 (1945), pp. 123–41.

Griffiths, Paul. 'Variation', in *The New Grove Dictionary* (London, 1980).

Hahl-Koch, Jelena (ed.). *Arnold Schoenberg, Wassily Kandinsky: Letters, Pictures and Documents* (London and Boston, MA, 1980).

Haimo, Ethan, and Paul Johnson. 'Isomorphic Partitioning and Schoenberg's Fourth String Quartet', *Journal of Music Theory*, 28 (1984), pp. 47–72.

Hall, Ann. 'Texture in the Violin Concertos of Stravinsky, Berg, Schoenberg and Bartók' (unpublished doctoral dissertation, University of Michigan, 1971), University Microfilms International.

Hill, Richard. 'Schoenberg's Tone-Rows and the Tonal System of the Future', *The Musical Quarterly*, 22 (1936), pp. 14–37.

Hyde, Martha. 'A Theory of Twelve-Tone Meter', *Music Theory Spectrum*, 6 (1984), pp. 14–51.

'Musical Form and the Development of Schoenberg's Twelve-Tone Method', *Journal of Music Theory*, 29 (1985), pp. 85–143.

Schoenberg's Twelve-Tone Harmony: The Suite Op. 29 and the Compositional Sketches (Ann Arbor, MI, 1982).

'The Format and Function of Schoenberg's Twelve-Tone Sketches', *Journal of the American Musicological Association*, 36/3 (1983), pp. 455–80.

'The Roots of Form in Schoenberg's Sketches', *Journal of Music Theory*, 24/1 (1980), pp. 1–36.

'The Telltale Sketches: Harmonic Structure in Schoenberg's Twelve-Tone Method', *Musical Quarterly*, 66 (1980), pp. 560–80.

Hymanson, W. 'Schoenberg's String Trio (1946)', *The Music Review*, 11 (1950), pp. 184–94.

Kelly, C. 'Declaration, Dissolution and Reassembly: A Creative Principle in the String Quartets of Arnold Schoenberg' (unpublished master's dissertation, Florida State University, 1970).

Krumhansl, Carol L., Gregory Sandell and Desmond C. Sergeant. 'The Perception of Tone Hierarchies and Mirror Forms in Twelve-Tone Serial Music', *Music Perception*, 5/1 (1987), pp. 31–77.

Leibowitz, René. *Introduction à la musique de douze sons* (Paris, 1949).

Schoenberg (Paris, 1969).

Schoenberg and His School, trans. D. Newlin (New York, 1975).

Lerdahl, Fred. 'Cognitive Constraints on Compositional Systems', in *Generative Processes in Music*, ed. John A. Sloboda (Oxford, 1988), pp. 231–59.

Lewin, David. 'A Study of Hexachord Levels in Schoenberg's Violin Fantasy', *Perspective of New Music*, 6 (1967), pp. 18–32.

'A Theory of Segmental Association in Twelve-Tone Music', *Perspectives of New Music*, 1 (1962), pp. 89–116.

'Inversional Balance as an Organizing Force in Schoenberg's Music and Thought', *Perspectives of New Music*, 6 (1968), pp. 1–21.

MacDonald, M. *Schoenberg* (London, 1976).

Mann, Thomas. *The Genesis of a Novel*, trans. R. and C. Winston (London, 1961).

Martino, Donald. 'The Source Set and its Aggregate Formation', *Journal of Music Theory*, 5 (1961), pp. 224–69.

Marx, Adolf. *Dr Marx's General Musical Instruction ('Allgemeine Musiklehre'): An Aid to Teachers and Learners in Every Branch of Musical Knowledge* (London, 1854).

Mead, Andrew. 'Large-Scale Strategy in Arnold Schoenberg's Twelve-Tone Music', *Perspectives of New Music*, 24/1 (1985), pp. 31–77.

'The State of Research in Twelve-Tone Music', *Music Theory Spectrum*, 11/1 (1989), pp. 40–4.

'"Tonal" Forms in Arnold Schoenberg's Twelve-Tone Music', *Music Theory Spectrum*, 9 (1987), pp. 62–92.

Neighbour, Oliver. 'Dodecaphony in Schoenberg's String Trio', *Music Survey*, 4 (1952), pp. 489–90.

'Schoenberg, Arnold', in *The New Grove Dictionary* (London, 1980).

Nietzsche, Friedrich. *The Birth of Tragedy*, trans. F. Golffing (New York, 1956).

Newlin, Dika. *Schoenberg Remembered: Diaries and Recollections 1938–76* (New York, 1980).

'Secret Tonality in Schoenberg's Piano Concerto', *Perspectives of New Music*, 13/2 (1974), pp. 137–9.

Peel, J. 'On Some Celebrated Measures of the Schoenberg String Trio', *Perspectives of New Music*, 15 (1976), pp. 260–79.

Peles, Stephen. 'Interpretations of Sets in Multiple Dimensions: Notes on the Second Movement of Arnold Schoenberg's String Quartet no. 3', *Perspectives of New Music*, 22/1–2 (1983–4), pp. 303–52.

Perle, George. 'Schoenberg's Late Style', *The Music Review*, 13 (1952), pp. 274–82.

    Serial Composition and Atonality: an Introduction to the Music of Schoenberg, Berg and Webern (Berkeley, CA and London, 1977).

    Twelve-Tone Tonality (Berkeley, CA and London, 1977).

    The Operas of Alban Berg (2 vols., Berkeley, CA and London, 1980, 1985): vol 1, *Wozzeck*; vol. 2, *Lulu*.

Perle, George, and P. Lansky. 'Twelve-Note Composition', in *The New Grove Dictionary* (1980).

Phipps, G. 'Schoenberg's *Grundgestalt* Principle: A New Approach with Particular Application to the Variations for Orchestra, Opus 31' (unpublished doctoral dissertation, University of Cincinnati, 1976), University Microfilms International.

Rauchhaupt, Ursula von (ed.). *Schoenberg, Berg, Webern: The String Quartets, a Documentary Study* (Hamburg, 1971).

Ratz, Erwin. *Einführung in die Musikalische Formenlehre* (Vienna, 1951).

Reich, Willi. *Schoenberg: A Critical Biography*, trans. L. Black (London, 1971).

    The Life and Work of Alban Berg, trans. C. Cardew (London, 1965).

Rochberg, George. 'Reflections on Schoenberg', *Perspectives of New Music*, 11/2 (1973), p. 56.

    'The Harmonic Tendency of the Hexachord', *Journal of Music Theory*, 3 (1959), pp. 208–30.

Rosen, Charles. *Arnold Schoenberg* (New York, 1975).

    Sonata Forms (London, 1980).

Rufer, Joseph. *Composition with Twelve Notes Related to One Another* (London, 1954).

    The Works of Arnold Schoenberg: A Catalogue of His Compositions, Writings and Paintings, trans. D. Newlin (London, 1962).

Samson, Jim. *Music in Transition* (London, 1977).

Schoenberg, Arnold. 'Analysis of the Four Orchestral Songs Op. 22', trans. and annotated C. Spies, in *Perspectives on Schoenberg and Stravinsky*, ed. B. Boretz and E. T. Cone (Princeton, NJ, 1968), pp. 25–45.

    Fundamentals of Musical Composition, ed. Strang with the collaboration of L. Stein (London, 1967).

    Letters, selected and ed. L. Stein, trans. E. Wilkins and E. Kaiser (London, 1964).

    Theory of Harmony (Harmonielehre) (Vienna, 1911), trans. R. Carter (London, 1978).

    Models for Beginners in Composition, rev. L. Stein (New York, 1942).

    Preliminary Exercises in Counterpoint, ed. L. Stein (London, 1963).

    Structural Functions of Harmony, ed. H. Searle, rev. L. Stein (London, 1969).

    Style and Idea: Selected Writings of Arnold Schoenberg, ed. L. Stein, trans. L. Black (London, 1975).

    'Vortrag/12TK/Princeton', trans. C. Spies, *Perspectives of New Music*, 13/1 (1974), pp. 58–136.

Smith, Joan. *Schoenberg and His Circle: A Viennese Portrait* (New York, 1986).

Stuckenschmit, H. *Arnold Schoenberg: His Life, World and Work*, trans. H. Searle (London, 1977).

Straus, Joseph. 'Recompositions by Schoenberg, Stravinsky, and Webern', *Musical Quarterly*, 72 (1986), pp. 301–28.

'The Problem of Prolongation in Post-Tonal Music', *Journal of Music Theory*, 31/1 (1987), pp. 1–21.

Travis, Roy. 'Directional Motion in Schoenberg and Webern', *Perspectives of New Music*, 4/1 (1966), pp. 85–9.

Westergaard, P. 'Toward a Twelve-Tone Polyphony', in *Perspectives on Contemporary Music Theory*, ed. B. Boretz and E. T. Cone (New York, 1972), pp. 238–60.

Whittall, Arnold. 'Schoenberg and the True Tradition', *Musical Times*, 115 (1972), pp. 739–43.

Schoenberg's Chamber Music (London, 1975).

Williams, C. F. Abdy. *The Rhythm of Modern Music* (London, 1909).

Wood, Hugh. 'Introduction for Round House Concert: Schoenberg, *Ode to Napoleon*, Op. 41', unpublished, broadcast on BBC Radio 3 (10 February 1975).

1922285R0013

Printed in Great Britain
by Amazon.co.uk, Ltd.,
Marston Gate.